Shaping Taxpayers

Shaping Taxpayers

Values in Action at the Swedish Tax Agency

Lotta Björklund Larsen

berghahn
NEW YORK • OXFORD
www.berghahnbooks.com

Published in 2017 by
Berghahn Books
www.berghahnbooks.com

Library of Congress Cataloging-in-Publication Data
A C.I.P. cataloging record is available from the Library of Congress

British Library Cataloguing in Publication Data
A catalogue record for this book is available from the British Library

ISBN: 978-1-78533-410-8 (hardback)
ISBN: 978-1-78533-411-5 (ebook)

To my preciously valued ones – N, J, G, F

Contents

Acknowledgements ix

List of Illustrations xi

List of Abbreviations xii

Introduction. On Tax and Treasure: A Fiscal Anthropological Approach to Taxes 1

- Creating and Retaining Legitimacy 5
- The Peculiarities of Swedishness 7
- Tax and Taxation in Sweden 9
- Fiscal Anthropology: Taxation Creates Relations 14
- How to Study and Understand Knowledge-Making? 21
- Tax Agency Employees at Work 29
- Secrecy and Anonymity 33
- Disposition of Book 34

Chapter 1. From Control to Compassion: A History of the Swedish Tax Agency 43

- A Very Brief History of Swedish Taxation 46
- Buildings as a Force of Form 51
- Who Rules (at) the Swedish Tax Agency? 56
- Working with Tax Compliance at the Agency 57
- Agency Strategies Creating Tax Compliance 66
- The Analysis Unit 76
- The Cost Deduction Project 79
- The Workings of the Agency 83

Chapter 2. Talking with People: What Can We Learn from an Attitudinal Survey? 88

- The Social Life of Surveys 89
- Surveys Are What We Usually Do 92
- Making and Framing the Survey Structure 94

Caveats in Theory, but Not in Practice 100
Disciplining the Survey 104
Executing the Survey 110
And the Results Are ... 113

Chapter 3. X Per Cent: The Birth of a Number at the Random Audit Control Department 119
Random Audit Controls: Core Practices at the Agency 121
The Random Method: Planning, Organizing and Sampling 123
At the Random Audit Control Department 126
An Audit 127
Reasonable Decisions 130
A Secured Result? 135

Chapter 4. To Publish or Not? Communicating and Legitimizing Concerns Regarding the Projects's Result 141
The Problem of the Who ... 146
... and the Why 149
Interpreting and Applying the Law 151
The Role of Analysis 153
Measures: What Can the Agency do? 155
To Control or to Communicate – What? 161

Conclusion: Values in Action 168
Knowledge Used in this Risk Assessment Project 170
How to Impact Tax Compliance? 173
Fair Interpretation, Fair Taxation? 176
Values and Valuations 178

Reference List 183

Glossary 193

Index 197

Acknowledgements

In an anthropologist's life, the second round of fieldwork has been both questioned and somewhat mystified. For me it was a very logical consequence of my earlier work on how Swedes justified black work – that is, a way of avoiding taxation. Given the Swedish laws on income taxation, I realized that the Swedish Tax Agency has large room for interpreting such laws. How does it do that? What makes for taxable income, and tax-free income for that matter, when every exchange of services having value, regardless of how it is compensated, ought to be subject to taxation?

There are many people who contributed to the shaping, as it were, of my original pondering on these matters and to whom I want to express my sincerest gratitude. Foremost, to my informants at Skatteverket, who were both courageous and generous in inviting me to follow deliberations and discussions in a project that proved far more difficult than initially anticipated. In addition they copied me in on all correspondence and even recorded meetings when I was absent, which is more than any ethnographer could ask for. The informants prefer to be acknowledged by their pseudonyms. My most sincere thanks goes to Lars in particular, to Julia and Gunnar and also to Per, Svenne and Gunilla. I am also grateful to Alice, Petra, Ulla and the SNO, who accommodated me while in Örebro. I also acknowledge the generosity of all other employees at Skatteverket, who welcomed me, asked many good questions and put up with my presence in their meetings.

Initial encouragement and intellectual support came especially from Bill Maurer. Thank you for believing in the strange ideas of, at the time, a half-baked Ph.D. candidate as well as welcoming me to a most gratifying stay at IMTFI, UC Irvine. Ulf Hannerz and Helena Wulff, thank you! When in doubt about developing the various knowledge an anthropologist need, I could, and can, always turn to you. Without the support, good advice and welcome to Tema T at Linköping University by C-F Helgesson this would have been a completely different book. Thank you and thanks for laying the groundwork for the lively, friendly and constructive seminar series ValueS. Warmest gratitude also goes to friends and colleagues Francis Lee, Johan Nilsson and Karin Thoresson. I am also grateful to Maria Eidenskog, Linus Krafve-Johansson, Lisa Lindén, Reka Andersson, Oscar Maldonado, Teun Zuiderent-Jerak and Steve Woolgar. The support of Ericka Johnson, Sonja Jerak-Zuiderent and Corinna Kruse has been inspiring and essential.

Andrea Ballestero, Ulf Hannerz, Åsa Gunnarsson, Håkan Malmer, Ingrid Melbi and Teun Zuiderent-Jerak have read and commented on this manuscript in its early stages. Lars, Julia and Per have read parts and provided much needed and important input. Thanks to all for pointing out errors and underdeveloped ideas as well as reminding me about the reality of what it means to be working with taxes and taxation in various capacities. In the making of this project I found like-minded researchers. I especially want to acknowledge Karen Boll's contribution to this project. May we continue exploring taxation from our diverse perspectives …

I want to acknowledge the following people who have contributed to this project in various ways: Susanna Alexius, Patrik Aspers, Boel Berner, Michael Blim, Benedicte Brøgger, Neil Buchanan, Kimberley Chong, Matilda Dahl, Nimmo Elmi, Rebecca Empson, Liv Fries, Staffan Furustam, Christina Garsten, Anna Gavanas, Bas Koenee, Marianne Lien, Monica Lindh de Montoya, Johan Lindquist, Michael Livingston, Roberta Mann, Emer Mulligan, Jose Maria Muñoz, Anette Nyqvist, Lynne Oats, Nina Olson, Jenny Palm, Ebba Sjögren, Göran Sundström, Eva Sönnerhed, Renita Thedvall, Lennart Wittberg and Caitlin Zaloom.

Early versions of this work have been presented at UCL's Social Anthropology Seminars on financial logics, regimes of value and forms of economic knowledge, at the department of Social Anthopology at Stockholm University, at BI Oslo's Seminar serie on interpretative methods, at Institutet för framtidsstudier, and at the Rethinking Value Group at IMTFI. Thanks to all participants for useful comments. At IMTFI, Smoki Musaraj, Ivan Small, Taylor Nelms, Julia Elyachar and Keith Murphy gave good input and reminded me about the peculiarities of Swedishness. To make this into *a book*, I am to indebted to the three anonymous reviewers who provided much needed and constructive critique. As crucial has been the efficient assistance and help of the lovely Pat Baxter and Eeva Berglund, Caroline Kuhtz and Sasha Puchalski at Berghahn Books. Riksbankens jubileumsfond has supported this endeavour throughout. They dared to grant a fiscal anthropological project in the call for new research on taxes and taxation. I am immensely grateful for the funding and for the trust they have shown me. Finally, this book is dedicated to my loved ones, who remind me that there are other values in life than research. Puss på er!

Illustrations

0.1	Skatteverket logo.	2
0.2	*Buried Treasure*: Illustration of William 'Captain' Kidd overseeing a treasure burial.	11
0.3	www.skatteverket.se	13
1.1	Francis Ward in 'Robin Hood', July 1919.	44
1.2	The bailiffs were seen as harsh and extorted the locals (author translation). From Olaus Magnus 2010 [1555, 1909], *Historia om de nordiska folken*.	47
1.3	Skatteskrapan, view from Bondegatan, Stockholm.	52
1.4	Skatteverket headquarters, Solna.	53
1.5	*Dags att deklarera* 1972.	68
2.1	Analysts making surveys.	95
3.1	Skatteverket Örebro office.	127

Abbreviations

ANT	actor network theory
ATO	Australian Taxation Office
Brå	Brottsförebyggande Rådet (Swedish Crime Prevention Council)
CFA	Communauté Financière Africaine (French colonial currency, also known as CFA-Franc)
COEN	A Commercial Entity – these were subject to scrutiny in this risk assessment project (my abbreviation)
CRM	commercial relationship management
CSR	corporate social responsibility
FAR	Branschorganisationen för redovisningskonsulter, revisorer och rådgivare (Professional Institute for Authorized Public Accountants)
IRS	Internal Revenue Service (US)
NACE	Nomenclature statistique des activités économiques dans la communauté européenne. Please also see SNI code.
NNR	Näringslivets nämnd för regelförenkling (Board of Swedish Industry and Commerce for Better Regulation)
OECD	Organisation for Economic Co-operation and Development
PAR	a commercial address register
RAC	Random Audit Control is a method that is commonly used at the Swedish Tax Agency. The purpose is to 'fill identified lacunas of knowledge', 'create an unpredictable audit mechanism' or 'set an example' (my abbreviation).
RC	private research consultancy that was hired to execute the survey (my abbreviation)
ROT	*reparationer, ombyggnad, tillbyggnad* (repairs, refurbishing, attachments)
RS	rationalization of tax administration reform

RSV Riksskatteverket (National Tax Agency. This organizational name existed from 1971 to 1991 at which point it was replaced by Skatteverket)

RUT *renhållning, underhåll, tvätt* (cleaning, maintenance, laundry). Subsidized governmental programme for domestic services for private persons. Rut being a female name, it is also a play on words and traditional gender roles in domestic work. Compare with the ROT deductions.

SAOB *Svenska akademins ordbok* (Dictionary of the Swedish Academy)

SCB Statistiska Centralbyrån (Statistics Sweden)

SIE file an open standard format data file containing the bookkeeping ledger

SKAT Danish Customs and Tax Administration, Denmark's tax authority

SME small and medium-sized enterprises (in terms of number of employees)

SNI code Swedish Standard Industrial Classification code. The SNI standard is modelled on the Statistical Classification of Economic Activities in the European Community, commonly referred to as NACE. The SNI standard is maintained by Statistics Sweden (also known as SCB), a Swedish government office. The most recent version of the SNI standard is SNI 2007, which corresponds to NACE Revision 2.

SNO *Skattenämndsordförande* (Chairman of the Tax Board). The Tax Board make all decisions concerning changes to a tax statement before a memorandum is sent out to the auditee. Since 2012 these have been abolished regarding income taxation issues.

SOU *Statens Offentliga Utredningar* (Swedish Government Official Reports)

SPSS file Statistical Package for the Social Sciences, a common file format for predictive statistical analysis

XOX A department at the Agency that works entirely with big data models and other quantitative means to identify risk (the name is anonymized, my abbreviation)

Introduction

On Tax and Treasure
A Fiscal Anthropological Approach to Taxes

On a gloomy Friday afternoon on 30 January 1976, two tax inspectors accompanied by policemen walk into the entrance of the Swedish national theatre Dramaten. They are looking for the director, the world-famous filmmaker Ingmar Bergman, who has just started the rehearsal for August Strindberg's *The Dance of Death*. An incredulous and aghast Bergman is led away and charged with tax negligence. It is for real: when they exit the building a third policeman, who had been posted on the corner to make sure that Bergman would not escape by a back door, approaches and greets the party. While Bergman is being taken away for an immediate 'conversation', his home is searched and a number of binders are secured. He is bewildered, afraid, upset. This event[1] throws him into a state of depression and he is hospitalized in a psychiatric clinic.

Two months later, his depression switches to pure anger as the charges are dropped. He is innocent but he finds it impossible to work and think in Sweden and leaves on 22 April for Germany promising never to return. The ensuing worldwide (adverse) publicity was aimed only at Swedish bureaucracy, as Bergman said that RSV (the tax collecting authority at that time) could do as it pleased with his estate. The issue for him was not the taxes he was said to have neglected to pay, but rather the treatment he had been subject to: a bureaucratic show of strength accompanied by threats and blackmail (Bergman 1987: 121). It did not help that the two tax inspectors[2] wore similar black leather coats, apparently in fashion at the time.[3]

Illustration 0.1 Skatteverket logo.

Bergman's emigration and all the brouhaha it created was one event that made decision makers at the tax collecting authority rethink their strategies on how to treat taxpayers and what the relationships with them should be. The prevalent view about taxpayers among RSV employees seemed to be one of cheaters: if a taxpayer was not already caught avoiding taxes, it was just a question of time.[4] Compliance meant enforcement. It is difficult to assess what the answer to the chicken and egg question is in such relations between tax collector and taxpayer – does the tax collector regard the taxpayer as a cheater from the very start or does the taxpayer err, intentionally or not, thus becoming a cheater? If the view is that controlling and auditing is the only way to relate to taxpayers, the latter will always be seen as prone to evade taxes to the largest extent possible. In line with this view of taxpayers, no one would voluntarily part with their hard-earned money unless there were sanctions (cf. Levi 1988). Starting with the Bergman affair, a long trajectory began towards making the Swedish tax collecting authority and its employees develop and apply a different approach towards the taxpayers.

The authority has apparently succeeded, as contemporary standing of the Swedish tax authority is very different. In surveys citizens currently hold this bureaucracy in the highest esteem of all the nation's government agencies (Arkhede and Holmberg 2015: 22, 24), despite the fact that Swedes pay among the highest income tax rates in the world. How it collects a considerable amount of money from each taxpayer while being the governmental institution Swedes are most positive towards – 69 per cent think it performs its duties well and only 5 per cent have negative views on this authority (Holmberg and Tryggvason 2014: 11) – makes it an interesting object of study.[5] It has worked diligently to change its way of working, so in its aim to collect taxes and minimize tax errors it says it mediates the application of law and fulfils the orders of government, while among the citizens it taxes it strives vigorously to be seen as legitimate in its practices (e.g., Skatteverket 2007b, 2008b, 2012).

How has the the Swedish Tax Agency, *Skatteverket*, which will be referred to as the Agency throughout this book made this transformation? With tax compliance issues vigorously debated all over the world, there are lessons to be drawn from an apparently successful national tax collector, both for implementing an effective tax compliance regime and for reimagining the kinds of persons who willingly pay their taxes. Thus, a well-functioning tax collecting authority has to be taken seriously when we talk about taxpayers' willingness to comply and to pay.

This leads to a second concern: if we are to understand why Swedes willingly pay their taxes, we need to know how they are made to do so. Important to note is that this book is not a mere reflection of what is going on at the Agency, a mirror as it were, but is an inquisitive account of the workings of this Agency in making Swedes comply. Be aware though: I am not negative about taxation per se, nor is the purpose to argue for a change of tax laws according to a political agenda or other (radical) ideas. This is an investigation based on curiosity about how taxation is made given the laws, and how this tax collecting authority has come to be and still is regarded as one of the most trustworthy institutions in Swedish society.

Obviously, there are many other issues than a well-liked collector that impact citizens' consent to pay taxes. For one, getting value for money paid. This means that taxes paid are spent on infrastructure, things and services that are in accordance with values held in society; they should not disappear into private accounts, be spent on corrupt practices or be used to construct megalomaniac installations. 'Taxes, after all, are dues that we pay for the privileges of membership in an organized society' as Franklin D. Roosevelt put it. Yet even in Sweden taxpayers still evade and avoid taxes, so the Agency continues its work to increase compliance in society. With its good standing among the population at large it has to be careful of not rocking the boat and diminishing its hard-earned legitimacy if it changes its practices. After all, if Ingmar Bergman RIP had been questioned by the Agency today, it is not preposterous to assume that he would have been approached in a radically different way. Things have changed at the Agency and continue to change, which means changing the gaze somewhat: from looking at the Agency's existing procedures and control practices to how it works to understand why some taxpayers comply and others do not.

Above all, it is this third concern that this book addresses; the knowledge the Agency applies to understand what makes people comply with tax laws and pay their dues. More explicitly it is an anthropological inquiry about a seemingly successful tax collecting authority and how it works and impacts the Swedish population's willingness, considerable by international comparison, to pay up. We will follow how knowledge about compliance is gathered within this organization, the insights each of these knowledge claims provide and the implications of this bureaucracy's view on society. It is a processual view (the Agency wants to increase compliance) that studies how new knowledge is created and in turn is treated. There is knowledge that reinforces previous knowledge, but also challenges the established strategies and values the Agency applies to society.

In this quest I followed the birth, upbringing, disciplining and finally burial of a report produced by this Agency. The report lived for three years, from initiation to final version. It was a thing in the making (Latour and Woolgar 1986; Marcus 1995); from an idea of aiming to understand how certain things matter in the world to recognizing what can be publicly communicated about such matters. Underlying this report is a risk assessment project coordinated by the Agency's Analysis Unit. It was one of the largest projects ever undertaken by the Agency and is a project that provides insights into the broader workings of the Agency and the many aspects of how it understands society; how it performs taxation and the relationships it aims to create with taxpayers. Apart from knowledge-making about tax compliance, work on the report allows us to gain some insights into how Agency employees work, cooperate and interact with each other in the workplace. As the project also engaged external corporations, we will briefly step outside the Agency and follow how a consultancy assignment is handled and how the concerns of the private business interests of excessive governmental investigation are articulated. In this way additional insights are given into how the Agency carefully tiptoes around so as not to negatively influence the attitudes on taxation issues. These collaborations provide yet another context that allows us to see how certain knowledge claims emerge as important, whereas others are rejected.

The report was after all never published, as some of its contents contradicted previous knowledge communicated to the public. I do not argue that the knowledge this particular report communicates shapes the taxpayer, but the work with this report reveals many of the issues that are currently at stake for the Agency when trying to increase compliance among Swedish taxpayers. When insights from the report were presented within the Agency, it learned lessons from its very creation and existence and changed taxation practices because of the message the report carried and the new audit measures it recommended. Through the report's making we will see how the Agency engages with taxpayers, the methods it uses to create new knowledge and how it imagines applying the new knowledge – all in relation to the Agency's concerns about retaining legitimacy while shaping tax compliance.

Creating and Retaining Legitimacy

Legitimacy is not easily secured. Bergman's engagement with the Agency showed us that an effective tax collector cannot just force a given tax law on citizens. It has been proposed that the foundation of a functioning welfare state is a tax system that is widely accepted and considered fair and legitimate (Lodin 2007; Nordblom 2008), yet to appreciate the legitimacy of the tax system it has to be understood more broadly. Our gaze has to reach beyond the structure and the aims of the actual law to see how the system is applied and interpreted (cf. Merry 1990; Valverde 2003). Here legitimacy is understood as based in historically produced and ways of accepting authority, as something that also expresses morale or that guides how society at large responds to law, politicians and bureaucracy (e.g., Pardo 2000). Legitimacy is therefore also steeped in tradition – like Rome, it is not built in a day.

The much sought after voluntary tax compliance requires a legitimate tax system where taxpayers and the tax collector must share an understanding of what the rules mean (Picciotto 2007: 11) – in practice. Legitimate tax regulations should for example thus be seen as simple and fair (Picciotto 2007: 24), have an 'appearance of objectivity' (James 2010: 575) but also be made to work efficiently (Björklund Larsen 2015; cf. Riles 2011). It includes an element of flexibility in the practised legal techniques that renders the near future 'workable' for taxpayers (cf. Riles 2011: 180). Yet, acquired legitimacy is by no means static; changes to the enforcement of laws, and by what means, risks impacting the legitimacy of the enforcer among those who are affected by the very same changes (Riles 2011: 65). This often means increased suspicion in the relationship between enforcer and law abiders, in effect decreasing legitimacy.

To direct focus onto a tax system's legitimacy is thus to study its acceptance by taxpayers.[6] In practice it means that licit and legal actions converge. This is worth making explicit, because the common association between the licit and legal, on the one hand, and the illicit and illegal, on the other, is often complicated in practice. There are many activities that in essence are illegal but are still commonly practised. Yet in Sweden illegal and illicit are often used as synonyms; for example, in the English summary of the reports on *svart arbete*, titled 'Illicit Work in Sweden' (1998). What in essence is svart arbete is not easy to pin down and therefore such practices are easy to justify and make licit (Björklund Larsen 2010). With the focus here on the workings of a successful tax collecting authority, the question becomes how the authority imagines taxpayers' understanding of these aspects of legitimacy.

I thus argue that when the Agency creates knowledge designed to increase compliance it is both shaping *and* being shaped by Swedish taxpayers. To make the legal licit is a balancing act which is easier said than done. Maintaining this balance is of utter importance in the Agency's continuous efforts to be seen as legitimate among the Swedish populace. There are thus lessons to be drawn from this propitious national tax collecting authority, both for implementing an effective tax compliance regime and for reimagining the kinds of persons who willingly pay their taxes.

Yet this book is also about Sweden. Although highlighting taxation from a tax collector's perspective might appear narrow, this book will give insights on values held in contemporary Sweden, following Joseph Schumpeter's claim: in order to understand any society and its political life, one of the best starting points is taxation (1954). The remains of this chapter will lay the groundwork for how taxation is seen and studied with an anthropological perspective – a fiscal anthropology. But first I want to situate this study with a very brief introduction to Sweden and to Swedish values according to how some fellow social scientists have identified them. We will then proceed to learn about the all-encompassing tax law that the Agency has to work with. The law provides much interpretational leeway for the Agency, and while it pays attention to legitimacy, this interpretation has to be handled with care. In order to take seriously the effect of the collecting strategies on the relationship between the state, the tax collecting authority and the citizens who pay, we have to investigate how such a collecting authority actually applies the law and to see what its employees do when they 'tax' (cf. Boll 2011) or create strategies to do so. I will then explain more specifically the methodological

– method and theory that I see difficult to separate – approach applied in this book.

The Peculiarities of Swedishness

Swedes like to refer to themselves and their usage of things as *lagom*. An untranslatable word, it means neither too much nor too little but just right (Barinaga 1999: 7). Lagom pinpoints the delicate balance between the individual and collective in Sweden, which Barinaga exemplifies with the Vikings' sharing of drink from the common bowl; there had to be enough *mjöd* (mead) for everybody when the bowl had made its round. Your sip had to be lagom (ibid.). Yet lagom sits ill with Swedish values relative to other countries. In the World Value Survey's measurements of cultural values – a survey that describes variations in such values among approximately seventy nationalities – Sweden has a particular position. The result is visualized on the 'Inglehart-Welzel Cultural Map of the World', showing one axis with 'traditional values' at the lower end escalating towards 'secular-rational values'. On the other axis, 'survival values' are set against 'self-expressional values'. If we are to believe such surveys, Sweden displays an extreme result on the graph compared with other countries, being situated in the extreme upper right-hand corner. According to this survey, Swedes are simultaneously particularly rational and the least prone to worry about survival issues; they trust their government and fellow citizens.[7] The World Value Survey argues that there is a continuous inclination towards these values, a fact that makes Sweden appear as a modern and somewhat trendsetting country. Or perhaps this extreme position is a sign of the peculiarity of being lagom?

Historians Henrik Berggren and Lars Trägårdh explain this seeming paradox as 'statist individualism' (Berggren and Trägårdh 2006: 49 ff).[8] They trace this notion from the history of a country that was never feudal and where common men have been relatively free in a comparative perspective. So although Swedes put much trust in the state, there is also an individualistic component. 'The striving for individual freedom and autonomy, rather than the more socially acceptable embrace, constitutes the fundamental drive that underpins the state-individualistic social contract' (Berggren and Trägårdh 2006: 54, my translation). The Swedish model, including the welfare state, is argued to emerge from these forces. The contemporary Swede has a direct relationship with the state, regarding both rights and responsibilities, mainly through the social security net. Swedes are thus seen as a people of individuals, no one worth more than any other, and a people that can depend on the state when in need, before having to turn to family and kin (cf. Daun 1989; Berggren and Trägårdh 2006: 43). Swedes are thus seen as being comparatively trustful of the society in which they live and of the state that governs them (cf. Möller 2007: 18).[9]

Sweden is one of the larger countries of Europe, and although sparsely populated there has been quite a large influx of immigrants over the last sixty years, yet resulting in only around ten million inhabitants. The large majority live in the south and the remaining population is scattered along the coastline on the western shore of the Baltic Sea; the dense forest in the north is sparsely populated.

This big country has mercifully been unaffected by war for almost two hundred years, making for peaceful development. In the second half of the nineteenth century it was still poor and mainly agrarian, which caused many of its citizens to emigrate towards the Americas in pursuit of a better life. During this time industrialization simultaneously took off; the emerging industry was based on rich national resources of iron ore and forestry, helping the country to grow wealthy. This fortuitous development moved forward rapidly after the Second World War, as the country was unscathed by the horrors of war that most of Europe had experienced, and an undamaged Swedish industry supplied material and products for the reconstruction of Europe. Sweden thus found itself in the 1960s as one of the globe's wealthiest countries. The growing wealth was the source for a development of the welfare state, while privately owned industry and the state cooperated and grew for the benefit of both (e.g., Allvin 2004; de Swaan 1988; Rothstein 1992).

Many countries consider themselves welfare states today, yet the Swedish version is still considered a role model (e.g., Svallfors 1995), perhaps due to being one of the first. It is subject to debate why the welfare state came to take the course it did in Sweden (cf. Bäck and Larsson 2006: 295), but its development is mostly credited to the Social Democratic Party that governed Sweden when the welfare state emerged.[10] Two governing ideas are part of the Swedish welfare state self-image; ideas that remain even if governments have changed. One such idea was *Folkhemmet*, literally the People's Home. Despite the concept's murky history, during the Social Democratic reign it became a notion of a place where all citizens would feel equal (Frykman and Hansen 2009: 80) and where no one would be dependent on or abused by any other person (Lewin 2008: 30). This idea of equality might have earlier historical roots than twentieth-century social engineering (Berggren and Trägårdh 2006: 52), but one of its consequences was an evening out of differences in income level (Bennich-Björkman 2008: 47).

The other idea was *arbetslinjen*, the Work Approach. Getting all Swedes to work is argued to be one of the main and most successful parts in the building of the Swedish welfare society (cf. Esser 2005: 14; Lindvert 2006: 18). The Work Approach fits well with the country's Lutheran religious history. Although Sweden is nowadays a very secular country, Lutheran ethics such as self-sufficiency (Rosenberg 2013) and the importance of work (Björklund Larsen 2010) are part of this self-image. It was 'an axiomatic policy of actively promoting, preparing and facilitating employment' (Rosenberg 2013: 184). The state took an active role in getting people to work and all Swedes ought to contribute to building the country.

It is not too far-fetched to say that the Work Approach and the idea of equality are central cornerstones in the construction of Swedish society, including its financing.[11] Taxes on personal income – from work – provide the foundation for Swedish welfare politics.[12] Personal income tax is by international comparison very high (cf. KPMG 2009) and constructed as marginal tax (with an increased percentage level on the last krona earned). High-income earners thus have higher tax rates than the average Swede.

This redistribution of income via taxation underpins the idea of equality as well as adding to the Swedish public discourse on the benefits of paying tax. It starts at an early age; the blessings of taxation are even addressed in children's TV programmes.[13] Although politicians, legislators and opinion makers might 'slightly' disagree on the amount of tax that should be paid, most seem to agree on the importance of taxes for Swedish society, including the idea of marginal tax rates as fair. It is hardly *comme il faut* in Swedish political debate to argue for substantially less tax, and tax issues seldom take a prominent place in Swedish elections.[14] As a former colleague born and raised outside Sweden shared with me: 'Being Swedish is very much defined by paying tax; then you feel included. Nationalism is (also) created when delivering the annual tax return Sunday evening [first Sunday in May] into the letterbox. Being a taxpayer is central for Swedish identity; you then become a worthy citizen'.

Tax and Taxation in Sweden

The Swedish word for tax, *skatt*, is of Germanic and Nordic origin; *schat* (tax) and *Schatt* (taxable); in old English it was *sceatt*. Interesting to note is that in contemporary Swedish, for the citizen, skatt has two quite contrary meanings. It is the burden imposed by the state; the *National*

Encyclopedia bluntly describes it as 'forced contribution to the public without direct redistributive obligation'. This levy is extracted from citizens to cover the costs of public needs. In war, there may also be charges imposed on a defeated country but then it is often referred to as a tribute. Synonyms for skatt or tax are often invented when its collection is seen as problematic. Studying Swedish tax history reveals the amazing ingenuity: *ledung, gengärd, jordeboksräntan, fyrmannagärden, silverhjälper.* Currently, Swedes can pay *inkomstskatt, skatt på kapitalinkomster, moms, värnskatt, fastighetsavgift, punktskatt, arbetsgivaravgift* or *egenavgift, vinstskatt, skatt på realisationsvinst, fordonsskatt, bensinskatt,* etc. It is not easy to discern the actual tax burden in percentage, but the verbal flair is most probably universal.

Another meaning of skatt is in the sense of treasure connoted to wealth, often hidden and of a value difficult to estimate. Think of the dream of Treasure Island where somewhere a mysterious hidden chest with gems and jewels of various kinds can be found. This skatt, treasure, often contains a mixture of all kinds of valuables.

The word skatt also occurs in the sense of property; a collection of valuables, money and in some languages can even mean cattle (cf. Muñoz 2011). Often kept hidden and referred to as a collection of something that can be used in dire times, this version of skatt is something in storage, an asset or something saved. Skatt is also the abundance that nature can provide. For example in Sweden lingonberries are referred to as the red treasure of the forest, and the much sought after chanterelles as the forest's golden variety. A skatt can include everything from collections that have a non-material value such as archives, books, poems and literature to the more tangible ones such as items made of gold or silver and incorporating gems and pearls. Furthermore, someone is a skatt if s/he has special attributes, and is especially used as a name for someone you hold dear, most often by women but also children. My husband, a Dane who retains his mother tongue in our daily conversation, calls me *skat* (yes, Danish is similar but has fewer consonants) in his more affectionate moments. Finally, *skatta* means to estimate, guess, gauge, or to value something. At the end of this book we will return to my argument that legitimate taxation reflects the values held by the Agency on the citizens from whom it collects taxes. Skatt thus goes full circle in this book – from the practice of taxation to enacting the values of the very subjects that it engages with.

So skatt is many things. The tax burden, mainly originating from people's work, is figuratively amassed in the state's treasure chest and the contents of this chest make the Swedish comprehensive welfare state possible. The Swedish state is often depicted as the very essence of a welfare

Illustration 0.2 *Buried Treasure*: Illustration of William 'Captain' Kidd overseeing a treasure burial.

state (e.g., Steinmo 2002; Svallfors 1995); yet welfare does not come free – the funding of it all derives from taxes. I will not go so far as to argue that it is the word itself that performs taxation (cf. Mann 2006), but the meaning of a word contributes to people's views of it (Barinaga 1999: 9) and perhaps thus also informs tax compliance in Swedish society.

There are currently four main types of Swedish taxes, and the Agency is responsible for administrating and collecting all of them. Income tax provides the main funding for municipalities and provinces and makes up about two-thirds of the total tax collected in Sweden. Income tax is basically applied to all types of personal income, including work, pensions and sickness benefits, and includes indirect tax on work in the form of social fees. This latter tax is typically paid by the employer on behalf of the employee and does not show in tax returns. The actual tax percentage on income is thus far larger than what is shown on individual tax statements. Second, there is VAT (value added tax – *moms*), which is included in all consumption prices for private individuals. It is a governmental tax and amounts to almost 20 per cent of total tax collected. The third largest tax comes from capital, mostly on surplus from corporate activity and amounts close to 10 per cent. Excise, import and some other small varieties make up the remaining 10 per cent.[15]

Contemporary Swedish tax laws date back to 1991 when the 'centennial tax reform' was agreed upon.[16] The main purpose of the reform of the century was economic proficiency and it was very radical in comparison to contemporary tax reforms of many other countries (e.g., Agell, Englund and Södersten 1996; Steinmo 2002: 840). The law itself was a political compromise yet built on a lengthy investigation process by various stakeholders (Sørensen 2010: 62) aiming to create a solid, simple, transparent and fair system. One result was to broaden the income tax base while lowering the rates, changes that were implemented both for employees and for corporations. The reform also emphasized neutrality in taxation practices in order to provide efficient financing of public spending while aspiring to create minimal distortion in citizens' economic decisions (e.g., avoidance, which had been possible for high-income earners under the previous tax regime).[17]

The 1991 change of principles meant a move away from global income taxation to dual income tax (Agell, Englund and Södersten 1996: 645). Income from salaried work and return from investments and profit from business were separated and taxed accordingly. All exchanges of work/exchanges of services having (economic) value were deemed to constitute income – regardless of whether the compensation consisted of money, a service in return or of material objects. Thus everything deemed income ought to be subject to tax assessment and any recompense from

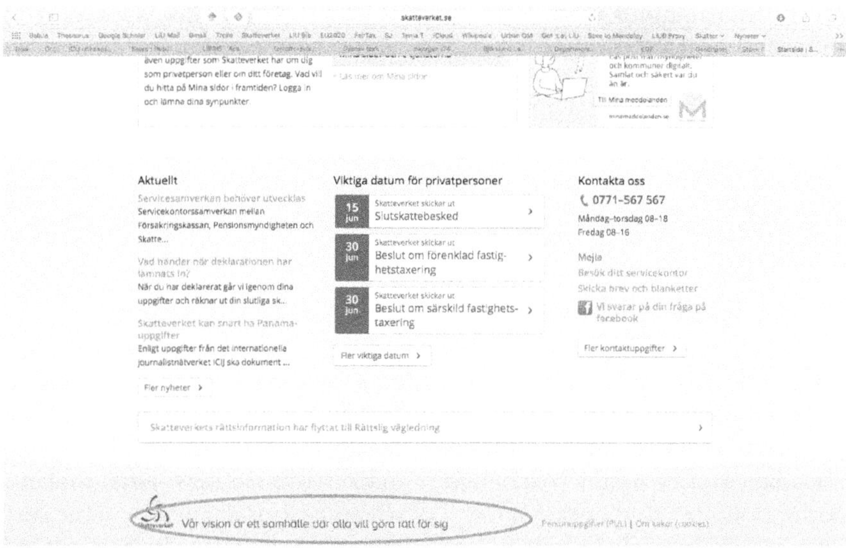

Illustration 0.3 www.skatteverket.se.

exchanges of services and goods was legally described as income. One aspect of this is that barter legally compares with cash compensation; another is that proximity of social relationships between exchangers is not relevant (Skatteverket 2006a: 21).

This consequence of the reform has been largely overlooked in public discussion; in fact it is the Agency's interpretation of tax laws that matters when Swedish income taxes are collected, which is a fact the Agency recognizes (e.g., Skatteverket 2006a).[18] The Agency has a daunting task and it is quite aware of its vulnerable position, as it recognizes that its interpretation of the tax laws and the way it performs its fiscal duty has an impact on the citizen's willingness to pay. The Agency thus continuously adapts the system aiming to be perceived as even more reasonable and equitable for the taxpayer (Skatteverket 2011c). 'Our vision is a society where everybody wants to do their fair share' (*Vår vision är ett samhälle där alla vill göra rätt för sig*) is the motto prominently displayed on its website. This somewhat intriguing message removes emphasis from the Agency as being a mere collector of taxes to its being a shaper of taxpayers' morality, and underscores the relational aspect of taxation. All Swedes have to contribute. Needless to say, this fact also attracts the attention of an anthropologist interested in the relationships that economic exchanges create.

To understand tax compliance in Sweden – or in any other country – it is thus vital to understand how taxpayers are made to contribute. If the Agency upholds its aims and mottos, its practice of tax law is subject to many considerations of 'what goes' in society. Although the law says that all exchanges having value ought to be subject to tax, the Agency is involved in quite considerable boundary work to distinguish between exchanges subject to taxation and those that are not (Björklund Larsen 2015). This means we also ought to look at the relationships created by exchanges having value.

Fiscal Anthropology: Taxation Creates Relations

So let us look at taxation from this angle, as exchanges that create relationships. From an anthropological perspective is an economy seen as made up of people who exchange and thereby create social relations. There is an abundance of economic exchanges – market transactions, gifts, robbery, corruption, just to mention a few – of which each is defined by some specific criteria, is made in specific circumstances, and creates its own type of relationship. The point is that the way people go about exchanges has to do with what could be called economic, social and cultural values.[19]

Tax is one type of economic exchange. In modern welfare states, tax payments comprise one of citizens' largest, if not *the* largest, economic relationship to anybody. Taxes can be viewed as where the state has greatest impact on the private lives of its citizens (Tilly 2009: X, XIII) and as such it is the most pervasive of relationships existing between citizens and state (Martin et al. 2009: 4). Thinking about taxes as yet another expense that Swedes pay – rent, mortgage, transport, food, clothing, membership fees, Internet and other communication expenses, entertainment – they make up a substantial part, taking into account all the different ways the state levies charges. Regardless of what it is called – VAT, income tax, capital tax, social fees – taxation brings in funding to the state. It finances defence, infrastructure and welfare and has as such at least the intention to benefit all citizens. It pays people in public employment. In a democracy, it is we – the citizens – who ultimately decide what taxes we should pay and how these resources should be collected and what they should be used for. As John Locke has already stated – taxes get into issues about democracy and reciprocity (Locke 1988: §§140). Yet, tax compliance not only depends on the level of tax but on many other issues (e.g., Hadenius 1985). An anthropological perspective on taxation not only hones our understanding of the explicit economic relationship between citizens and the state but also the implicit economic relationship with all other citizens. All citizens (supposedly) pay taxes and all (supposedly) benefit from living in a welfare state. In this light, tax collection in practice has an impact on how taxpayers view their relationship with the state and ultimately with other citizens. This is a holistic view on taxation – a view that intimately connects the spheres we call economy and society (cf. Maurer 2005b).

Consider the concept of 'tax competition' between countries that came to prominence in the 1990s. Tax competition makes for an imagined future, writes Bill Maurer (2009), and shows that it does not describe an actual condition but is a 'logical outcome' of contemporary economic theories about market behaviour governing all economic decisions. This is regardless of whether it is humans, corporations or countries that make them. The fact that some people move their wealth to societies with lower tax rates is not necessarily a result of a competition between countries. There can be many other issues at play for moving money than the mere emphasis on competition of tax rates between states. Maurer's point is that the emphasis on competition takes away the taxation issue itself. What might we discover if we for example see tax payments as exchanges instead of pure payment? Seen as exchanges, we expect something in return, but seen as payments they alter our relation to the state.

Whilst only a few anthropologists have written explicitly about taxation, more have looked at cheating and evasion (e.g., Mars 1982; Maurer 2010; Roitman 2005), perhaps in an echo of a more popular focus on avoiding taxes rather than on paying them (e.g., Capecchi 1989; Leonard 1998; Pardo 1996; Scott 1999). Circumventing tax might be the consequence of ideological or religious convictions when economic matters are organized. Anthropologists often have a concern for the powerless and vulnerable in society, and if our gaze includes the tax collectors it is in the role as despicable representatives of power (Lin 1948) or as ignorant bureaucrats, who do not spend tax receipts democratically (e.g., Guano 2010; Gupta 2012; Pardo 2004). It is not only Italians who can justify tax cheating as a result of their state's lack of fiscal fairness and universalist spending on the one hand and the same state's 'seemingly capricious application of rights, duties and entitlements' (Guano 2010: 488) on the other; Swedes too can find similar reasoning and excuses (Björklund Larsen 2010, 2013a, 2013b; Laurin 1986). Taxation is reciprocal and the act of collecting taxes is closely connected, yet not exclusive, to the redistribution of the same (e.g., Gudeman 2008).[20]

Inspired by Schumpeter but articulated as an economic anthropological question, I study taxation as a relationship between citizens and between citizens and state. In sociology the fiscal sociology movement has revived Joseph Schumpeter's original concern about the enormous impact of taxation on most societal features (1954: 6). This is the branch of sociology that deals with questions about how the state, through its tax laws and regulations and the practice of these, creates a fiscal dynamic that affects people's ways of exchanging and the economy in a broad sense (Campbell 1993; Marques 2004; Martin et al. 2009). One pertinent question within traditional fiscal sociology concerns when and why states can raise taxes (Tilly 2009) and still make their citizens comply with the law. Often, the acceptance of tax increases among the population at large is on account of wars and the necessity to fund resistance (Feldman and Slemrod 2009). As mentioned, for two hundred years Sweden has not been at war and we have to look for other explanations for Swedes' relative willingness to comply and pay up under changing tax regimes.

From a sociological point of view, the new fiscal sociology moved away from paying attention to the spending of taxes – who benefited from the spending of taxes, for what reasons these taxes were spent and the consequences of such expenditures – to looking instead at the effects of taxation on various social categories and at what fiscal practices were applied by any given state (Campbell 1993: 180).[21] The 'new fiscal sociology' addresses three broad issues (Martin et al. 2009). First, its proponents want to move the focus to informal social institutions; in part to underline that taxation is part and parcel of social relationships. The opportunity to tax is not only a political issue that depends on a country's legal structure but is shaped by diverse social institutions such as family, friendships, trust, work and religion. Second, fiscal sociology takes note of a country's history, the unfolding of events and the financing of those. An explanation of social phenomena has to pay attention to history and traditions. Third, focus is set on the impact of taxation on a societal level rather than on the individual.

This approach to the study of taxation thus encompasses a wide set of questions including the impact on and of economic, cultural, political, institutional and historical factors (cf. Oats 2012 for an overview of various interpretive fieldwork approaches to the study of taxation). A sociological approach 'differs from other approaches by focusing explicitly on the complex social interactions and institutional and historical contexts that link state and society in ways that shape fiscal policies and their effects' (Campbell 1993: 164). If we take seriously the reciprocal relationships as an outcome of taxation, one could argue that this link must be even more pertinent in states with high tax rates – that is, where a large part of the price of a private purchase, as well as net personal income, is tax. There are different explanations for why high tax rates have been accepted: due to war, as some historical research has indicated (e.g., ibid.: 167), but also to the building of a welfare state. High taxes can be said to originate in the organizational strength of societal groups and of the institutional structure of the state (ibid: 168), and it has been shown that

Swedes actually became more content with taxation from 1960 to 1980 despite the almost exponential increase in tax pressure during the period (Hadenius 1985: 362). Axel Hadenius's research showed that it was not taxation per se that Swedes appreciated, but the benefits provided by it.

This book acknowledges the importance of the questions raised by the fiscal sociology movement – the focus on informal institutions and history and taxations – but strives to get an even closer look by examining how a successful tax collecting authority works in practice; being there, talking with its employees, observing how they apply their knowledge and usage of software and other devices, reading the documents they write, seeing how they engage with taxpayers and so forth. These ethnographic questions could be slightly adapted to fit any study of a group of people; being there, talking with them, observing how they use their tools, studying what they produce, seeing how they engage with the outside world. It is what anthropology at its core is all about.

There are a few noteworthy anthropological studies of taxation that have indeed already been carried out. Building on anthropological holism, they show that the organization of taxation both reflects and maintains societal values. For example, Janet Roitman has examined the relationships forged through taxation in the Chad Basin, Cameroon, and demonstrated that they cannot be separated from the development of broader economic relations. She shows how tax evasion and the development of the political terrain have both resulted from French colonization. By applying the concept of 'tax-price', Roitman shows how Cameroonians simultaneously became consumers and taxpayers (2005). The French introduced the colonial currency CFA that became a source of European wealth as a result of colonial trading while simultaneously creating tax subjects. People who trade make profits that can be subject to tax; knowing that they are subject to both market exploitation and tax, they also find ways to avoid it. In Roitman's words 'conflicts over regulation and redistribution mean taking issue with the very rules that organize and govern economic life, such strife can only be understood by examining the very conventions that give rise to the concepts and objects of an economy' (ibid.: 6). This is made explicit in the concept of tax-price; it simultaneously refers to CFA as both a means of exchange as well as a valuation rule.

Concentrating on the efforts performed by a tax collecting authority in the Adamawa Province of Cameroon, José-Maria Munoz shows how this authority tries to create taxpayers of individuals and businesses (Muñoz 2010). The preferred tax is on wealth and as livestock makes up the lion's share of people's wealth it is livestock that is subject to tax. Muñoz point out that we cannot understand 'tax effort' only by looking at how the state tries to control taxpayers' activities or through a tax office's administrative efficiency. Taxation, or the avoidance of it, must be viewed through a historical gaze of what has value. In Cameroon, tax avoidance has been described as a cat and mouse game (cf. Braithwaite 2002) where people are trying to hide what the tax offices ought to find – in this case with reference to how people manage their cattle, how they document their stock and the way their wealth, in this case cattle, is transacted.

Both these studies see taxation practices and tax compliance from an anthropological perspective. They show the problems taxation regimes confront and depict a larger picture than the legalities of a tax system or its economic outcome. It can be proposed that taking account of historical arrangements – what is seen as having value, how this 'what' is exchanged, who is seen to benefit from these exchanges and people's response to them – make an impact on contemporary tax compliance in any given society.

Two other studies, from very different societies and times, direct the gaze to values held in society. Taxes collected and taxes spent have to be in accordance with those values in order to be seen as legitimate. Melville Herskovits (1952) shows how tax collection maintained a social structure in several places in West Africa. There was always a cost for the chief, king or government for ruling – a cost that had to be collected from some sort of surplus among the governed people. Societies with more complex political organization have a 'sharply differentiated system of taxation and public expenditure' (1952: 417). For example in the historical kingdom of Dahomey, taxes were collected in various ways but the way taxation was organized reflected values in society. Such 'taxes' could originate in various types of valuables: money, foodstuffs, cowries and cattle. All villagers had to bring taxes as 'gifts' to the king, but as he also was a villager even he had to pay the same type of taxes as his subjects. The message that all people were equal was conveyed when all could see what everybody else, including the king, contributed. Although stories from these preliterate societies cannot recall how much or the way taxes were collected (1952: 417). Herskovits argued that any ruler who wants to obtain legitimacy has to make sure that *all* contribute and that the 'gifts' are spent in a way that accords with the cultural values in any given society. The king could either give them to a group or to all ruled subjects to win loyalty or he could spend lavishly in order to enhance his status.

In contemporary society it is vital for any functioning tax system to be perceived as fair (Rawlings 2003). The Australian tax system at the beginning of 2000 was viewed as two-tiered, favouring the wealthy, yet most citizens regarded compliance with the system as an important social responsibility. In order to sustain compliance, it was therefore of the utmost importance that authorities pursued fairness and retained control over income subject to tax. Measures were taken to restrict income from escaping to overseas tax havens or to places where taxes were lower. Not surprisingly, his overarching argument for fair taxation is that all citizens ought to pay their dues and all citizens should be treated according to the same rules (Rawlings 2003: 291).

Although people might be unequal in the market and in their economic life, fairness and equality appear to be important tax collecting values, whether in contemporary Australia or in historical Dahomey. If you pay tax, everybody else seen as a member of society should also pay – including the ruler(s). This argument chimes loud and strong with the contemporary revelation of the Panama Papers and the following worldwide public outcry. Taxation has to be organized according to prevailing sociocultural values.

I end this short exposé of fiscal anthropologies with a study from one of the most economically equal nations in the world, Denmark. Ethnologist Karen Boll studied 'tax compliance' in Danish society. She approaches taxation as a set of practices and keeps both the 'economy' and the 'law' in the background. The outset for her analysis is the work performed at the Danish Tax and Customs Administration, SKAT, and the way it involves taxpayers – in this case small Danish companies. She describes how tax compliance is effected in practice in a variety of settings, but always as a laborious feat involving the active participation of auditors and taxpayers, and the knowledge, technology, rules and regulation and enforcement of these (Boll 2011, 2014a, 2014b). Her 'study therefore shows that the "source of government" in relation to tax compliance does not reside (only) inside the state but it is also the effect of a heterogeneous assembly of other actors and practices' (2011: 225) – what tax collectors do when they make citizens pay up (seemingly voluntarily). Her work, especially in the methodological sense, provided much inspiration for this book.

The foregoing studies of taxes and taxation and their implications for societal relationships and institutions underscore the importance of taking a broader, holistic approach if we are to understand *why* people pay tax (or avoid it for that matter). It does not need an anthropologist to say so: 'Taxation is intimately connected with the form of the state and the nature of the economy' (Daunton 2001: 6; cf. Heckscher 1935). However, a distinction between sociological and anthropological approaches to fiscal relations is worth making. To sum up, I see this study as exemplifying the latter for the following reasons. First, I see taxation creating relationships, as the focus is on the impact of taxation or more explicitly the perceived impact on society as we look at these practices from *within* the Agency. What type of relationship is taxation seen to create; what is its impact on society – and more explicitly on the taxpayers that constitute society

– deemed to be? Although the Agency is the place for this study, this is neither a study of the 'culture' of an organization or a bureaucracy per se, nor anthropology of policy. It can perhaps be seen as a slight shift of focus, but my aim is to pinpoint what the Agency and some of its employees actually do – their practices and the processes they undertake – when they try to understand society as a taxpaying entity and how society should be made to comply even more. This is about the knowledge the Agency creates and applies, affecting taxpayers' economic exchanges. Analysing processes aligns with the Agency's continuous aspiration for increased acceptance by Swedish taxpayers. In this quest it is not always successful, but the point is that the Agency also recognizes that the tax system is evolving. Behind the Agency's practices is always its concern about being seen as legitimate in Swedish society and that means reacting to events in society as well as continuously trying to ameliorate its own position (e.g., Skatteverket 2007b, 2013). From this perspective taxation does become an expression for an ongoing social relationship with society at large.

Second, my approach is curious and investigative, but also acknowledges that there are many ways to approach taxation and tax compliance. Taxation takes place at the nexus of law and economy. If we, inspired by Schumpeter, see a tax system evolving from and affecting social and cultural values in order to make people comply voluntarily, this means that both lawmakers and especially tax authorities need to make their actions legitimate. They have to understand the social and cultural implications of their actions and have to pay attention to what people think is, if not acceptable, so at least tolerable. In turn, we taxpayers have to accept the principles of tax legislation (Lodin 2007: 490) and the way taxation is implemented in practice (Björklund Larsen 2013c; Boll 2014a, 2014b). Although performed by a bureaucracy, it is the workings of a national tax system that is in focus – how the collectors practise it and how they see its (economic) impact on contributors/citizens. The insights from a legal perspective will, in this study, intersect with social studies of finance. A fiscal anthropology thus finds inspiration from economic *and* legal anthropology.

Third, for applying anthropological methods: this book is based on multisited ethnographic fieldwork (Falzon 2009; Hannerz 2006; Marcus 1995), following a report 'in the making'– wherever and whenever work was collectively done to it; well, almost – I did not after all have access to all instances, a point I will return to. In addition, the fieldwork was also performed in what can be described as a para-ethnographic perspective (Björklund Larsen 2013c; Holmes and Marcus 2006, 2008; Nyqvist 2008) (see below) in the sense that my informants were also researchers in their own right and used varieties of what can be called ethnographic methods but did not always acknowledge them as such. Their acquired data also included insights from the ethnographer studying them.

How to Study and Understand Knowledge-Making?

To study up close what knowledge this Agency applies and how this knowledge in turn is used to create compliance – shape taxpayers as it were – I followed one of their risk assessment projects. This approach has allowed me to acknowledge a holistic view on the Agency and to distil where and when certain values are pronounced while also retaining my original curiosity on how the Agency manages to be seen as legitimate in its practices and make us, the taxpayers, comply. How do they do it? How do they imagine a compliant Swedish taxpayer? Bear with me while I explain why this particular project was a good way in for looking closely at how the Agency produces and applies knowledge and how I studied it.

The Agency performs a number of these risk assessment projects yearly in order to address issues that put it at risk of failing in its duties and to collect the taxes as ordered by the Swedish Parliament (and more explicitly instructed by the Ministry of Finance). It is the Analysis Unit of the Agency that is responsible for the projects. These are mostly carried out by groups of analysts as a task force. This particular project concerned incorrectly claimed cost deductions among certain types of small corporations, here referred to as COENs (COmmercial ENtities). It was one of the unit's largest projects ever undertaken and grew well beyond its initial purpose. Apart from taking much longer than originally planned, it provided a good illustration of how a number of broader taxation issues are addressed within the Agency: how well it understands a particular problematic issue and how it informs taxpayers about it, the quantification and estimation efforts within the scope of such phenomena, and concerns about the impact on other citizens/taxpayers. The project can highlight the knowledge used to understand how the Agency views tax compliance in a broad sense.

The questions posed within the project were addressed through various 'field studies', as the analysts commonly call their research. The project collected information and created knowledge in many different ways and engaged many other departments within the Agency for their input, as well as decision makers on various levels and external providers. The project, and thus requests for analysis, knowledge and data, originated from the Analysis Unit to which the task force members belong, but was carried out at different localities, with each applying their method(s). Though this risk assessment project only involved a handful of analysts, who needless to say had an impact on the forming of knowledge, there were many others throughout the organization who had their say, including top management and the Director General. Through this risk assessment project I was therefore able to obtain a view of the broader workings of the Agency and the many aspects of how it works to understand society, and more specifically change taxation practices that are not complied with.

I followed this risk assessment project for its entire duration of three years: from its initiation, through the research phase, the writing of the report intermingled with presentations of its conclusions within the Agency, to seeing the report finally buried. I was not there full time but rather when work was done to it collectively. Although I am inspired by ethnographies following a 'thing' (Marcus 1995), I see the report rather as a thing in the making. Geographically, the project took me to four main localities. Foremost, I was at the Agency headquarters in Solna, a suburb of Stockholm, where I spent most of my time with the task force following physical and online meetings. They also invited me to the annual national analysts' meeting in Malmö where the task force collectively presented the almost finished project. Second, I conducted participant observation and interviews at RC, a private research consultancy, which conducted an extensive telephone survey. Third, I was introduced to the Agency's Random Audit Control department in the city of Örebro. Last, I was copied into all email correspondence between the task force participants throughout the project. My fieldwork took place when work was done collectively to the report.[22] The result is not *one* view but many competing and reinforcing views from within this bureaucracy of what is seen to make people comply, and not, with taxation.

It is thus what the Agency does in creating new knowledge that is in focus; the questions it poses; how they amass data to respond to these questions; and how they come up with answers. Each piece of collected data can be traced chronologically, since each document, field note and interview has its specific origin – the image of putting together a puzzle, to which the Agency used to refer in an earlier project about informal work (Skatteverket 2006a: 5, 2007a), is not really apposite. However, I find it hard to imagine a defined, set picture that makes up tax compliance; a picture that can be looked at to say that *this is* Swedish tax compliance from the Agency's point of view. Like Karen Boll in her (2011) study of Danish tax compliance, I am intent on avoiding the 'perspectivist' assemblage of a piecemeal ethnography ready to be seen, collected, transcribed, analysed, and written about.

There are thus two interrelated questions here. On the one hand I have an abundance of various material following this risk assessment project about how knowledge is made that needs to be made sense of, yet on the other hand this is not a seamless picture about a project at a successful tax authority. Presenting such an analysis would just be reifying attitudinal surveys (Skatteverket 2012, 2013) or stories from within (Stridh and Wittberg 2015). The report was, after all, buried, as the insights and conclusions of this project were not deemed publishable.

This is why I take inspiration from ANT (actor network theory) (Callon 1986; Latour and Woolgar 1986; Law 1992), which is perhaps not so much of a theory as a research strategy (Latour 2005). This 'theory' aims to identify actors that in different constellations make up knowledge that shapes our world yet without taking the constellations for granted. My motivations in studying knowledge-making about taxation through an ANT lens are numerous. Importantly, it allows me to retain my 'wonder' at how the Agency makes Swedish taxpayers comply while not taking *anything* as a given fact or for granted. ANT is at the outset agnostic about who and what makes action possible (Hardie and MacKenzie 2007) and starts out with a clean slate studying a given societal phenomenon where no specific scientific theory has an upper hand. This is also one of the reasons for the fierce criticism it has encountered (cf. Ingold 2008; Miller 2002). The chosen acronym ANT is playfully yet forcefully argued against in its perceived flatness (Ingold 2008); that all actors are 'there', having equal weight and qualities instead of being embodied within different powers. In theory, tax collectors certainly have a lot of power to exert, but can this fact alone explain a successful and legitimate tax collector? Many governmental tax collectors are often seen as powerful, but rampant tax evasion in many countries questions such power. In addition does contemporary tax compliance research suggest otherwise (see Chapter 1)? I want to give the Agency the benefit of the doubt and take the flatness as an outset and not as a result.

To take this multifarious explanatory stand in earnest means, at least at the outset, to recognize all the various things, theories and technologies used to make an economic action like taxation possible (cf. Callon, Millo and Muniesa 2007; Hardie and MacKenzie 2007).

The seminal work of Bruno Latour together with Steve Woolgar (1986) addressed practices in a biology laboratory; they showed that it was not only scientific theories that created new scientific knowledge (as references in publications might indicate), but that what went on in the laboratory's social world was also crucial when new scientific facts were created. Latour and Woolgar were in the lab; they saw what was going on and took account of all the different types of knowledge – even the most mundane ones. A range of ethnographically inspired studies at other sites followed, always emphasizing all issues, including sociocultural ones, which can be said to constitute knowledge. At the Agency, we will see how including internal systems and procedures (Boll 2011) – such as academic research and economic valuation models (Callon, Millo and Muniesa 2007), statistics, media stories, hunches and anecdotes and other tacit knowledge of various sorts (Elyachar 2012); and even the physical locations – (Murphy 2013; Zaloom 2006) matters when knowledge is created. It will be made apparent through this story that contemporary Swedish taxation practices are not possible without all the technical means that computers, Internet and various software programmes provide.

What makes taxation possible and what creates knowledge about it may from this perspective be many different things. All these new-found facts have to be related to something else to have impact. Latour, one of ANT's main proponents, has pointed to the theory's unfortunate choice of name; as a study of practices it is rather a worknet than a network. Regardless of whether we call the connections network, worknet or meshwork (Ingold 2008), it is the relationships between bits and pieces of knowledge that show what goes and what does not from the Agency's perspective when shaping Swedish taxpayers.

Such problematic findings were presented in the risk assessment project's resulting report as to why it was decided as not being fit for external publication. I argue that the report was definitely not a failure, as the Agency learnt from its insights. Deemed unpublishable, it rather makes explicit that knowledge that is problematic is impossible to make public. Therefore '… to regain some sense of order, the best solution is to trace connections *between* the controversies themselves rather than try to decide how to settle any given controversy' (Latour 2005: 23). I have therefore chosen to follow this project and the report 'in the making' to make explicit the insights that are problematic and how they came to be seen as such.

This leads to my final point of being able to gather all disparate knowledge that shapes Swedish taxpayers into one frame. Taxation is an interpretation of law that influences citizens' economic practices. Although there is only one ANT-inspired study about taxation practices (Boll 2014a, 2014b), there are ample studies of knowledge-making in the economy, a few in the law[23] and also some studies of methods like surveys, which play an important role in this project.

To start with things economic; an ANT perspective precludes the economy as an existing domain ready to be investigated (Çalışkan and Callon 2009). Instead it acknowledges how various things and theories in networks can be seen as constructing economic matters: how exchanges are carried out and settled; what the compensation consists of; who participates; the resources they have and by what means the exchanges are carried out; and how ideas and research about the economy make an impact on its functionality (e.g., Callon 1998; Garcia-Parpet 2007; Hasselström 2003; Kjellberg and Helgesson 2006; MacKenzie 2008, 2009). Thus economic theories are not a description of how we should understand economic matters, but are in themselves vehicles for change for how economic practices are done; for example these theories both shape and make the market and market practices (e.g., Callon 1998). Using economic theories sometimes had political motives and was sometimes unintentional, but there was a unanimous faith in approaching economic occurrences in society in this way. Knowledge from the discipline of economics was thus performed in the reality it was seen to model. Performed thus meant uttering and doing something while it was simultaneously happening (cf. Cochoy 1998; Kjellberg and Helgesson 2006; MacKenzie 2008).

Perhaps 'mutate' is a better way to describe the application of research models to reality (Neyland 2013)? The economic models are never used exactly as intended; instead they take on a slightly different appearance in practice for a number of reasons. To know how something performs we need to know the state of it prior to it being performed, and how other practices are used in coordination with the economic knowledge used – that is how the model is applied in practice, so that we can exactly predict the outcome of such a model, and how much of the reality a performative action accounts for. This is not hair-splitting and I find Neyland's questioning economic models as performative most helpful; if they are seen to mutate the human capacity is taken more seriously and this is regardless of whether we humans talk or engage with things and tools. For example, economists seldom see their models as explaining everything. At the very outset for this discipline, making models of certain economic practices in society is vital in order to explain or predict the result of such practices. Economists have a realist approach to occurrences in the world and model them accordingly. The problem is that the models the discipline of economics provides have for many different reasons and in very many places been made into the truth, yet they are very seldom performative as an exact copy, but applied with provisions. As already hinted above, the task force applies many other types of knowledge within this risk assessment project: newspaper articles, personal anecdotes, colleagues' tales, etc. Regardless of whether these are seen as true facts or complete fables, they are part of what shapes their risk assessment project and thus also the knowledge emanating from it. To know the origin of such knowledge in order to see it 'perform' or 'mutate' is impossible.

As been hinted above there are many origins of the knowledge used. Perhaps it is better to think of the dispersal of ideas in terms of 'creolization' (e.g., Hannerz 1997). Obviously the concept originates in the mix of languages spoken in the Caribbean islands and has a heavy colonialist connotation. The very idea that no culture is 'pure' but is always subject to influences resonates well with what is of concern at the Agency. Although it has the law on its side and the governmental/state power to enforce it, the Agency has to listen very carefully to what people find legitimate to tax, given the room for interpretation of tax laws. As Ulf Hannerz proposes: 'a creolist view is particularly applicable to processes of cultural confluence within a more or less open continuum of diversity, stretched out along a structure of center-periphery relationships which may well extend transnationally, and which is characterized also by inequality in power, prestige and material resource terms' (Hannerz 1997: 14). Creolization underlines a process; knowledge is never static or well-defined but open to influences from new arrivals, as are the Agency with regards to what makes people comply with taxes. Perhaps we can see existing research knowledge performing – that some of the models are mutating when they are applied to reality, but this is mostly creolized, creating new insights when combined and intertwined with other types of knowledge. This is not a study of an economy where taxation is performed according to a set formula but of the processes through which behaviour, organizations and institutions are constituted as being taxable.

Taxation is also an interpretation of law that influences citizens' economic practices. If anthropology has recently ventured into finance and taxes it has also been drawn into studying law, not least as an element of how taxation in democracies operates. In *The Making of Law* Bruno Latour (2010) tackles law as a crucial type of knowledge that makes up contemporary society. He describes a location where the law is not read to the letter – the French Conseil d'Etat [24] (Council of State) – and shows us that the legal reasoning between the advisers who work there is precedence-based. What appeared especially important in Latour's analysis was the view of law as a world of its own in society. 'One should be able to say that law is there at birth. It precedes us and survives us' (ibid.: 276) and he adds 'Yet it says nothing, informs us of nothing; we have to do all the work' (ibid.). The making of law is in this view the practice of it. Although tax law is not directly the object of my study, it is always there and is referred to and obeyed yet in certain circumstances subject to interpretation. Law constitutes one type of knowledge, and this type of knowledge will have the upper hand when specified in enough detail.

Latour's book is also a fine-grained ethnographic detail of law at work – or rather of the people who do the work. He makes us understand that inside the famous and much-adorned buildings in central Paris there are people working. There are real people who go about their duties, discuss the issues at hand, and blend a deep knowledge of the intricacies of law with prior decisions that shape the law; but who also have concerns for the everyday life of the citizens they rule. Although they express occasional disdain for 'common knowledge' (Latour 2010: 23), my overall impression of his ethnography is that different types of knowledge need to be blended in order to make a legal decision possible within the Conseil d'Etat, which is the highest authority in France for legal appeals. As you will see, there is a great deal of knowledge-blending at this Agency you are about to visit.

In addition *The Making of Law* has managed to reach a much wider audience than the cohort of legal anthropologists or ANT researchers. Through the ethnography at the Conseil d'Etat, Latour manages to give us a picture of how lawmaking is done in practice, an invaluable insight for all not being able to be there yet interested in aspects of law. It has been argued that Latour is not very helpful with either theoretical insights or analytical concepts (cf. Boll 2011), yet the description he provides is most valuable for all people that learn about or have to deal with decisions made at the Conseil d'Etat. My ambition is to provide similar insights through the study of the work among some employees at a tax collecting authority.

Finally, Latour reminds us of the eternal yet interpretative stance of law. After drawing on historical accounts and the very detailed ethnography of the 'ceaseless, patient, stubborn and pedestrian piece-working' (2010: 69), he concludes that the law is always there but we have to do all the work (Latour 2010: 242). This is a statement I will revisit, as I see the Agency is actually doing most, if not all, of the work with the law at hand. As a Swedish politician and academic rhetorically asked at a presentation of mine, 'perhaps it is at the Agency that tax politics is actually made?'[25] I am not sure how to respond to such a question, but in the Agency's interpretation of a fairly all-encompassing law, it certainly draws attention to what people find legitimate.

Indeed, whereas ANT emphasizes the potentially equal standing of actors making up networks (cf. Valverde, Levi and Moore 2005: 89; cf. Ingold 2008), what is interesting about law as a type of knowledge is its capability to make a radical change to a given issue. When contested cases are brought to court, a specific legal decision will precede any other knowledge (Latour 2010; cf. Riles 2010). A carefully moulded taxable/not taxable status for certain exchanges in society can change very abruptly when a court decision is made. Yet there are always some aspects of law that are subject to interpretation and the Agency certainly has the potential to make its own interpretations. So with the Swedish income tax laws, the Agency certainly does a lot of work on its own, although seldom all of it following Latour's claims.

Numbers are another particular type of knowledge. Numbers per se might be innocent, but when the new-found numbers relate to earlier findings we will see how such relations can make them problematic (Crump 1981: 77). Certain combinations and relations, or rather comparisons between numbers, unsettle the message the Agency wants to convey to citizens (see especially Chapters 3 and 4) and these numbers often derive from statistical calculations. Statistics has a particular status at the Agency; both as method and a range of knowledge that is frequently used and referred to by the analysts, also in this project. For some at the Agency, statistical data is even the very core of knowledge (Björklund Larsen, Johannesson and Thoresson forthcoming). If an analysis poses questions to which answers are not quantifiable in relation to other quantifiable data, for some it is knowledge not worth knowing. I would argue that although many employees at the Agency would adhere to the view that 'modern statistics is the strongest language of all' (Asad 1994: 78) in the sense that producing numbers according to approved statistical methods is convincing and reliable, this project also proved them wrong. Statistics, and the comparisons those numbers render possible, is needed if we are, in time and space, to reconstruct 'moral and material conditions for target populations' (ibid.).

Finally, my ANT approach is also emically inspired. Håkan Malmer, a retired veteran from the Swedish Tax Administration as well as participant of several governmental inquiries regarding taxation, emphasized that a tax audit is made possible due to five different components: the tax system and the inherent obligation of citizens to provide information; the authoritative capacity of the Agency; its human resources – (i.e., employees); technology; and how all these matters are organized (Malmer 2003: 50). He thus recognized that there are many aspects at play when trying to understand how the Agency in practice makes sure that citizens in their role as taxpayers comply with rules and regulations.

In sum, I find ANT a good approach to studying the making of meaningful knowledge at the Agency. The Agency's way of operating and creating tax compliance *is* heavily dependent on technical devices and ideas about what makes people pay tax – and avoid it. Yet anthropology also offers other tools, like the concept of creolization, to help understand the creation of knowledge I witnessed as part of the risk assessment project. The project we are about to follow exemplifies the Agency's many means to understand tax compliance among the citizens and is an example of how physical agency, technical devices and knowledge coalesce.

Tax Agency Employees at Work

Within the concept of physical agency is a human in full and it is important to pay tribute to a person's diverse capacities for action. For one, due to the Director General's intervention, the report was not published. Like the Agency that acknowledges that taxpayers make errors but can never say for sure that they are intentional or not, I can only suggest reasons for why he decided not to publish it, but I will never know for sure. As we will see, most of the Agency's employees that we meet throughout the book are genuinely interested in differing approaches to taxation. Research about taxation, tax avoidance and tax compliance is important for them, but so is understanding the driving forces as to why taxpayers actually do as they do. Even if I do not follow the Agency employees outside their workplaces (cf. Boyer 2008), I pay attention to their way of being, their different ontological capabilities, and how they influence each other in meetings. I can only bow to Boyer's manifesto attempting to know the humans behind the expert shield, follow their professional development and pay attention to the various forms of knowledge – not only the rationalist argumentation – they provide (Boyer 2008: 44).

A type of knowledge seldom recognized as such is the talk, anecdotes, stories and hunches from the media and everyday life, and this fieldwork provided many such examples. These play an important if not decisive role but are often taken for granted and seldom credited as knowledge on par with the more scientific, economic or legal references. In fact, the way the analysts told such stories resembled an ethnographic gaze. In other anthropological studies of experts in contemporary society Douglas Holmes and George Marcus grappled with similar issues (2005, 2006, 2012). They introduced the notion of 'para-ethnography' that draws inspiration from the historical roles of anthropologists but applies it to contemporary settings. Ethnographers aimed to understand aspects of 'cultures' among people living far away from themselves and their academic cohorts. These cultures often consisted of illiterate peoples that lived more or less secluded from other cultures and had very few, if any, opportunities or possibilities to understand ethnographers' society. These people had seldom travelled, never been where the anthropologists came from nor knew anyone who had. When anthropologists study experts operating in complex societies ethnographically, the outset is very different.

The concept of para-ethnography was introduced as a way to study experts; not in their entirety as social beings (cf. Boyer 2008) but in their professional role. It is a way to critically assess the type of knowledge professionals use and to at least indicate how to deal with, in my case, tax and taxation expertise built up over many, many years: in disciplinary education and by practical work experience. This anthropological study of the work of and values held and practised by taxation experts should not be a mirror, yet should acknowledge *all* the knowledge they apply. A para-ethnography moves emphasis from employee discipline epistemology to the 'anecdotal, hype, and intuition' (Holmes and Marcus 2005: 237). It is also a way to include 'common knowledge' (cf. Valverde 2003), such as stories, hunches and examples from the media and everyday life.

A para-ethnographic stance means that the knowledge the analysts invoke includes participant observation in the sense that they live in the society they attempt to understand. As we will see, they reflect on society in referring to friends and acquaintances and how they go about their daily economic activities when they infringe on issues that are of interest to tax compliance. The way the analysts in the core project group, here referred to as the task force, carry out their chores is thus a striking example in itself of an application of para-ethnography (Holmes and Marcus 2006: 35). Its members certainly make use of the disciplinary knowledge within which they are trained (economics, political science, management), and of previous research reports that have built up the Agency's knowledge of tax non-compliance as well as a few external research reports. But they also cite newspaper articles, refer to friends' practices (though perhaps not explicitly), take up examples of discussions at coffee breaks and in general try to keep up with what is going on in the society in which they live.

For example, Lars and Julia, two of the analysts who will be properly introduced in Chapter 1, had been to an international conference on tax research in August 2010 and met Benno Torgler, a well-known tax scholar. Their discussions are just one example of how Agency staff reflect on the different explanatory models offered of compliance and draw on their own 'ethnographic' experience. As Lars said:

> The classical model looks for individual behaviour, and tax compliance is explained as dependent on the risk of being caught and the consequences if caught. Then someone introduces morale, which is said to increase compliance among some people, whereas other people find satisfaction in getting away with cheating. What is lacking in this research is that taxpayers operate in different circumstances. Employed taxpayers have no chance to get away with non-compliance, as their employer pays the tax. Thus the risk of detection is 100 per cent. There is no way to avoid paying tax. And this view is what I miss.

According to Lars, Torgler recognizes that Swedes have a well-developed taxation system, but such a system is not present in the research he has done. And Julia added her view that for a start we have to define what the norms are; what is the culture we, and the taxpayers, inhabit?

Para-ethnography also takes into consideration my own (potential) impact on knowledge creation. An ethnographer can never be a fly on the wall (cf. Blomberg et al. 1993) and the analysts also read and referred to my earlier work (Skatteverket 2011b: 98–101), which was my admission to this otherwise fairly closed organization. From a naive positivist standpoint, this fieldwork would thus be considered contaminated. However, this fact points out a reality that many researchers of contemporary institutions and organizations have to address (Holmes and Marcus 2008: 98), as well as an awareness of (Swedish) academia's so-called third task.[26] My informants read and reacted to what my colleagues and I wrote and also made use of our presence when we undertook research. There were numerous directly posed questions during the meetings I attended and we had many informal discussions at luncheons and coffee breaks. They also asked for lectures and discussions about qualitative research methods, which even resulted in a course introducing social scientific 'tools' for all analysts at the Agency (Björklund Larsen, Johannesson and Thoresson forthcoming). Thus both a collateral (cf. Maurer and Mainwaring 2012: 182) and collaborative (Holmes and Marcus 2012: 127) type of knowledge can evolve when doing fieldwork among curious experts. In thinking about this study in terms of para-ethnography it resolves a number of issues concerning the various origins of data, including the presence of the ethnographer and his/her knowledge about tax issues.

There are thus many varieties of knowledge and ways to attain them. To take cognizance of all of them, yet acknowledge that certain set-ups of knowledge have precedence over others when affecting tax compliance in society, I return to ANT to pursue my analysis with the help of the concept of *agencement*. Certain combinations of diverse physical agency, technical devices and set-ups of all the types of knowledge hinted at above can create different agencement, 'arrangements endowed in the capacity of acting in different ways depending on their configuration' (Callon 2007: 320).

Agencement is often referred to as socio-technical, as it then comprises both 'human beings as well as material, technical and textual devices' (Çalışkan and Callon 2010: 9).[27] How this capacity can act depends on its configuration (ibid.) while not establishing precedence between different types of agency. Thus laws, ideas, knowledge, calculations (not forgetting the people applying these) are seen as having reflexive competencies and possibility for deliberation. This concept has sometimes been translated to technical arrangement or assemblage in English research literature. Although socio-technical agencement is a Frenglish expression, I will stay with it to keep the processual and shaping component that it provides. An arrangement seems more static and an assemblage quite loosely connected, whereas agencement underlines the activity (cf. Hardie and MacKenzie 2007: 57). To my mind it also remembers and recognizes whatever action has to deal with the never-ending changes in society. And these are changes that a tax collecting agency has to pay attention to in order to retain its legitimacy and keep compliance high.

Thinking with socio-technical agencement also teases out the collectivity in the actions. It is seldom one person or one thing acting alone that makes a specific impact. An employee collaborates but also pays attention to colleagues' views, what other stakeholders are up to and also, which is very important for the Agency, what society at large would think about its actions. And although a person needs to decide to put any technological device into action, at least at initiation, s/he needs it to perform the actions. As we will see, this collectivity is expressed, as employees mostly talk about the Agency as 'we' in action. Socio-technical agencement resists the temptation to contrast individual and collective action or to let a specific technique or knowledge take all the blame or credit for actions.

> All action is collective since it is distributed; what vary are the mechanisms for attributing the source of the action. The shape, content and architecture of the agencement, with equipment that facilitates the action to a greater or lesser degree, from a distance, decisively influence the modalities of attributing action. So does the inclusion of specific legal or regulatory texts that distribute responsibility or property. (Çalışkan and Callon 2010: 10)

One part depends on their own capacity to act, their knowledge about research and theories as well as about people's social practices and habits. In particular, agencement is here used to think about combinations of knowledge that impact tax compliance.

In following this project – all the applied knowledge, the usage of various technical devices and its resulting report in the making – I will explore why and how certain selection processes came about; why certain set-ups of knowledge have agencement and what that says about the Agency's view on tax compliance in society. My original curiosity about how this bureaucracy makes us comply goes well with Steve Woolgar's and colleagues' adequate reminder when writing this up: could it have been otherwise (Woolgar 2014: 330)? Looking back at this project, could it have taken other turns and posed other questions, or could other knowledge have been selected for the report? Could the content of the report have been otherwise and thus have been published? And why was it not? We will see throughout this book that certain set-ups of knowledge the project assembles are assumed to be more plausible than others and what the Agency does with this knowledge is always against a backdrop of previous knowledge and practices. In the end, it is, however, humans that decide what will be published or not. The socio-technical agencement makes explicit what can be communicated, as it has to enforce the Agency's strategies, and it excludes other set-ups of knowledge when it goes against established ideas about what makes taxpayers comply.

Secrecy and Anonymity

Anthropologists have often looked for a contained field, where supposedly both the people to be studied and the researching anthropologist find themselves in a natural, social environment (e.g., Gupta and Ferguson 1997). This somewhat naive and idealistic view of containers seldom exists in contemporary society. Instead I have followed this 'thing' (cf. Marcus 1995: 106–108; Mintz 1985), an intellectual work endeavour within an organization, the result of which was a report. As hinted, it is not the report in itself I am interested in, but rather the knowledge that was used in creating the report, the new knowledge that emerged from the project with the taxpayers in focus, and what of that knowledge could be publicly communicated given the Agency's aim to be seen as legitimate.

Following a thing, in this case a thing in the making, allowed me to visit many places where knowledge about taxation is practised and gathered. This risk assessment project, which eventually resulted in a report, although not published, is a thing that holds the fieldwork together. The field became multilocal, as it took place in different professional environments, each demanding various field methods (Hannerz 2001, 2006).[28]

The analysts were very helpful in providing me with material and included me in their communications and even recorded the occasional meeting when I could not attend. I can only express my serious gratitude to the task force members for their help in making all this material available to me and I hope this account makes sense to them. They were also subject to a quite intimate exposure of their minds when they let me follow their reasoning and deliberations, as well as their successes and setbacks. Arguments over issues are perhaps toned down due to my presence, but throughout my following of the project there were very few disagreements in these consensus-driven deliberations. However, I also know that for more disputed issues or in their communication with top management I was left out (see more about this in Chapter 4). This was, of course, for both political and personal reasons, and the curse of the participant observer is always to miss out on 'something'. One place to which I was at first denied access says more about the Agency's work as such than about the limits of observation.

My visit to the Random Audit Control office in Örebro was not easy to arrange. The confidentiality issue regarding my following the project had been debated on several occasions and at different levels within the Agency.[29] I mention this, as the confidentiality question takes place verbally at the very nexus of identifiable and physical contact between the Agency and their audited subjects. It is somewhat contradictory how searching for hidden transactions is not only an issue when dealing with the tax cheaters, as in my previous fieldwork. After all, they spoke willingly about their illegal yet licit purchases in order to justify them (cf. Björklund Larsen 2010). Also at their foe's (the Agency's) den, the same, questionable types of transactions were hidden from me.

This secrecy manifested itself in various ways. As a start, in the tax auditor Alice's office I visited, a set of binders (there was one for each entity subject to audit) had been turned so their spines faced the wall. Alice also ensured that I did not overhear any conversations taking place in the corridor outside the office. The reason, I found out, was not to protect the auditors, although they were, as mentioned, subject to quite intimate exposure of their thoughts when they let me follow their reasoning and deliberations, as well as their successes and setbacks. Second, I signed a confidentiality agreement, as all employees do, which prevents me from disclosing any type of sensitive information. Third, in Sweden information on income and taxes paid is publicly available;[30] however, any audit under way is strictly confidential until it has been completed, so any individual has a legal right to identity protection until a verdict is agreed upon and made public. Fourth, and in light of the above, I was told that it was out of the question for me to accompany the auditors on their visits to the selected entities, as audit visits are one of the most sensitive tasks the Agency performs. Having two visiting auditors can be seen as an intrusion, so bringing a researcher along posed too much of a risk. A compromise was finally proposed; since I could not follow a 'live' audit within the department I had to make do with being shown the guidelines and other material they used when auditing. To pursue the auditors' practices throughout an audit was thus not possible. I was, however, allowed to sit in on the discussions regarding specific cases, where the identity of the taxed person was not revealed.

Disposition of Book

To understand a legitimate tax system includes seeing how a tax collecting authority makes people comply. Such a study requires interpretation of the law *and* an understanding of economic issues, while paying attention to how this is done in everyday practices. This study is thus an ethnography of practices concerning economic matters while being an interpretation of a tax collector's – the Agency's – legal boundaries.

In this quest I followed how a risk assessment report came about: its birth, upbringing, disciplining and burial within the Agency. The ANT approach is chosen, as this is an investigation of knowledge that shapes our everyday life. It pays attention to how certain set-ups of collective knowledge – things, theories, technology – create agencement that can be used by the Agency to improve compliance. That the tax collecting authority in question is seen as legitimate in its practices means that it observes the values held by Swedish citizens. I argue that these set-ups of knowledge make explicit certain values that are said to govern the Agency's communications with taxpayers. By studying taxation practices and teasing out the socio-technical agencements that make contemporary taxation possible, we can better understand the values the Agency says it places on Swedish society.

Such values are thus seen as a result of work (cf. Dussage, Helgesson and Lee 2015) performed by the Agency. Needless to say, Agency valuations do not only concern economic estimates of exchanges made, but follow the initial proposition that the Agency is concerned with maintaining legitimacy within society. This legitimacy must be based on some sort of shared values with taxpayers on what type of exchanges can be and ought to be subject to tax. Seeing set-ups of knowledge as agencements will tease out problematic situations so that the law may be applied equitably, at other times it identifies tensions between laws and regulations. We will also find situations where the values this Agency publicly pronounces are invoked yet contested.

Throughout the book we will see situations where combinations of people, things and ideas pronounce values the Agency places on Swedish taxpayers. The study will show that these values have changed over time, differ in various contexts and are definitely *not* the same held throughout the Agency. The book aims to describe the knowledge this governmental authority applies in making citizens comply with taxation and how it works with such knowledge in order to be seen as legitimate in its practices.

The emphasis in Chapter 1, 'From Control to Compassion: A History of the Swedish Tax Agency', is twofold. First it depicts the Agency and its history, organization, structure and place in Swedish society. We will visit the Agency and its offices, and see the impact of place and space as an example of how design impacts social interaction (Murphy 2013; Zaloom 2006). Seeing a working place in this way contributes to the reader's understanding of 'the critical mechanics that drive Swedish politics and society but also the more general, often uneasy, relationships subsisting between people, power and the things of the world' (Murphy 2013: 129). It situates the Agency as the backbone of the Swedish welfare state.

Second, the chapter looks at different views on how tax compliance has been aimed for and also created. Historically, a tax administration collects taxes and verifies tax filings to ensure that the correct taxes are being paid. In the workings of this Agency, the role of such an audit control and what can be controlled (i.e., controllability) have been subject to debate. This is especially so regarding the seminal model proposed by Michael Allingham and Agnar Sandmo (1972) and the somewhat contradictory insights from Valerie Braithwaite and her colleagues in their cooperation with the Australian Taxation Office (ATO) (Braithwaite 2002). Both of these strands of research have provided inspiration for the Agency. The chapter looks at how these and other models influenced views on audits and what the implications were for the Agency's everyday practices. Inspired by this research on tax compliance, we will follow how the Agency has adapted its work over time in order to be seen as more legitimate. I discuss what tools and knowledge were used and how the Swedish tax law is applied regarding the controllability of income and expenses. The Agency's trajectory to greater legitimacy among Swedes could not have been achieved without the simultaneous technological development and the implementation of such solutions.

Finally, the chapter introduces the reader to the Analysis Unit and the people who work there. We will then look closer at risk assessment projects in general, their role within the Agency and more specifically to the project we follow in this book. It describes the questions and considerations that made this project about cost deductions for a specific type of commercial entity come into being and how the task force leading the project was formed.

In Chapter 2 'Talking with People: What Can We Learn from an Attitudinal Survey?', we will follow the work the task force first took on – creating and executing a survey. The chapter identifies how questions addressed within the survey were composed, how the survey was planned and performed by a call centre, how the results were used, as well as the type of knowledge an attitudinal survey can provide. We briefly step outside the realms of the Agency to visit a private RC hired to conduct a survey regarding taxpayers' attitudes towards cost deductions.

The chapter also follows the objections made by intermediate bodies representing civil society and the thresholds that had to be passed by the Agency to talk to, collect information about, and audit these commercial entities. Thus emerges a somewhat disparate view on the role of the Agency in Swedish society, one that is different from the rosy picture initially depicted in this book.

The third chapter, 'X Per Cent: The Birth of a Number at the Random Audit Control Department', addresses numbers. This chapter describes a random audit control that is the backbone of a risk assessment project and how it arrives at statistically secured results in terms of amounts and percentages. Such numerical results are seen as a reliable 'truth', but the practices of the Random Audit Control department show that there are many societal considerations influencing such a calculation. The claims to legitimacy are articulated within this department as a negotiation between values of reliable statistics and values held by the audited taxpayers.

First, this chapter describes how the taxpaying commercial entities were selected and what impact this sample made on the resulting numbers when the details were shaped in collaboration between the task force members and the managers of the Random Audit Control department. Second, the reader will learn what auditors look for in this random audit and how they do it, including which type of knowledge they apply. Third, the chapter describes how established praxis is articulated vis-à-vis tax faults – that is, every exception to the 'correct' tax, which includes cheating, evading, and plain ignorance. Finally, the chapter reveals how the quantitative results are interpreted and the conclusions drawn, and what these considerations say about what is at stake for the Agency.

The third chapter pays special attention to the role of statistics, which has a long history in Sweden. The discipline of statistics started out as a qualitative method but developed into sophisticated quantitative calculations (Sjöström 2002). This chapter reveals the qualitative aspects of performing statistics but also discusses it as a way of trying to control citizens' practices. This is contradictory to the intent of the random audit control method, which is seen as a democratic and equitable tool. In the Agency's audit practices we see how the values of Swedish society emerge, values that are based in the Agency's legitimacy claims. Theoretically, in this ANT-inspired approach, the legal interpretations meet economic knowledge. There cannot be any incorrect cost deductions, or any deductions at all for that matter, without considering the law.

It was a long and rather strenuous project and in the final ethnographic chapter, the fourth, we will see how the various versions of the report were greeted among the Agency's management. In 'To Publish or Not? Communicating and Legitimizing Concerns Regarding the Project's Results', the reader will meet the decision makers at various levels at the Agency and see how they receive and react to the 'new knowledge' provided by the numerical results and the interpretations of these that the task force presents. The results from this random audit control prove very problematic in contrast to the strategies laid out by the Agency in its quest for legitimacy. The chapter reveals how the management questioned the results, how and why the communication department feared the publication, and most importantly how the Director General stepped into the process – the objections he raised after reading the report in a very detailed and knowledgeable way, the drastic changes he proposed, and finally his decision to stop the report from being made public. The consensus-driven way of working stopped short here because the management was concerned about the Agency's legitimacy claims. This case also raises questions about the aim of analysis done at the Agency and for whom it is done.

In the concluding chapter, 'Values in Action', I will discuss the different values that have appeared throughout this book and return to the question of how the Agency tries to impact society. This chapter reviews not only how more than one type of knowledge is found in a particular locality or milieu, but how diverse types of knowledge compete and reinforce, make and shape, and support and contradict each other to provide new insights. In the end, concerns about the legitimacy of the Agency won out regarding what knowledge could be revealed to the public. The insights from the report that are applied internally are a different matter. Thus, in Sweden, the taxpayer and the Agency shape each other, but on different levels and in diverse ways.

Second, I argue that an equitable interpretation of the law brings out certain values, values that can be both enforced but also contradicted by the Agency's practices. All taxpayers should be treated equally, which is most easily done by an impartial reading of law and a commensuration of exchanges; yet some exchanges cannot be subject to tax, given the Agency's legitimacy claims. The chapter distinguishes what makes up exchanges that should not be considered for tax and thus be left, non-taxable, to the private realm and outside the Agency's curious eyes. The reasons given pose a dilemma for a bureaucracy that on the one hand aims to earn acceptability from all citizens in its actions, and on the other hand ought to ensure equitable treatment and thus investigate all expenditure and incomes in detail.

This book provides an account of the knowledge that shapes citizens' everyday economic behaviour – implicitly and explicitly. It is a story about Sweden that provides an example of how a state, working through one of its main bureaucratic institutions, cannot govern its citizens only by enforcing the law. In order to be found legitimate, such a tax collecting authority has to pay attention to values in the broadest sense, which has an impact on economic exchanges in society.

Notes

1. Press conference Los Angeles, late April as recorded in radio programme 'Ekot'. http://sverigesradio.se/sida/artikel.aspx?programid=1602&artikel=813302. Retrieved 25 April 2015.
2. Presentation Lennart Wittberg, Almedalen 30 June 2014.
3. Ingmar Bergman depicts both tax inspectors as altogether unattractive: they are plump, have impure complexions and dirty fingernails and wear flowery shirts (1987: 105).
4. Presentation Lennart Wittberg, Almedalen 30 June 2014.
5. This survey also found that governmental bodies that give out money are the least likeable – for example, CSN, the Student Aid, and Försäkringskassan, the Swedish Social Insurance Agency.
6. Willem van Schendel and Itty Abraham (2005) make the following distinction: licit, and its contradiction illicit, exist in the views of people, where illicit refers to behaviour that is not in accordance with common values and accepted norms. What is legal and illegal is negotiated within the state and/or political domains and refers to behaviour that adheres to, or breaks, formal laws (ibid.: 20).
7. http://www.worldvaluessurvey.org/. Retrieved 12 January 2016.
8. Statist individualism comes out of a deeply rooted and popular democratic view within society, based on the 'the Jante Law' rather than originating in people's natural rights of universal equality (Berggren and Trägårdh 2006: 43). This 'law' originates in a book about Danish (and more broadly, Scandinavian) culture written by Aksel Sandemose in 1933, *A Fugitive Crosses his Tracks* (English translation in 1936), and consists of ten commandments, all determined by jealousy and habits and ways of living in a small town, where contact with the larger world was restricted and social change slow. In common parlance, the Jante Law is unwritten but carries the message that 'thou should not regard thyself as better than any other'.
9. To nuance this homogenous picture of a trustful and law-abiding people, Swedes have also claimed that the state meddles too much in private concerns (e.g., Ahrne et al. 2003: 173).
10. The Social Democrats held power almost exclusively from the 1930s to the 1970s, with interruptions from right-wing coalitions during the last forty years.
11. This is despite the fact that the collection of revenue and the spending of it are kept strictly apart in Sweden.
12. Swedish welfare today basically consists of four different parts. First, there are public services, such as schools, healthcare and provisions for the elderly and children. Second, there is a compulsory social insurance system based on income from work. General subsidies connected with citizenship are a third component, and finally there are contingency-tested subsidies when all other sources are inadequate (Rothstein 2002 [1994]: 25).
13. A foreign-born colleague amusedly told me that his child had seen this on *Barnkanalen*, a programme for children on SR, the Swedish Public TV channel. February 2016.
14. Except for the debate about taxation on housing in the 1979 election.
15. http://www.ekonomifakta.se/sv/Fakta/Skatter/Skattetryck/Skatteintakter-per-skatt/. Retrieved 15 January 2015.
16. Many of the regulations and the principle of assessing income at source for tax goes further back, to kommunskattelagen, the municipal tax law of 1928. The background

for the centennial reform was a floundering tax system in need of structural change (Agell, Englund and Södersten 1996: 644; Sørensen 2010; Lodin 2011). For one, the previous system had evolved into very progressive income tax rates where the idea was that high-income earners should pay more of their income in tax. But with 80 per cent at the margins, it was a system that was seen to thwart work. The incentive to work more or aim for higher income did not provide much additional net income, and recompense for work came in the form of fringe benefits that were often tax free (Sørensen 2010: 62). Any increase in tax rates meant that all citizens were affected and so the high marginal rates also affected low-income payers. A patchwork of specific taxes as well as incentives had created many possibilities for tax arbitrage, or tax planning schemes, an activity that increased among taxpayers as the marginal rates rose. The increase and spread of many loopholes perhaps allowed this system to last as long as it did (Webber and Wildavsky 1986), but in the end it was seen mainly to benefit the very rich, a contradiction in terms of the original idea of who should pay for the Swedish welfare state (Agell, Englund and Södersten 1996: 644). The change of tax system meant that the principle of paying taxes according to ability was changed to the principle of uniformity; although for higher income earners a state tax *(värnskatten)* was introduced in 1995 (cf. Agell, Englund and Södersten 1996).

17. However, the outcome of the tax reform was not as hoped. The economic cycle turned downward in 1991, when Sweden was hit hard, and in order to balance the budget adjustments to the tax reform were directly implemented. Those additional fees were seen to distort the structure.
18. From an economic anthropological perspective, this law also directs our attention to the types of exchanges that ought to be subject to tax and which ones ought only to be socially constituted. If we see exchanges creating social relations this is obviously a dilemma for the good welfare state. When does a 'helping hand' become a market transaction?
19. For those readers not familiar with economic anthropology, here are just a few of the many, many interesting works on how to understand human economic behaviour in a variety of settings: Befu 1977; Callon 1999; Davis 1992; Granovetter 1985; Gudeman 2001; Holmes 2014; Malinowski 1922; Maurer 2005b; Mauss 1990; Miller 2002; Narotzky 1997; Roitman 2005.
20. Karl Polanyi (1944) proposed redistribution (the others being reciprocity and householding) as one of three mechanisms making up an economy prior to the arrival of the market economy and its supposedly rational economic behaviour. Although his emphasis in the analysis lay on the redistributive act, it is implied that the means were freely given to the ruler. People knew that taxes would eventually be of use for the entire collective and the redistribution was used to maintain the social structure within the group that contributed.
21. Compare this fact with the vast amount of studies on the welfare state. Yet these welfare states are financed by taxes, a fact that is taken for granted and is most often omitted from such studies. We can imagine the almost endless questions that a fiscal anthropological or sociological approach could pose.
22. More specifically, input also comes from my participation in about fifty meetings originating in the Analysis Unit, lasting from thirty minutes to two consecutive days. These make up more than 100 hours of recorded and transcribed deliberations of task force discussions and manifold meetings with the analysts and various colleagues: tax auditors and managers and sometimes also outsiders from academia, as well other governmental agencies and external corporations that were invited to participate.

In addition to the participant observation, I followed the analysis work and saw it progress into various versions. I have read most of the research material, background reports and written communication between the analysts, as I was copied into almost all emails. The content of these emails varied, from invitations to meetings, long discussions about specific topics, and notes from meetings summing up the conclusions and next steps to take. With this material at hand, I can present employee views from within this bureaucracy that differ on taxation practices and the impact they have on society and taxpayers. The work of a tax collecting authority is regarded as a relational phenomenon and as such an achievement and the effect of an assemblage, or network, of various different actors. To explore certain issues and events more specifically, I conducted more or less formal interviews with about twenty employees and engaged in numerous discussions at lunch and at *fika* (coffee breaks) throughout the fieldwork.

23. I aim to sketch if not a bridge then at least the hazy contours of one between the work within social studies of finance and Bruno Latour's view on law as the practice of it.
24. Conseil d'Etat is a body of the French national government that acts both as the legal adviser of the executive branch and as the supreme court for administrative justice.
25. Comment made at a presentation at the Institute for Future Studies (IFF), 26 October 2011.
26. The university's responsibility to share and disseminate research insights, apart from the more recognized tasks of teaching and research.
27. Socio-technical derives from Michel Callon's work with John Law on hybrid collectives (1997).
28. As fieldwork, it could be said to be a type of 'polymorphous engagement' (e.g., Gusterson 1997: 116) that takes me wherever the project is professionally carried out. In contrast to the approach by Gusterson, who tried to discern the work among scientists in American nuclear weapons laboratories, I was invited to follow the project at the Agency.
29. Those involved in the debates were the project coordinator, the head of the Analysis Unit, the head of the Random Audit Control department, and a legal expert at another regional office.
30. This means that, for example, anyone can visit their local tax office and use the public computer to access income statements as well as tax payments. The tabloids often make use of this information, listing the 100 highest paid individuals in 'your municipality' as well as publishing other, similar rankings. These rankings often make the headlines in order to increase sales, leaning on the law of Jante.

Chapter 1

From Control to Compassion

A History of the Swedish Tax Agency

If the tax collector is not a bore, his historical role is often that of the evil guy. He (seldom a woman) is a greedy misanthrope without any human feelings, only occupied with extracting as much money as possible from citizens. The more destitute a person is, the more he seems to rake in. We have seen the rotund Sheriff of Nottingham, the city's tax collector, in a shiny outfit, confidently knocking on the door of a small dwelling. A poor workman in rags opens the door. He leans on a pair of crutches and excuses himself, as he is well behind in his work. And so are his tax payments, the sheriff adds with a grin. As the workman limps away, the sheriff hears the rattle of a few hidden coins. His grin widens and he offers to help the poor man get into his rocking chair. When he has sat down, the sheriff takes the workman's plastered foot and with a sneering smile pulls his leg up so that the few coins trickle down into his fat, collecting hand. Just to make sure nothing is left, the sheriff hits the plastered foot – needless to say it hurts – and the last coin goes the same way as the others. Although from a Disney movie, this illustration mirrors our perception of the historical tax collector – a ruler's mean and often corrupt subordinate who while executing his duties represents the worst in human behaviour. Either he follows the rules to fulfil the wishes of the ruler by any available means in order to reach the taxation goal and /or he retains a share for himself. Regardless, the tax collector is a person who bows to the powerful and has nothing but disdain for the poor. Exercising his duties, he comes across as inhuman.

Illustration 1.1 Francis Ward in 'Robin Hood', July 1919.

The humanity is depicted differently with a contemporary tax collector. Here is a nitpicky bore, difficult to identify and remember. It is someone to avoid by all means at social events and you would feel very sorry for yourself if placed beside such a tedious person at a dinner party. It is therefore no coincidence that in David Foster Wallace's *Pale King* (2011), the astonishing novel on contemporary irksome and undignified behaviour, the focus is on a local branch of the U.S. IRS (Internal Revenue Service). There, employees are dressed in bland clothes with, for men, an obligatory tie in similarly nondescript colours, whose knot is never untied. They seem in the same way tied to their desks and blend easily into an equally bland environment. Their daily work tasks of control and audit procedures take away any remaining human feelings and dignified behaviour. These tax collectors are inherently prosaic, lacking in personality and initiative to start with, and seem trapped in a true Weberian iron cage (1978) in different shades of grey. The book ends with the newish employee subsiding into a different office, an office as difficult to depict as his previous one at the IRS, but probably a psychologist's, or the like. He needs help.

Regardless of how the tax collector is illustrated – whether s/he is depicted as greedy and amoral or as a rational machine – s/he is not viewed as charming and compassionate. In what follows I will introduce the governmental administration where Swedish tax collectors work – and actually like to work.[1] We will gain insights into how the Agency's fiscal duties have changed simultaneously with changes in Swedish tax law. Although it is a sketchy background, its aim is to present how the Agency has developed into one of the most revered governmental Agencies among the Swedish population today.

The emphasis in this chapter is threefold. First it describes the Agency: its history, organization, structure and place in Swedish society. The reader will first pay a visit to the Agency and its offices. The physical impact of place and space is acknowledged as an example of how design impacts social interaction (Murphy 2013; Zaloom 2006). Seeing a workplace in this way contributes to the reader's understanding of 'the critical mechanics that drive Swedish politics and society but also the more general, often uneasy, relationships subsisting between people, power and the things of the world' (Murphy 2013: 129). It situates the Agency as the backbone of the Swedish welfare state, in its physical as well as invisible presence.

I then proceed to look at how the Agency works, emphasizing its role in the control and creation of tax compliance. Historically, its task seems simple; a tax administration collects taxes and controls and audits tax filings to ensure that the correct taxes are being paid. This chapter discusses what tools and knowledge have been used and how the Swedish tax law is applied regarding the controllability of income and expenditure. In the workings of this Agency, the role of audits and what can be controlled (i.e., controllability) have for legal reasons been subject to debate due to the law.

Third, the chapter summarizes ideas that are said to make taxpayers comply – research that provides and provided inspiration for the Agency. The chapter looks at how these and other models influenced views on audit and compliance and what the implications were for the Agency's everyday practices. Inspired by research on tax compliance, we will follow how the Agency has adapted its work in order to be seen as more legitimate. Finally, the chapter introduces the reader to the Analysis Unit, the work it performs and the risk assessment projects and their role within the Agency. We will see what questions and considerations – about cost deductions for a specific type of commercial entity – helped this project come into being and how the task force leading the project was formed.

A Very Brief History of Swedish Taxation

The first time it was noted that taxes were being collected on a more organized basis in Sweden was during the thirteenth century (Odén 2008: 3). The aim was, as elsewhere, to finance the King's army and the warfare quests it undertook. Although some cash could be collected, the bulk was paid in kind: butter, oxen, grain, fish and hides. Already from around this time there was a difference between on the one hand the yearly taxes and on the other hand *bevillningar*, taxes extracted when needed – a difference that continued until modern times (Borg 2008). Taxes in the Middle Ages consisted mainly of what could be had from farms or what of value could be extracted from beneath the soil. Anything in the ground or bedrock was seen as property of the king, whereas what grew in the soil belonged to the person owning the land.

The ground tax (*grundskatter*) – tax that is based upon owned property – was instituted quite early on. It was made possible when the enterprising King Gustav Vasa in the sixteenth century introduced *jordeboken*, a book where all taxes collected were noted (Ekman 2003b: 72). He called this tax *jordeboksräntan*, as he saw such tax as interest; people who lived on the land that belonged to the king ought to pay interest or rent. During his reign, he actually reverted to an increasing levy of in-kind tax that was contrary to what went on in other European countries at the time (Odén 2008: 7).[2] The monetary economy among Swedes was underdeveloped compared to other European countries. In the few

Illustration 1.2 The bailiffs were seen as harsh and extorted the locals (author translation). From Olaus Magnus 2010 [1555, 1909], *Historia om de nordiska folken*. Sala: Gidlunds förlag, p. 355.

records that exist, focus is on the amount of taxes and not on how they were collected. Yet Gustav Vasa seems to have understood that in order to tax, one has to know what can possibly be extracted. Gustav Vasa is thus an early example of a ruler who knew his subjects and could also tax them (Crump 1981; Miller and Rose 2008; Porter 1995). Knowing how much people owned was a rough but still robust way of extracting a sort of fair tax and collecting it in kind quelled most complaints (cf. Odén 2008: 9).

Although the control, collection, organization and levels of the ground tax changed throughout the centuries, it remained in use until the beginning of the twentieth century (Löwnertz 2003). The ground tax was difficult to reform, as it was intimately connected to the defence of the country; for example soldiers were given a small estate (*torp*) instead of salaries. All farmers throughout Sweden were grouped into *roter*, which were obliged to provide these small estates for soldiers. The fiscal duties were thus not always directly in the hands of the state. Instead it delegated them directly to small communities, one efficient way to collect and spend taxes in kind. This example of providing a living for soldiers is just one illustration of how the fiscal aim at the time was almost exclusively to finance the wars in which Sweden was engaged. It was not the only tax though; in peace time the tax was lighter, but the burden grew when disturbances occurred among geographic neighbours or when Sweden directly participated in wars. Taxes were sometimes calculated based on heritage or on wealth.

The fiscal aim already had an early impact. For example, tolls and customs excises were introduced over the centuries in order to steer trading practices and control markets. Taxes could be extracted on luxury consumption, such as the tax on glass windows, which was introduced in 1743 (Löwnertz 1983). Such taxes were smart and efficient, as glass windows could not be hidden. The king also recognized that income differed between the regions, so, for example, a glass window was taxed at a higher rate in Stockholm than in the countryside. Other taxes and tolls were added through the years; the list is very long (see p. 10 on etymology) and provides an interesting insight into both old Sweden and the many ingenious ideas about extracting income almost exclusively from the poor. Needless to say, the poor did not always appreciate this fiscal attention.

It was not until 1869 that the government decided that taxes solely had to be paid with money. This came some years after townships, municipalities and regional boards had been given the right to tax in order to finance basic education and provision for the poorest (Borg 2008). Sweden was, at the end of the nineteenth century, a country where industrialization was well on its way; an increasing population of city-based industrial workers started to demand rights, and public funding was heavily dependent on indirect taxes (Löwnertz 2003: 65), which have the harshest impact on low-income earners (ibid.: 59). Taxes collected amounted to 8 per cent of GDP (gross domestic product) and half of this amount came from tariffs (Tarschys 1988: 5), mostly from customs and taxes on the production and sales of *brännvin* (potato schnapps). What the land provided was still the foundation for taxation, although the economy was increasingly driven by industry and manufacture. Industrialization created new challenges in terms of demands for very basic welfare services (Borg 2008: 7). The time was thus ripe for changes in tax legislation and taxation practices.

In 1903 the first national income taxation law came into effect. From now on the basis for taxation was explicitly income, which for the majority of the people came from work. This is still the case; income tax today provides for almost two-thirds of all tax paid. The introduction of income tax was followed in 1909–10 by at least a paper reform of progressive taxation (Löwnertz 2003: 69). Both these institutions survive to this day although the content and the practice have been subject to many changes throughout the years. However, in order to tax work there is a need to know how much people earn. With jordeboken, rulers knew the land citizens owned and used, which provided the basis on which to calculate the ground tax. With the much needed change to tax income from work instead of owned land, the state needed to know the income for all who worked. Simultaneous with the introduction of national income taxation in 1903 came the duty for all citizens to declare their yearly income (*allmän självdeklaration*).[3] The aim was obviously to get a more detailed specification from each *skattskyldig* (tax indebted individual) while simultaneously increasing the controls to monitor whether or not proper tax had been paid.

The control mechanisms have obviously changed over the years. Audit hardly existed and formerly there were harsh sanctions if the tax declared was proved wrong (Malmer 2003: 28). With the introduction of income taxation in 1902, the diverse monitoring institutions of the time were made more efficient and in 1907 they became one, entitled *taxeringsnämnd* (the taxation board). Each district had one (Ekman 2003a: 12) and most Swedish municipalities had at least one district. These taxation boards existed for most of the last century; but the constitution changed over time as well as the power to appoint the board members.[4] Over the years the taxation boards developed from being a truly lay body to being increasingly staffed by experts. This had implications for monitoring practices. For most of their existence, the boards relied upon personal knowledge of taxpayers. Needless to say, the quality of the control work of these boards varied; from not being knowledgeable enough about economic matters to executing personal vendettas by checking enemies' statements with overt exactitude. However, the main criticism against the tax boards was that the system strained gnats and swallowed camels (Ekman 2003a: 19). Taxation boards finally disappeared in conjunction with the centennial tax reform in 1991,[5] having been made redundant after the simplified tax return was introduced for all in 1987. Instead came *skattenämnder*, tax boards that handled issues that had been contested by taxpayers. Members of a tax board were elected, but an employee from the tax authority chaired it. The tax boards could be said to reflect a qualitative turn for taxation; from the taxation boards' legal verification of faulty amounts, to the tax boards' focus on why the amount was incorrect (Malmer 2003: 50). However, since 2012 these boards have also ceased to exist and have been replaced by specially qualified tax auditors within the Agency, who handle these contested cases.

Now, however, not all taxpayers complied; for those who did not register their tax returns, or who were seen by the taxation boards to have understated their income on their returns, *skönstaxering* (discretionary assessment) could be used as an alternative. It has been described as somewhat of a poker game (Malmer 2003: 41); it was not unusual for a taxpayer to avoid stating his income, claiming that the bookkeeping records had been stolen from the car, eaten by the dog or disappeared in other ways and instead await the estimated tax amount from the tax authorities. If the proposed tax was higher than the actual income suggested, s/he could appeal stating that the bookkeeping records had reappeared. If the tax amount proposed by the authorities was less, well, it was a winning hand. Discretionary assessment is still applied by the Agency if the annual tax return is missing. Approximately 150,000 taxpayers considered their yearly return in 2011 to have been subject to disadvantageous discretionary assessment.[6]

Although the creation of the taxation boards took care of tax at the local level, prior to 1971 Swedish taxation was divided among several administrative entities. Following a decision by the Riksdag, the Swedish parliament, in 1971, several governmental agencies that previously handled different taxes[7] were merged into one – Riksskatteverket or RSV, the National Tax Agency (Ekman 2003b: 76). This new organization consisted of a headquarters and four regional offices and became especially responsible for the audit of corporations that had activities in different regions. The reorganization did not mean much for the actual control and auditing work. However, the local tax administration offices that emerged could now assist the tax boards. Emphasis was still on the audit of personal income (Malmer 2003: 42) and calculations were often made manually. Håkan Malmer recalls that when he started out at the RSV audit department in 1972 he was given two pencils and one eraser (ibid.: 43), materials that were, however, subject to being replaced when worn out.

The RSV now had overall responsibility for taxation in Sweden, but the daily tax administration was until 1987 part of *länsstyrelsen* (the provincial council). With scattered institutions on diverse governmental levels, much effort went into the coordination of work between the different tax authorities.[8] A reform was long overdue and came after the internal so-called Plan-projekt report that stated vital issues in need of change. Insights from this project ordered the future organization and work tasks of what became the Swedish Tax Agency (Skatteverket).

There were four official issues that precipitated the reorganization. First, everyday tax administration needed to be part of the RSV and not the responsibility of the provincial government. Second, citizens had to deal with a difficult and time-consuming annual tax return form that proved similarly difficult and time consuming to audit. Third, simplification and modernization of the laws that steered taxation were long overdue. Fourth, actual audits needed to be undertaken by professional employees and not by the appointed lay tax boards (Ekman 2003b: 78). A fifth issue, not mentioned at the time but understood in hindsight, was that taxation practices needed to be applied in the same manner throughout Sweden; citizens should receive the same treatment and be taxed in the same way regardless of where in Sweden they lived (Björklund Larsen 2013c: 214). The time was ripe for yet another organizational change, this time even more thorough than the previous one in the early 1970s.

It was finally time to gather all Swedish taxation into one structure. The 120 independent local offices were thus reorganized into independent agencies, one for each province but all answering to one head office. This decision took effect during 1991–92 (Malmer 2003: 50). Citizens now had one place of contact for all their tax issues, a 'one-customer relation' (Ekman 2003b: 80). In addition, the quality of audit was upgraded by introducing hierarchies among auditors; an experienced auditor could now be promoted to tax auditor.

At about the same time the Agency was merged into one national organization in 1991 the 'centennial tax reform' was agreed upon. This was a huge makeover of the entire tax system (as was described in the Introduction). To repeat, one of the new tax law implications was that all exchanges of work/exchanges of services having value were deemed to constitute income – regardless of whether the compensation consisted of money, a return service or gifts in kind. This encompassing approach obviously leaves room for interpretation (Skatteverket 2006a: 145) and everyday interpretation was, and is, left to the Agency. So the Agency has to do if not all the work (cf. Latour 2010: 273) then most of it (there are court decisions that overrule praxis at the Agency) due to this all-encompassing law.

Buildings as a Force of Form

Before we are presented with ideas about tax compliance escalating at the Agency and we walk into the Analysis Unit and become acquainted with the people who participated in the risk assessment project this book follows, we will in this trajectory also take note of the environment in which taxation takes place. Like the etymological ventures, the buildings also add to the story of how the Agency has seen its role in society over the years and how it embodies a very Swedish image (cf. Murphy 2013). The following few extracts are from Stockholm where the HQ is located and where most of the ethnography has been performed, but we will eventually also become acquainted with the local office in Örebro (Chapter 3).

The Stockholm tax authorities resided for many years in a high-rise building that could be said to embody the modernist turn Sweden took in the late 1950s. It was given the Swenglish nickname Skatteskrapan (the tax-scraper). The architect was Per Hedqvist, who was inspired by Mies van der Rohe's U.S. high-rises and Italian office[9] constructions. With its twenty-four floors it was not only the highest building in Sweden but the highest in Europe, a record it held for five years.

Illustration 1.3 Skatteskrapan, view from Bondegatan, Stockholm. Photo by Holger Ellgaard.

The scraper was the first of its kind with 'curtain wall facades'. As the name implies, this is a non-structural covering of the facade; a curtain designed to keep the main structure untouched by the weather. The 'curtains' are made of lightweight material such as glass or aluminium, although the first varieties were made of iron. When glass is used, natural light can penetrate deeper into the building. Yet the curtains also keep out inquisitive glances. It is perhaps no coincidence that such an imposing building was the headquarters for the Swedish tax authorities – the creation and enthusiasm for building the welfare state, and transforming old and decrepit city districts, was high in the 1950s. Located in the heart of Södermalm, a former working-class neighbourhood of Stockholm, and constructed in the shape of a cross, Skatteskrapan can easily suggest a Lutheran ethic of work, as tax on income makes up the largest part of

Illustration 1.4 Skatteverket headquarters, Solna.

Swedish taxes. This imposing skyscraper, fifty metres higher than any of the surrounding buildings,[10] was said to incorporate the gaze over if not all Swedes then at least over many Stockholmers. So not only is Skatteskrapan surveying the city of Stockholm, in its design it is also impenetrable from the citizen's view; by height and by construction. 'We see you' seems to be the message that auditors and controllers working inside it silently communicated.

For many years Skatteskrapan's address, Götgatan 78, hosted an almost party-like event on the eve of the annual tax return date. Excitement rose as the clock moved towards midnight. We can speculate about the reasons for such a party feeling; I doubt that the general feeling was a celebration of the Swedish welfare state, but rather one of sheer relief of finally having handed in the return.

So what does the move in the mid 2000s to an adjoining but less glamorous building, and since 2013 to Solna, a suburb of Stockholm, indicate? The Stockholm regional office is now almost seamlessly incorporated within the HQ, yet another sign of the Agency's national consolidation. When one wanders the corridors in this building complex the only visual change from regional 'Stockholm' offices is the colour of the carpet.

In Solna, the Agency occupies almost an entire city block as well as a large building next door. According to Agency lore, when the building was under construction in the late 1960s as a factory for light industry, Gunnar Sträng, one of the architects behind the reorganization of the Swedish tax authorities and the Minister of Finance at the time, passed by in a car. He apparently exclaimed 'this is what I want for headquarters' and for Mr Sträng, being who he was, the state subsequently acquired the construction site and the half-finished building was adapted for office work.[11]

When I followed the risk assessment project, the Stockholm office had not yet been established in the new offices and there were only about 1,000 employees in the old interior layout. The initial purpose of the building was still apparent, as the floors sloped and there were pieces of wood and cardboard, thin books or other sorts of supports under many bookshelves to prevent them from falling over. Evening out the slanting floors would have required so much floor filler that the building would have collapsed under its weight. The original purpose of the building, its location in a former industrial area, and the red brick facade common for factories, seemed all the more fitting, as two-thirds of all Swedish taxes collected derive from salaries.

In this building the physical meetings of the task force take place. Either its members convene in a meeting room at HQs or meet up over the internal online meeting system to which all Agency offices are attached. I am picked up at reception where there is a pre-printed visitors' badge with my name waiting for me. After introducing myself and naming my host I am given this badge and admitted by the security guards. I am then made to wait in a well-lit and open visitor's area. From the quite dark, narrow and basement-like reception desk area, the atrium unfolds to give an impression of space and unlimited thinking. However, after only five flights up, the glass ceiling abruptly intervenes. As a result, the initial impression of limited space is quite fleeting and quickly changes to the reality of an enclosed space, surrounded by the same red brick walls that make up the atrium. It is a noisy environment. Employees and visitors pass, alone or in groups, with folders or the occasional laptop or iPad tucked under their arms. A door is clicked open with an employee's pass, footsteps shuffle and the conversation abruptly becomes inaudible as the doors close shut.

In the middle of the atrium, one broad flight of stairs invites employees and visitors up to the coffee hall (*Nöterian*, a literal translation is 'the Nut Place')[12] where I am usually invited to grab a coffee on the way to meetings. Skipping the elevator, we walk up two flights and into the corridors that surround the atrium. Tiny office cubicles or smaller areas of office landscape align the corridor, interspersed with meeting rooms of various sizes. All offices and meeting rooms have windows out onto the corridors, making the place look larger and more transparent than it is in reality. Most meeting rooms are occupied and one or two bored attendees glance at us as we pass by outside. It is a very typical Swedish office milieu; well-lit, a mixture of colours on the walls, curtains and decorations that do not offend the eyes but leave no impression and are awfully difficult to remember. The office furniture has the common beech-coloured laminate with adjustable chairs in brightly coloured fabrics. This is an office milieu that does not stand out and connotes to historical meanings of work.

The premise of the Agency is thus an example of how design impacts social interaction (Murphy 2013). First of all, the buildings connect to work and industry in a broad sense; both in location and the red brick the building is made of. Remember that income from work provides more than 60 per cent of Swedish fiscal income. Second, it is not particularly an example of aesthetic Swedish design (ibid.), but displays a worn, contemporary, everyday Swedish office and thus a milieu that most Swedish office workers are accustomed to. These points together can make the building an illustration of the Agency's vision of Sweden as 'a society where everybody wants to do the right thing' or perhaps more specifically 'do one's fair share'.[13] Third, as we will see, given knowledge cannot be articulated publicly as exemplified by the building's glass ceiling. I thus agree with Murphy and Zaloom on the importance of place on the people who work in it; 'it is something with a social life of its own that can be pointed to and articulated and argued' (Murphy 2013: 129). Seeing a place in this sense contributes to our understanding of it as an infrastructure that is the backbone of Swedish society, both in a political sense but also for the people engaging with such structures (cf. Murphy 2013).

The Analysis Unit has since moved next door, as all buildings in the entire block have been refurbished with completely new interiors. The HQ is now adjoining the Stockholm regional tax administration. If the impression of entering the former reception was like going into a cave, this one is open, but more impersonal. Glass, steel, grey carpets and a more secure entrance makes for an extraordinarily unwelcoming feeling. The boring impression is, however, countered by the many employees that happily go back and forth through the entrances, interspersed by the occasional taxpayer who has got the wrong address. No, tax returns cannot be delivered here at the HQ. No, civil registration has to be addressed at the local tax office; the receptionist takes out a crumpled piece of paper and shows the citizen how they can walk over to this office, located about a kilometre away. No, passport issues have to be dealt with at the police station. Every other time I visited the Agency and waited at reception to register there were people in the queue asking similar questions only to leave confused and trying to find their bearing in this suburban landscape of office buildings.

Who Rules (at) the Swedish Tax Agency?

Although there are different types of taxes that are executed at different levels of society – municipal, county and national – there is today only one tax administration – the Agency – that organizes all Swedish tax collection. This organization is managed from the buildings described above. Besides collecting taxes and controlling taxation, the Agency's main responsibilities consist of population registries[14] and estate inventories.[15] Yet, it is the democratically elected politicians in the Riksdag, in municipalities and in county councils that decide on what taxes – and how much tax – Swedes should pay. The Agency is, as all Swedish governmental authorities are, governed by the yearly *regleringsbrevet* (appropriation directives issued by the government). This public document states the government's objectives and performance requirements for the authority in question as well as the financial conditions, including the budget for each authority. These appropriation directives are more or less detailed in content, but they spell out the aims for each authority and can also demand specific status reports. For example, in the Agency's reglerïngsbrev for 2014, the government asked explicitly for a report about the status of the tax gap (Finansdepartementet 2013). In addition, the appropriation directives asked what measures had been implemented to reach the Agency's stated goal: 'The taxes and fee revenues sought shall be guaranteed to be correctly and safely calculated for society in an economically efficient manner and for citizens and businesses in a cost efficient and simple way. Tax crime must be prevented and combated. Citizens and businesses should have confidence and trust in the Agency's activities' (my translation).[16]

To formulate strategies and carry them out in practice as a response to the appropriation directives are thus an important task for the Agency's leadership. The Agency talks in terms of 'we'. It could be interpreted as a 'royal we', but seems to be expressed more in terms of a collective – a body of employees. According to the document *Skatteverkets inriktning* (Direction of the Tax Agency), 'we' aim to provide four strategic contributions: to make sure taxpayers do the right thing; to earn the trust of citizens and corporations; to work for all who pay the right tax; and to simplify the taxation process for all. The values 'we' have are active, trustworthy and helpful (Skatteverket 2013b).

The Agency is thus accountable to the government, but operates as an autonomous public authority. This means that the government has no (direct) influence over the tax affairs of individuals or businesses. However, the government does appoint the Director General (*generaldirektör*) and the Deputy Director (*överdirektör*). Sweden is a small country and there are close personal connections between top managers at the Agency and in the finance department as many have worked in both places.[17] The headquarters contain a management team/board of directors and six internal departments: IT, Administration, Legal, Production, Communication and Accounting. Seven tax regions are directed from the HQ. As we saw at the start of this chapter, the organization of Swedish taxation has altered over the years and is quite a messy story entangled with changes in tax law, the advancement of IT, and legitimacy claims for the entire tax system. The authority to tax has been merged on and off with similar governmental responsibilities, and perhaps simultaneous development of the tax system can be seen as a sign of the times – reflecting how views of society have changed. The practical changes in how taxation operates have been accompanied by the reorganization of authorities collecting the tax. From emphasis on the need for personal knowledge about the taxpayer in control and audit work, to the increasing automatization of income statements that moved control from municipalities to provinces to finally arrive at the contemporary organization at the national level.

In the following section we will get to know more intimately how the Agency has worked on ideas of how to increase tax compliance and how these ideas have changed ways of working within the Agency. It is work that has paid off, as during the last ten years the Agency has increased its legitimacy among the Swedes and now rests at the very top of governmental authorities Swedes find trustworthy.

Working with Tax Compliance at the Agency

The start of a more service-minded approach is said to have coincided with the charge of tax neglect made against the famous film director Ingmar Bergman, which we learned about in the introduction to this book. The ensuing worldwide (bad) publicity was aimed only at the Swedish tax authorities, as Bergman said that the Agency could do as it pleased with his estate. Bergman's sortie made decision makers at the Agency rethink their strategies when collecting 'the right tax'. A long trajectory began towards making the Agency and its employees apply a different approach towards the taxpayers.

The Bergman affair crowned a decade of applying increasing tax rates, and the RSV started to reconsider its work and relation with taxpayers. The prevalent view about the taxpayers among Agency employees at the time, the 1970s, was one of cheaters: if a taxpayer was not already caught avoiding taxes, it was just a question of time.[18] Tax compliance strategies at the Agency emphasized control of taxpayers; the pure threat of a possible audit would make them pay. And if the view is that control and auditing is the only form of relating to taxpayers, then it means they believe that taxpayers are prone to evading taxes to the largest extent possible; there is no way someone would voluntarily part with their hard-earned money unless there are sanctions (cf. Levi 1988).

From being a mere fiscal collector and auditor of tax returns, the RSV started to provide informative and instructive services. The timing was also ripe to be inspired by research on societal tax compliance (the first memorandum was published in 1983) and by the escalation in service-mindedness that had started to inspire corporations, organizations and bureaucracies throughout Sweden (Johansson 2003).

The Agency's compliance strategist Lennart Wittberg suggests the following chronological trajectory over the last five decades of this transformation from, in the citizens' view, an ugly and despised duckling to a revered swan. In the late 1970s insights from the Bergman affair made the Agency realize that control and sanctions were not enough, but perhaps even counterproductive. The Agency thus put emphasis on information during the 1980s. During the following decade, it strove to find a balance between the wealth of information that surged forth from the Swedish population on the one hand and its earlier experiences of audits and control on the other. In the new century, the Agency's strategic work put in during the previous decades started to pay off. Swedish citizens were now seen to express increasing trust in the Agency and its work, and emphasis turned to pre-emptive measures and development of IT services. Since 2010 this work has continued, although an emphasis on audit and control has also made a return.

I could at this point try to indicate a trajectory of how specific research on tax compliance has been applied at the Agency, to connect these ideas to the changing strategies in the Agency and the reorganization of the tax collecting practices, in order to sketch a background to the Agency's current position of being seen as trustworthy in Swedish society. Somewhat naively one could, for example, look at all research reports and note the references used. Apart from references in the Agency's reports to previous internal reports and documents, there are very few actual references made. The main external references are from other governmental reports such as *SOU*[19] and from analysis done by Riksrevisionen[20] and Brå[21] as well as from the occasional newspaper article. An exception is the future scenario report *Vår förvaltning år 2010* (Skatteverket 2000).

I will not do it. In a para-ethnographic vein I see ideas coming from a variety of sources (as will be further underscored in the risk assessment project we are about to follow). Second, there are also many reports and strategies that are unavailable to a broader public where citations might have been made. Third, as the analysts repeatedly point out, we are not researchers at the Analysis Unit; we are analysts preparing decision support for management. People working with research all know that the input used to understand society around us comes from numerous sources, although not all of it can be referenced and cited. Instead we will see how different ideas flow when examples from reality meet so-called theories. One example is the first memorandum composed at the Agency, which is an overview of a selected number of foreign tax authorities' control and audit work (Skatteverket 1983). The aim was obviously to learn from others' experiences. I explicitly state 'are seen to increase tax compliance' as there are many opinions as to which strategies work and also how to evaluate various measures. While looking into diverse strategies, we will also encounter insights where it could have been otherwise (cf. Woolgar 2014), as the journey towards the Agency's contemporary revered status among governmental bureaucracies has been somewhat bumpy, rather than smooth and straightforward.

That citizens, corporations and organizations comply with taxes and voluntarily pay what they owe is a most sought after condition for governments and the authorities that carry out fiscal duties. Tax in its broadest definition is what politics is all about: how should the state spend the money collected from its citizens and other taxpayers? As the focus for this book is about a tax collecting authority, I leave aside the politicians and their arguments over which type of taxes should be used and at what percentage that dominate the public discourse on taxes. Yet, the types of taxes citizens pay are obviously more or less easy to collect and more or less legitimate, depending on what they are levied on. So focus is kept on taxation, regardless of the specific national laws the taxation process follows.

Tax compliance has been analysed through several disciplinary strands of tax research reflecting various definitions of the concept (cf. Oats 2012). The major difference between these studies, though not always easily identifiable, is that some aim to understand causes for tax compliance and thus find measures to increase it, while others apply a critical stance to the societal effects of compliance measures (Boll 2014a; Braithwaite 2002; Gracia and Oats 2012). The following is an attempt to point out diverse research that could have inspired the Agency in its endeavour. Although the research quoted is often looking for remedies to increase compliance, it is not immune to a more critical stance of tax research (exemplified by the Agency having let me follow this project). I start with the broader views of actors engaged in societal tax compliance then narrow in on studies of the tax revenue authorities and see how they actually go about their work.

The seminal article within economics by Michael Allingham and Agnar Sandmo (1972) has often been cited as an inspiration for why Swedish taxpayers evade income taxes (e.g., Engström and Holmlund 2009; Lindbeck, Nyberg and Weibull 1999; Schneider and Enste 2000; Slemrod 2007). A very simplified conclusion of this model is that a taxpayer is always calculating profit and will therefore attempt to maximize their economic outcome by paying enough tax without being caught by a control and thus pay penalties. These insights have been used to create strategies against evasion in order to increase compliance (Skatteverket 2006a), but as will be apparent in what follows there is much more than economic benefits that makes taxpayers pay up. And this is something the Agency acknowledges.

Margaret Levi's (1988) starting point is also from rational choice theory, regarding both the tax collecting state and the taxpaying citizen, but she casts a wider net. Levi proposes three ways to create compliance: by coercion, by ideological conviction and by quasi-voluntary compliance. The first way is argued to be too costly, and although ideological conviction is argued to be able to bring costs down, the quasi-voluntary method is her preferred option. This method implies that a tax collector should create a structure where people choose to pay and those who do not are coerced – if caught (Levi 1988: 52). At work here are ideas of taxpayers' rational calculation of paying vis-á-vis their perception that others pay vis-á-vis being caught if cheating. A ruler can increase compliance by showing that the system is fair to all taxpayers; that all are treated equally and that all are subject to coercion if caught misbehaving (ibid.: 54).

From a purely legal standpoint 'reporting all income and paying all taxes in accordance with the applicable laws, regulations and court decisions' (Alm 1991: 577) was an early definition of tax compliance. It is quite a primitive view of citizens that they follow the law to the letter. Legal scholars increasingly emphasize issues outside the law.

> Research shows that tax compliance is affected by (social and personal) norms such as those regarding procedural justice, trust, belief in the legitimacy of the government, reciprocity, altruism and identification with the group. Cognitive processes, such as prospect theory, also influence an

> individual's reaction to tax issues. Studies also indicate that certain demographic factors such as age, gender and education correlate with the tax morale. (Kornhauser 2007; cf. San Juan 2013)

These legal studies confirm that the study of taxation says much about a given society (cf. Schumpeter 1954), and willingness to pay tax indicates many aspects about what it is to be a citizen.

Taking a broader stance and looking at how people understand principles of tax laws and taxation regulations, Sol Picciotto (2007) argues that in order to increase compliance, attention has to be redirected to the tax system's perceived fairness. Governments create greater compliance by aiming for a tax legislation that can be understood and agreed upon by *all* in the tax field. The implications are that principles behind the tax law should be purposive and supported by detailed regulations that govern everyday taxation work (Picciotto 2007: 12). As I understand his argument, tax collectors, tax advisers, taxpayers – and perhaps also tax researchers – ought in a democracy to agree upon what should be subject to tax in order to increase compliance. People have different norms, so instead of the often-elaborated discussion about technical details and intricacies of tax law specificities the focus in tax law should be on fairness and equity. 'Unless the tax code itself is built on a sound foundation of principles generally accepted as fair, compliance will be problematic' (ibid.: 11). Picciotto's approach mirrors a processual view on the interpretation of tax laws. Society around us changes and so do the issues that are subject to tax. If a tax collecting authority has sound legal principles to rely on in tax law, it can more easily navigate and contain its legitimacy instead of always having to change the specific regulations that taxpayers have to comply with.

Looking closer at the actual practices that form compliance, Valerie Braithwaite draws a distinction between cooperative and compliance-related actions (2002). She describes it as a 'dance with authorities', recognizing the interaction between the implementation of responsive regulation and the resulting behaviour of taxpayers (2002: 15). Her starting point is that responsiveness to paying taxes is shaped by two dimensions: one broad and attitudinal and the other specific and behavioural. Do taxpayers evaluate their compliance effort when actually paying taxes? And how do they regard the tax system in terms of motivation (2002: 34)? If taxpayers attempt to increase the social distance between themselves and a tax collecting authority (e.g., by denouncing it), it is an indication of increasing dislike, and less status is ascribed to such an authority. However, giving consent, Braithwaite claims, is different from obeying a request. Therefore we have to do away with the often assumed consistency between attitude and behaviour. When dealing with non-compliant behaviour, it is important for the authority to show these people and the rest of society (e.g., other taxpayers) that it will not happen again. This is a way 'to deal with the wrongdoing today, while nurturing consent for tomorrow' (2002: 35).

The model Braithwaite helped create for the ATO (Australian Taxation Office) stipulates both rights and duties for taxpayers. On the ATO side, the emphasis is on services for citizens – to explain, assist and treat fairly – to respect citizens' rights to privacy, to be accountable in all its decisions as well as effectively manage the expenditure when collecting taxes. The duties of the citizen on the other hand are to be truthful, careful and responsible, and follow rules and regulations laid out by the ATO.

Taxpayers are often seen to evaluate their benefits relative to the tax burden (Folger 1986); whether the tax paid somewhat accords to what they perceive they are receiving in return (cf. Cowell 1990; Falkinger 1995). The idea of fairness is moved from equitable treatment of the taxpayer in relation to other taxpayers (cf. Taylor 2003) and embraces a broader, reciprocal view of taxes paid and welfare benefits received. Compliance can in this perspective be described as a tit-for-tat relation (cf. Björklund Larsen 2010) and something a tax collecting agency has difficulty in making an impact on, unless it is seen as corrupt with its officials lining their own pockets (Aidt 2003). Obviously these are perceptions; although a citizen might calculate how much tax one pays including VAT, social fees, etc. there is no way to estimate the pay-off – how much welfare and other governmental services are given in return (for taxes paid).

The more psychological/behavioural explanations follow experiments where individuals or groups of people have been studied 'doing' taxes (Torgler 2002). In these experiments theories about tax compliance are tested and/or additional facts about the impact of certain tax behaviour are assembled (Torgler 2002: 659) in order to understand more about what tax morale is. 'Realistic settings' are created where taxpayers engage with diverse taxation control strategies and different propositions about taxes themselves or fiscal behaviour. For example, what impact do fines and audits have on tax evasion behaviour compared to certain tax rate levels (Friedland, Maital and Rutenberg 1978)? Or how do taxpayers comply, knowing full well that the audit is performed by random selection models (Alm and McKee 2004)? These experiments are mainly constructed in an attempt to expand on traditional economic models, as it is 'shown that many taxpayers seem to have a more refined motivation structure than that assumed by traditional economics' (Torgler 2002: 678). Thus have economists created models where 'social norms', as for example those identified by the World Value Survey, are seen to impact the level of tax compliance in various countries (Knack and Keefer 1997; cf. Slemrod 1998). Torgler provides an impressive overview that underlines that there are many, many aspects to tax compliance. He sums up this strand of tax research: tax compliers see avoidance as immoral; people that are friends with tax evaders tend to avoid tax; moral persuasion increases compliance; and compliance is higher in countries with larger social cohesion (Torgler 2002: 664). It all makes sense, as most people usually do what others do, but as Valerie Braithwaite reminds us, consenting is quite different from complying (2002). And what do experiments really tell us? Experiments are a constructed reality that can be more or less close to reality and that people have to relate to. As work in the social studies of science has shown, the empirical framework and approach of a study often dictate the answers research produces (Barad 2007; Haraway 1998; Harding 1986). 'How you know is what you know' directs our gaze to see what really is going on.

Engaging with actual taxation cases is done by critical tax scholars who use social theory, for example inspired by Foucault and Bourdieu, to sort out how different stakeholders relate to each other in tax compliance issues. In a famous U.K. case of presumed tax avoidance, the usage of Bourdieu's social practice can throw light on how different stakeholders (a tax authority, tax professionals, taxpayers) negotiate both their actions and motives regarding tax regulatory practices (Gracia and Oats 2012). This view makes explicit the boundary work between compliant and non-compliant behaviour in which the diverse stakeholders are engaged and shows how this particular case was framed both to be set inside or outside boundaries of regulatory practice.

To more explicitly relate to the actual doings when complying with taxation, Karen Boll makes us understand that the law is something most taxpayers do not know about in great detail. In a critique of common tax compliance definitions, for example those that almost exclusively emphasize the black-letter legal understandings, she underlines that many of the institutional explanations are based on a reductionist stance (Boll 2014a: 296), for example seeing compliance as a cause for trust. Boll proposes that we look at what is actually done when paying/complying with taxes; 'tax compliance denotes the practices of reporting income and paying taxes to a tax administration' (ibid.: 293). Actor network theory (ANT) enables her to show how social, material and relational aspects (see also Boll 2011, 2014a) make up tax compliance in the everyday work of taxpaying corporations – also when they fail to comply.

The definitions, and the remedies more or less explicitly proposed to increase tax compliance, thus go mostly hand in hand with researchers disciplines: legal scholars want to improve the law; economists emphasize economic incitements and punishments; behavioural economists test various social norms; and sociologists and anthropologists apply a more holistic view on taxes emphasizing the relationships created between taxpayer, ruler and other citizens (cf. Roitman 2005).

Directing the gaze towards the tax collecting authorities, Roberta Mann suggests somewhat humouristically ten strategies for the IRS, and the U.S. tax system, that ought to improve compliance among U.S. taxpayers. She emphasizes simplicity and common sense; she argues that her suggestions would make life easier for the already honest taxpayer and are intended to make the usually hassled process more pleasant. I selected those suggestions where the tax authority can have an impact, and the compliance issues boil down to four – which are actually her top four contenders. Starting with her list in reverse order, her fourth point is that compliance should be rewarded, instead of non-compliance being sanctioned. People are more prone to regard carrots as fairer than sticks (Mann 2006: 925). Her third issue is that the information provided should be meaningful; helpful and correct information can increase compliance, instead of what has previously been suggested (in the United States). The proposal is for IRS-sponsored tax return preparation software (Mann 2006: 926). Her runner-up is to actually inform taxpayers on what services the IRS provides. Citizens do not always know what they can get help with. If the IRS communicated a message like 'we will make sense of the mess Congress has imposed on you' (Mann 2006: 926), taxpayers might actually do the returns themselves instead of using tax accountants, who often take the combative stance; we fight the IRS for you (ibid: 927). And her proposed winner is for the IRS to make the return process as simple as possible. By letting the tax authority prepopulate the return with as much information as possible, tax return time would for wage-earners be less stressful and thus is a truly compliance-increasing issue (ibid.: 927). As Martin Daunton reminds us, the introduction of self-assessment in the United Kingdom has worsened the Inland Revenue's public image, for example by losing over five million taxpayer filings in 2000 (2002: 253).

OECD (Organisation for Economic Co-operation and Development) has through its Forum on Tax Administration's Compliance Subgroup compiled insights from different tax authorities' experiences since 2004. Although these experiences vary, the forum encourages each tax collecting authority to develop methods and tools, measures and indicators, to monitor taxpayer compliance over time (2008, 2010). This forum underscores the difficulty in finding ways to understand what makes people comply and therefore encourages the collecting bodies to document what strategies and tools work, noting those that are less efficient, and share those insights with other national tax collecting bodies. Noteworthy is their encouragement of developing an array of indicators that can be comparable over time. But there are neither recipes for making specific indicators, nor a list of recommended ones to be used. Instead the forum emphasizes the need for each tax collecting agency to articulate indicators that to the largest extent possible address the issues at risk that might impact compliance (2010).

The Swedish contribution to the latest OECD report derives from the large project about work performed and bought within the informal sector (cf. Skatteverket 2006a, 2006b, 2007a). The OECD report summarizes the insights and especially those indicators that are seen to tease out who is at risk of non-complying and what indicators to compare to find out if non-compliance is suspected. Interesting to note is the forum's emphasis on the inadequacy of methods to supply a correct answer. To this particular question they note that not everything is brought out in interviews; not everything can be revealed in tax audits; and some people do not know what can be classed as illicit work (OECD 2008: 77). Many indicators do not mirror actual compliance. In focus are attitudes *and* perceptions among taxpayers towards compliance, and research doubts that such approaches mirror actual behaviour (OECD 2008: 77), thus reinforcing Braithwaite's work (2002).

Although research on tax compliance is abundant, there are many diverse suggestions for strategies and measures that impact tax compliance. Obviously, at the outset there should be a law with stipulations to create compliance (e.g., Lodin 2007; Mann 2006; Smith 1776), yet what creates compliance differs between countries. In the application of tax laws, the problem is to understand which of all these suggestions work; in the long and short term, on an individual and societal level, and among different categories of taxpayers. With the evaluation tools at hand, we are never 100 per cent sure if instituted compliance measures do their work.

We have already been introduced to how a number of academic disciplines approach tax compliance and thus implicitly to some suggested remedies. There are many insights, yet two main points emerge. We can on the one hand see the constraints of methodology in research about compliance and on the other the many normative assumptions about compliance. The idea with the above section is not to provide a complete overview of all research about tax compliance, but rather understand what types of knowledge and ideas have flowed within the Agency and inspired the various changes in strategies and resulting practices. So let us continue to focus on what the Agency has done in order to increase tax compliance in Sweden.

Agency Strategies Creating Tax Compliance

In this section we turn from academic articles and books to a discussion of different strategies, where possible referring to research that the Agency has applied to increase compliance during the last five decades. The emphasis is on the leeway the law permits the Agency as a tax collecting authority. Changes to the tax legislation, or other issues that lie outside the authority of the Agency to impact, are therefore omitted.[22] We will see examples of how audits, information, service, pre-emptive work, trust, prepopulated information and perhaps surprisingly how the changes in wording when talking about taxation and taxpayers have been deployed as strategies by this Agency in order to increase compliance.

The development of IT solutions and E-technology has revolutionized the Agency's work with compliance. The Agency has come a long way from the manual calculations with pencil and paper that Malmer started out with when he became employed (2003: 43). This depiction does not only include analysis, controls and audit (see also Chapters 2 and 3), but IT also makes it possible to communicate with the Agency in a simpler and quicker way. Agency information on the Web is always available, technology has simplified the annual return forms and IT has also made a greater impact on analysis work when attempts are made to model and understand taxpayer behaviour (Skatteverket 2006a, 2011a, 2014a) as well as identify potential tax avoiders.

Taking into account the materialities, tools and help for the taxpayers is an important aspect of compliance. Karen Boll shows in her study of the Danish equivalent to the Swedish Tax Agency, SKAT, that tax compliance can never be pursued in isolation; there are always many different actors, things and theories (according to the ANT approach) that work as a distributed action (Boll 2014a). Danish companies' tax compliance takes place in a variety of settings but is always a laborious feat involving the active participation of auditors and taxpayers and the knowledge, technology, rules and regulations, and the enforcement of these; 'the heterogeneous assembly of actors and practices'. She points out the importance of recognizing both the technical resources and social practices of the collector, the Danish SKAT, and the taxpayer, in order to understand how compliance is achieved (Boll 2014a, 2014b).

Historically, the emphasis of the Agency's compliance work was, and is, on the threat of audit control. Prior to the 1980s, there was no service policy, so it was up to the individual auditor to decide on the extent of his or her service-mindedness in contacts and communication with the taxpayer (Johansson 2003: 114). During the 1980s, the idea of service-mindedness grew in society and so also, although slowly, at the RSV. In 1987, a law was passed in the Riksdag[23] that required all governmental agencies to provide information, help and advice concerning all issues within each authority's domain of responsibility. Noteworthy was the need to provide such advice in as easily accessible a language as possible (ibid.).

The emphasis on providing service and information to the taxpayer started in 1970. There is hardly any documentation available that such work existed before then (Johansson 2003: 111) and the information void might have been due to a lack of resources. In 1940 there were only 180 tax administrators employed throughout the country – today there are more than 10,000. To provide service on top of all other duties was not easy, even if an employee wished to do so. Until 1960 service from the tax authorities consisted of answering the phone and if necessary setting up meetings with taxpayers. Waiting times were thus lengthy. Compare this with today. For example, I called the Agency's service phone on 2 May 2014, the day before the annual return forms were due. The automated message informed me that 279 employees were currently busy taking phone calls and that the waiting time was eleven minutes. Actually, someone answered after nine minutes.

From the 1970s onwards we find the first memoranda addressing organization changes and rationalization efforts within the RSV as well as results about cooperation with other governmental agencies. These memoranda generally have two aims: to describe the many reorganization efforts and to make such endeavours known within and throughout the Agency. One memorandum described the reorganization of the regional agencies into the RSV, in 1972, which made it possible for the first time to seriously address information issues (Johansson 2003: 113). This was the largest tax return reform since 1903 and the Agency invested heavily in a nationwide information campaign. The main attraction of the campaign was the *Dags att deklarera*, 'Time for tax return', a document that exists to this day. The first issue was a twenty-four-page brochure illustrated with drawings in 4-colour print and written as an aid to taxpayers in filling out the four-page annual tax return. Mirroring the immigration land Sweden had become, the first brochure was also translated into Finnish, Serbo-Croat, Turkish, English, German, Greek and Italian, as well as in Braille, and sent to taxpayers they imagined would be helped by such information (Thärnström 2003: 120). The Agency's ambition to help with the tax return in diverse languages has differed over the years, but all in all, the RSV, and later the Agency, has consistently been aware of the problem

Illustration 1.5 ***Dags att deklarera*** **1972. Photo by Björn Thärnström.**

for all taxpayers in understanding what a tax return is all about and how to complete one. Perhaps *Dags att deklarera* was too radical for its time, as the brochure became subject to media critique. It was said to be written in too simplified a language (Ekman 2003a: 15) and even called a 'Donald Duck' brochure (Thärnström 2003: 128). Citizens' appreciation of the entire concept was however deemed almost unanimously positive at 91 per cent (ibid.: 121).

Research on taxation has shown that to increase compliance one should minimize taxpayers' manual entries on the tax return forms (e.g., Daunton 2001). The Agency aims to make this procedure as automated as possible and such tax returns are obviously easier to verify and cheaper to audit. Since 1987, the annual tax return has been increasingly automated and adjusted to ameliorate the rights of the individual taxpayer. The innovation here is that some information started to be prepopulated, a content that has increased over the years. Contemporary income tax reporting and payment is a simple task for most Swedes and to a substantial extent an automated process. The yearly tax return for employed people is now highly automatized and they usually have very simple filing to do. Salaries are directly transferred into employee bank accounts as net income, and employers pay the deducted tax amounts monthly to the Agency. Employers provide a standardized form – a control income statement – early in the year to all employees in Sweden. The form states income, taxes paid, taxed fringe benefits, and other related information for the previous income year. There is thus seldom any manual reporting to do; figures for wages and income tax deducted are provided by the employer, and mortgage institutions and banks report interest received and paid, and even some subsidized service deductions such as repair work in private homes and domestic services (so-called ROT and RUT)[24] are already in place.

In April, a prepopulated tax return is delivered to all those who have reported income. In addition to the amount of income and taxes paid, this form includes information such as interest income and expenses supplied by financial service providers. The great majority of individuals are only required to confirm this information electronically – by telephone, text message, an app, or at the Agency's website – by early May. There is obviously the opportunity to add income or deductions, but most employed Swedes just authorize the information once they have checked the figures on the pre-filled tax return and simply accept it with an electronic signature, in some cases after making a few changes to the return over the Web. The Agency encourages citizens to confirm their annual tax returns electronically by promising that any tax repayments from returns will be confirmed in this manner by midsummer.[25] I have not been able to find contemporary estimates of how much time a Swedish taxpayer spends on average on their tax return, but it is definitely much, much less than the American average of twenty-seven hours (Lepore 2012). After the tax reform, the average time spent was significantly reduced from two hours and twenty-one minutes in 1992 to one hour and forty-two minutes the following year. There is no reason to think that it has increased, but rather the opposite. If the IRS was able to automate its tax return forms, U.S. compliance would perhaps improve following Roberta Mann's suggestions (2006: 927).

For self-employed people and other commercial entities, the tax return procedure is different and much more complex. Compared to employees, self-employed taxpayers have to manually fill in all information on the tax return. These taxpayers themselves or with the use of an accountant have to prepare their yearly returns. The propensity to make errors but also to deliberately cheat is therefore greater and these taxpayers are therefore more prone to be subject to explicit audits and controls. As a result, the self-employed have been depicted in the media as potential wrongdoers, making their interest organizations accuse the Agency of singling out entrepreneurs as cheats (see Chapter 3 for an explicit example of this type of discussion).

From the tax revenue collectors' perspective, emphasizing tax compliance (instead of maximizing tax revenue) has changed employees' ways of working and also their skills within tax authorities. Penny Tuck argues, for example, that the contemporary tax auditor does not only have to have a thorough technical knowledge of taxation procedures and tax law, but also managerial and communicative skills, as the emphasis on tax authorities providing information to taxpayers has increased direct contact (Tuck 2010). This is recognized by the Agency, which has continuously worked via internal courses and memoranda on how to be more approachable to taxpayers, in order to change tax auditors' views on the taxpayers as plausible, if not eternal, cheaters (e.g., Skatteverket 1985, 1997, 1998), and has evaluated such strategies (e.g., Skatteverket 1995).

One such internal campaign identified attitudes among Agency employees.[26] Type A stands for an old-fashioned fiscal approach. They read the law to the letter and are inflexible in their ways of working. There were apparently many such employees in the 1970s when the transformation work started. Type B has a softer approach and is very Swedish lagom. Finally type C stands for the new employee that is pedagogic and helpful in his/her contact with taxpayers. For a while the attitude was more important than background when the Agency looked for new employees. A good example of a C attitude seems to be held by Alice (the tax auditor you will meet in Chapter 3). Yet throughout the book it will also be apparent that for the Agency there is still work to do on these issues.

Another strategy of the Agency has been to show how efficient it is in its collecting endeavours. It repeatedly describes and measures the tax gap while simultaneously presenting its work in diminishing it. The gap is thus a measurement of tax compliance. Estimating the tax gap is a task that is performed by many OECD tax authorities, for example in Denmark, Holland, the United Kingdom and the United States (OECD 2008). The methodologies differ somewhat among nations, but in essence the Swedish tax gap is the calculated difference between the amount of tax that ought to be paid if all taxpayers accounted for their economic activities correctly and the tax that is established in practice after audits by the Agency. In the best of worlds the tax gap would be nil if the calculation and the audits of amounts actually collected were equal. The tax gap has thus nothing to do with the actual amounts collected and is a pure calculated construct where no consideration is made of the actual fiscal income. Yet the tax gap estimate, or portions of it, is widely used in society.

Important to note is that the tax gap does not only consist of cheats, but also of unintentional errors in reported income as well as cost deductions. To narrow the tax gap, the Agency argues that citizens should be made to understand how the tax law is applied. It is argued that citizens' willingness to comply depends on the perception that all other taxpayers pay their share; the tax gap is then small. A decreasing tax gap number represents the success of tax collection. Estimating the tax gap is a reoccurring task for the Agency; today it is even stated as one of the Agency's two superior aims[27] (Skatteverket 2012: 7). The tax gap result for 2007 was 133 billion krona, published with a repeated caveat of being calculated with great uncertainty (Skatteverket 2008a). The result from 2007 was an often-cited number or percentage (5 per cent of GDP or 10 per cent of total tax income) that was used in political debates singling out cheaters, or as input to other economic models when bragging about the Swedish welfare model, or as a quality assessment of how well the Agency was fulfilling its purpose (Skatteverket 2014c). As mentioned, in the 2014 *regleringsbrev* the Agency was explicitly asked to quantify the tax gap and describe any changes from the last estimate from 2007 (Finansdepartementet 2013). Much work went into this new estimate but in the end the Agency courageously stated that it was impossible to come up with a number because of the worsening quality of data (Skatteverket 2014c: 5). The guesstimate for 2013 became a non-number. Reliance on the estimates making up the tax gap has thus decreased and time will tell if the strategies of the Agency will change.

How the Agency has transformed its treatment of the taxpayer can be seen in how the latter is referred to. Thus we turn to communication and more explicitly the wording used when referring to the taxpayer. At the beginning of the last century when modern taxation laws were introduced, the citizen was still considered a minion (*undersåte*). The right to vote in elections depended on income; the elections to the first chamber were indirect but based on municipal votes. Being a voter was directly connected to how much tax the person had paid (taxation started at incomes of 500 krona) and not having tax debts. This concerned men, unmarried women and widows, and even corporations. Voting to the second chamber[28] was for men only and based on a different income estimate. Yearly earnings had to amount to at least 800 krona (in 1910, the amount had been lowered from 1,000 krona in 1907, when the average income for a worker in industry was 750 and on farms 350), and taxpayers ought to have paid the relevant tax (*bevillning*) on this amount. Alternatively, the male voter had to show ownership of property worth at least 1,000 krona (Löwnertz 2003: 62). Democratic citizenship was thus for the wealthier in society and was closely connected to the ability to pay tax. This is probably where the concept of the tributary (*skattskyldige*) originates according to the SAOB.[29] The literal translation, tax indebtedness, connotes more correctly to seeing the citizen as liable. The concept probably originates in the fact that taxes were paid in retrospect, based on actual earnings. A citizen with a job or income from capital was by definition indebted to the state and such a liability needed verification to ensure that the right tax had been paid.

Compare this to today when most citizens pay a preliminary tax. An employed taxpayer does not pay directly anymore; the wage is transferred net into the employee's bank account while part of it, the preliminary income tax, is paid directly from the employer to the Agency. The taxed amount is then adjusted in the annual tax return, which includes other, non-reported income as well as various deductions such as additional work-related expenses. Simultaneous with the Agency's increased service-minded approach the question of talking about the taxpayer as the tributary arose. Some advocated the concept of customer (*kund*) (Johansson 2003). In the Agency's plan for 2003, they stated 'We are a modern and efficient administration and we work from a processual and customer oriented approach. The citizens and corporations can make use of our service at their leisure'[30] (Johansson 2003: 117, my translation).

Even if skattskyldig still lingers here and there in contemporary documents from the Agency and in discussions among employees, we can see how this term has over the last forty years been transformed into a citizen-customer who pays tax (*skattebetalare*) – the taxpayer. Having paid, s/he has certain rights; if nothing else these rights include being given the correct information and help to pay the taxes due. But perhaps it is going too far for the Agency to adopt the business slogan that 'the customer is always right'? Views on the taxpayers can also be deduced from looking at the Agency's mottos and diverse campaign slogans over the years. The contemporary motto 'Our vision is a society where everybody wants to do the right thing', or perhaps more specifically where everybody wants to 'do one's fair share', emphasizes the Agency's move from being a collector and auditor of taxes to being a shaper of taxpayer compliance. Always in focus is that the taxpayer should want to pay taxes.

The first motto was probably introduced in 1955 when the department of finance ran a national advertising campaign in forty-three different newspapers (Thärnström 2003: 119). The slogans were both economic-political, as the wording emphasized what taxes 'should pay for' but also proposed that the citizen got something in return for taxes paid. *Skatterna bär upp försvaret* (Taxes support the defence); *Våra skolor danar framtidens Sverige* (Our schools fashion Sweden's future); *Att bli sjuk utan att bli ruinerad* (Being sick without going bankrupt); or *Att få åldras utan oro* (To age without anxiety). The intention was obviously to make citizens pay due taxes making sure that they realized that they got something in return. But they were also modern messages; the slogans showed that the taxpayer lived in a welfare society and did not only pay for national defence, the historical reason for taxation; we Swedes received schooling and would be taken care of when we could not earn money – if sick or old. The mottos underlined the taxpayers' reciprocal relation to the state; we get what we pay for. Another slogan was *Vår åsikt om skatter ska vi uttrycka med vår röstsedel – och inte genom felaktig deklaration* (Our tax opinions should be voiced in voting, not by faulty tax returns) (Thärnström 2003: 119). Regardless of political opinion, Swedes should obey the democratic order and pay the taxes due.

Despite catchy campaign slogans, taxes did not pay themselves and audits had to be performed. Director General Gösta Ekman's attempt in the 1970s to marry the somewhat contradictory concepts of audit control and service-mindedness was apparently not well received. His motto *Kontroll är en del av servicen* (Control is part of the service) did not in the least appeal to the media. It became subject to contempt among journalists and the bantering articles were many (Ekman 2003a: 19). In the 1980s, mottos like *Rätt skatt på rätt sätt* (Right tax [collected] in the right way) and *Balans mellan kontroll och service* (Strike a balance between control and service) were easier to fathom. The Agency now focused on its own practices, which in the next decade changed again. In the late 1990s, then Director General Anitra Steen introduced willingness in the efforts to increase tax compliance. The motto was *Folk ska vilja göra rätt* (People should want to comply), and the Agency has in various ways since the early 2000s proposed measures to increase the willingness to pay tax – to comply. The somewhat more clumsy Swedish term, however, moves emphasis from a passive to a more active taxpayer. This person is just not someone who obeys and follows the law. Willingness expresses a more positive attitude towards paying up what is due following the law, perhaps exemplified by the former Social Democratic Party leader Mona Sahlin: 'If you are a Social Democrat, then you think it is cool to pay taxes. Tax is for me the finest notion of what politics is all about'.[31] Per Schlingman, former chief strategist to Moderaterna, the Swedish conservative party, agreed with her (although many years on), writing: 'To contribute to the commons is right and responsible and to be unsolidaric is limp'.[32] Once again we get a hint of the values within Swedish society from these views on taxation; it is also an illustration of Schumpeter's insight from fifty years previous that in order to understand any society and its political life one of the best starting points is taxation (1954).

In this vein it is perhaps not surprising that the incumbent Director General has promoted the idea that tax compliance ought to be part of CSR (corporate social responsibility). During the last couple of years he has emphasized that the Agency's motto for Swedish taxpayers, 'Our vision is a society where everybody wants to do one's fair share', should also include corporations and organizations. The CSR message seems especially addressed to those that by diverse tax planning measures evade taxation in Sweden. The idea is to make tax compliance explicitly part of corporations' and organizations' CSR work, which would also mean a change in internal structures. The Director General argues that tax planning should not only be an issue for the accounting department, where taxes historically have been kept to a minimum like any other cost within a corporation, but that the issue should solidly belong at a corporate board level. Tax planning is an ethical question and should be talked about as such and on the same level as environmental sustainability, social responsibility and fair foreign production conditions (Hansson 2011).[33]

The image of the Agency started to change among Swedes as it worked on providing adequate information and personal service when additional questions arose. Technological developments provided increasing means for both better control and a more equal treatment of all citizens, and also simplified the yearly tax return procedures for most taxpayers. These measures taken together with the diverse moral messages finally paid off. At the start of the twenty-first century, the work that had started in the 1970s came into full effect. Since 2006, the Agency has been among the top contenders of governmental authorities that citizens find most reliable (Ekonomistyrningsverket 2012). In 2011 the Agency was found to be, together with the police, at the very top of the governmental authorities that citizens found most reliable. And this is regardless of respondents' political opinions, gender, class, or age (Engelbrecht and Holmberg 2012: 9). Knowing that the Agency does its job well has created a perception among the Swedish population that everybody else is paying. An efficient and friendly Agency has to be doing its job right, no? The Agency is perceived to be doing its job well and is therefore trusted.

Even if the Agency has very high tax rates to administer by international comparisons, paying these is not something Swedes seem to worry too much about. Never more than 14 per cent of the population has thought that taxes are among the three most important societal issues over the last twenty years (from 1987 to 2005) – perhaps not so strange, as most Swedes do not see the taxes they pay – they are deducted before the (net) salary hits their bank account. The top score of 14 per cent was noted just before the big reform in 1991; most of the time the score shifted between 3 and 7 per cent of the population[34] (Holmberg and Weibull 2006: 24). Although it seems as though most Swedes pay their large amount of tax without objection, there are objections and safety valves (see also Chapter 5). For one thing, with the Swedish tax law at present, it is almost impossible to pay the correct tax (e.g., Riksrevisionsverket 1997: 27; Skatteverket 2006a: 17) and thus it is very easy to justify tax cheating in various ways (Björklund Larsen 2010). Still, almost none of the close to fifty people interviewed in a project about how purchases of informal work can be justified referred to the workings of the Agency. Only one person denied participation, as he was fed up with the Agency; he was very resentful, as he had been taken to court and felt mistreated (ibid.: 46).

Although the Agency is mostly a well-respected governmental institution, there are of course other views. There are loud voices from all corners of society such as entrepreneurs, ordinary and well-off people who have a disdain for tax authorities either through their own experience of being singled out and receiving unfair treatment or through hearsay. A few of these have fled the country and relocated to where authorities have less control and demand less in taxes. However, the Agency's success during the last ten years, recorded in attitudinal surveys, belies these occasional voices.

We can also speculate whether the Agency's pragmatic and commonsense interpretation of the law (Björklund Larsen 2015) makes room for barter and other ways to obtain cheaper services while still being compliant. As long as most people have this opportunity, they perhaps feel that the Agency does not control their affairs in the most intimate detail but allows for a certain margin for mischief (cf. Scott 1990). Another issue is the growing number of small businesses during the last decade.[35] Performing such business activities also allows for certain deductions of costs where the mix of private and business expenses is not always easily discernible.

Although level of taxation, spending of taxes, and taxation practices themselves are three different issues, they seem in public discourse and also in discussion at the Agency to interconnect and blur what is real. This is despite the fact that the Agency is careful to clarify what they measure as citizens' views (*synpunkter*) on various taxation issues (e.g., Skatteverket 2012). It is therefore very difficult, if not impossible, to assess the connection between the level of taxation, tax compliance and the spending of taxes with these surveys on how citizens perceive the Agency.

So the Agency has, by being pragmatic, been able to create a perception of itself as one of the most trusted governmental institutions in Swedish society. It repeatedly asks about its own standing in its own annual surveys about the population's diverse views on tax, taxation practices and how the Agency is perceived to be working (e.g., Skatteverket 2012). Other governmental surveys reinforce this image (e.g., Ekonomistyrningsverket 2012). The Agency understands that in hindsight stupid decisions such as the much written about arrest of Ingmar Bergman did not accord well with Swedish opinion. It complied with, and to some extent was at the forefront of, the information surge in the 1980s, with brochures such as 'Time for tax return', and has increased the service to taxpayers by being more respondent and helpful. The Agency has used insights from research and technological innovation to its advantage. For example employees' automated tax returns are a feat. The Agency has managed to simplify what for most citizens is the dull and mandatory task of an annual tax return through increased automation, leaving the employed taxpayers increasingly outside the process of paying tax. Errors and cheats are thus increasingly minimized. This is an extraordinary accomplishment, as it makes both audit and control for the Agency much simpler; taxpayers spend less time on 'boring' issues and thus view the Agency in greater esteem. It can be seen as a true victory for audit society (cf. Power 1999, 2000), although in a slightly twisted way. Here it is not the governmental institutions we citizens have lost trust in (Power 2000: 118) if we are to believe the surveys to do with Swedish governmental authorities and how citizens regard them. Swedish taxpayers 'allow' themselves to be audited so that they can trust that everybody else pays up.

Obviously, the above insights are mostly depicted as a view from within; these are mainly based on the Agency's own perception of what has made its strategies – as well as the practices implemented to fulfil these strategies – successful. But by being perceived in various surveys as reliable and trustworthy, the Agency reinforces this by posing relevant questions about its own work in its own yearly surveys to the population. Important to note, once more, is that this work says very little about the tax law structure itself and also what taxpayers actually do when they have the chance to alter income and costs.

To alter the gaze from the somewhat idealistic mottos, academic theories and verbal altercations the Agency has engaged in, we will now get closer to see what is actually going on in these buildings. In the rest of this chapter you will get to know those within the Agency who create and assemble knowledge about taxpayers. The analysts and the group who undertook the risk assessment project takes us around the Agency. In this way we will look at what is happening, instead of what is perceived as happening from the outside.

The Analysis Unit

The risk assessment project I followed was carried out in the Analysis Unit at the HQ. The unit's task is to prepare decision support for the

Agency. As the term 'analysis' implies, the unit's aim is to go beyond hard facts and develop new insights from the often quantitative, but also qualitative, material these facts are based upon. Analyses should address issues that might put the Agency at risk of not being able to carry out their instructions and collect taxes as ordered by the Swedish Parliament and instructed by the finance department. The analysis work is clearly grounded in both quantitative and qualitative scientific methods, but the analysts themselves do not consider their work as research. Their tasks could address anything from very specific issues such as the impact on tax evasion due to the decreased VAT in restaurants (Skatteverket 2014e) to broader recommendations and strategies as to what the Agency should concentrate on in the upcoming year given the instructions from the government in the appropriation directives (regleringsbrevet).

There are more than fifty analysts working at the Agency out of a total of more than 10,000 employees. Although most analysts work at the HQ, there are many dispersed in the regional offices. Those located in the regions sometimes carry out their own projects. Certain regional offices also have specific duties; for example Intelligence Analysis (*omvärlds-bevakning*) is carried out in Gothenburg. Often analysts from several offices are involved in larger projects such as the one followed in this book. Selecting analysts for a project depends on knowledge and availability, but it is also a way to share knowledge between offices. All analysts gather at least once a year for two 'Analyst Days' where strategies for the Analysis Unit are presented, work in progress is reported on, qualitative issues are addressed and 'food for thought' is presented, such as a presentation by an author who has written about the Swedish Mafia.

The analysts have different educational backgrounds. Some have solid experience in the Agency's control and audit work; others have a more academic background from statistics, economics or political science. Almost all have a university degree and there are also a few Ph.Ds. An analyst is typically involved in several research projects simultaneously and depending on the stage of the project works more or less intensively with it: reading, analysing, organizing, or writing up the results as well as sometimes disseminating their insights throughout the Agency through verbal presentations.

Their main production is reports. Some are for internal distribution, a handful are published in book form, and most are made accessible on the Web for the public. A few are even translated, often in a shortened form, into English; for example, the studies made on the tax gap (Skatteverket 2014d) or on the informal sector (*svart arbete*) (Skatteverket 2006b). The annual *Tax Statistical Yearbook* is the Agency's most read publication, and is a summary of diverse economic statistics about the tax system and taxation in Sweden. The intention is to supply facts for debates about this very political issue. The Agency thus takes seriously its view not only on performing fiscal duties, but also educating other interested parties on Swedish tax matters.

The types of analyses the unit performs have recently been somewhat narrowed in descriptive terms with the aim of improving quality: to be more specific, to apply scientific methods and to delve deeper into the issues investigated (Skatteverket 2014d). Various types of analyses, six in all, loosely relate to what the Agency deems the Risk Cycle. Their aims somewhat overlap and each can apply one or several methodologies. First in the risk cycle is the Intelligence Analysis (*omvärldsbevakning*), which is a type of analysis made to monitor and assess the future development of the Agency's position in relation to actors, situations and phenomena in society. An intelligence analysis seeks to identify trends but the focus is particularly on uncertainties. It provides decision support for Risk Assessments (*riskanalys*). In these assessments, identified risks are further investigated and evaluated in greater detail. A risk assessment appraises the probability of a phenomenon occurring and if so its consequences. The difference between a risk assessment and a Consequential Analysis (*konsekvensanalys*) is the latter's emphasis on positive and negative consequences – for certain actors or for the entire society– if the Agency was to implement certain measures. These types of analyses are often prepared prior to introducing new measures; noteworthy is that there is emphasis on including an analysis of the zero alternative – that is, what would happen if no measures were taken.

A Sample Analysis (*urvalsanalys*) is used both as input to other analyses and also to create samples of taxpayers that are considered more prone to evade taxes – regardless of intention (planning, evasion, cheating, but also categories of taxpayers that might have problems understanding the rules). Next comes the Impact Analysis (*effektanalys*), which is an evaluation of the introduction of changes to certain taxes or control measures. The effect of the reduced VAT percentage on restaurant services on tax evasion within the restaurant sector (Skatteverket 2014e) is an example of an impact analysis. The final analysis type is an Attitudinal Survey (*attitydundersökning*) where a statistically selected group of respondents reply verbally or in writing to a specific set of questions (see Chapter 2 for an ethnographic example of such an endeavour).

The analysts are both at the forefront and also somewhat on the periphery of core Agency work – to collect taxes and monitor that the right taxes have been paid. 'What we think and talk about as important issues at the unit is not necessarily what the rest of the Agency talks about', Julia explained to me the first time I met her. So in order to engage properly with the knowledge the Agency needs, there is emphasis on the instigation dialogue (*beställardialog*). It is called dialogue, as it is not just an order from decision makers to be executed by the analysts. The instigator for any report is ultimately responsible for using the resources to make such analyses, but it is said to be of vital importance that the analysts understand properly what is being asked for and that the instigator understands the limitations of what is feasible to analyse given the methods the analysts have at hand (Skatteverket 2014d). Yet, this is not always easy, as insights can come up during the analysis itself; insights that could not be foreseen at the initiation of a project (as all social scientists know …).

The analysts seem aware of what impact their reports have. Wera, a seasoned analyst, experienced too much success following an analysis she had carried out on deductions made as other costs in the yearly tax return, an issue that was really minor. She and a colleague had used a new method that was very easy to apply in random audits. As a result did a number of very large (in the sense of encompassing many people) audit controls take place that were way out of proportion to the extent of the implications of these illicit deductions, she said.

The Cost Deduction Project

The project I came to follow mainly resembled that of a risk assessment and this is how I will refer to it in this book, but discussions about what the project's actual identity was occurred throughout its life. The definition of risk at the Agency is quite extensive and issues are described as originating both externally as well as internally (Skatteverket 2005). Internal risks consist of topics such as a 'wrong' interpretation of the law, requests originating from other departments – especially the legal one – as well as lacunas in the control procedures and organization. External risks are events in society that are deemed to impact the ability and will of citizens to pay taxes. These could be, for example, the financial crisis, changes in laws that might create loopholes, or structural changes like the rapidly expanding number of self-employed. The initiation of risk evaluation projects derives from many sources: inquiries from authorities, tips or questions from the public and even from discussions at coffee breaks. A risk evaluation usually runs throughout the Agency as a longer project involving diverse knowledge, assessments and evaluations.

This risk assessment project came about for several reasons. Lars thought that it started with an analysis from the Danish Tax and Customs Administration, SKAT. A few of the analysts had been at a meeting in

Denmark where they heard a presentation of a report.[36] The Swedes thought its content interesting, but perhaps being too rigid in its categorization of taxpayers as either teammates or opponents. About the same time, a few of the analysts had discussed similar issues at coffee breaks. The problem with illicit cost deductions among commercial entities of various sorts (COENs) had been brought up at unit meetings. As Ingela said: 'Many of us have friends who work as COENs.[37] They travel with their family, they buy computers and mobile phones and all these acquisitions are paid for by the COEN'.

There was also a general feeling among the analysts that the Agency had concentrated its audit efforts on incomes over the last five years, somewhat neglecting the cost side when it analysed risks. So with these three issues at hand, the time was ripe for conducting a survey of such cost deductions among COENs.

Gunnar, the head of the Analysis Unit, encouraged this project so it would also address issues that had escalated as a result of the large svart arbete (informal work or working off the record) studies that were made from 2004 to 2006 (Skatteverket 2006b, 2007a). One of the conclusions was that small corporations were active in what was seen as svart arbete. But the issue that surfaced was not informal income, but deductions of certain costs. So the Agency was curious as to how the distinction between costs in private and public, or formal work, was made in practice. The Agency still notices a rapid increase in registered small corporations; at this point the question arose as to whether these deductions would increase to the same extent. 'We want a better picture of the situation', said Gunnar. There were thus a number of merging interests that could be investigated by this project. Perhaps it was also the reason for its protracted life and in the end the burial of it, as the conclusions were too complex to be fathomed by society at large.

So Gunnar obtained a formal order and granted a group of analysts – the task force – significant latitude in carrying it out. It started with two analysts from HQ, Lars and Julia, together with two colleagues, Svenne and Gunilla, from two regional offices. The two women, Julia and Gunilla, participated at the start and at the end of the project only, due to parental leave and sickness respectively. Along the way Per joined, from yet another regional office. The constitution of the task force underscores the homogenizing knowledge endeavours of the Agency.

They met for one to two days monthly at HQ, interspersed with hour-long video meetings, a common way to communicate between the Agency offices. Their meetings consisted of long discussions on information collected and how to go forward, given the insights that they had concluded so far. The meetings were as informal as the environment, as was the dress code of the attendees. Lars, the meeting organizer, is a gentle theoretician who never pushed his opinion until he had listened to all the other participants and had thoroughly considered any issue. Per came in a year into the project and from the start worried about methodologies in order to perform proper/real research. He repeatedly asked me, the ethnographer, how research is done in the academic world. One avenue he proposed was to re-examine all issues previously agreed upon as hypotheses. The others were initially reluctant, but as they are always eager to gain new insights, they agreed and all attained insights were reformulated into hypotheses. The guy from the North of Sweden, Svenne, repeatedly dug out anecdotes and episodes from his long experience. His accent betrayed where he was located; he is street-smart and a word equilibrist. In the beginning he found everything 'very interesting', not mockingly but truly intrigued by the smallest of issues. He continuously offered examples from reality, as well as new metaphors to elucidate the issues they discussed. In his own increasing insight of their quest, he once proposed: 'Before I felt like this project consisted of 40,000 islands with shitty communications. I feel that they get increasingly connected and that there are regular boat services between some of them'. Lars smiled and proposed that there were perhaps even bridges between the islands. 'Not yet, but in due time', Svenne objected. 'There will be bridges. Right now, some of the islands only have a rowboat that departs monthly'.

What seemed so obvious at the start (incorrect cost deductions among a certain type of COENs) turned out to be a tricky subject to work with. The task force's deliberations for finding definitions is an illustration of this point and also serves to illustrate how the Agency looks at different ways to address compliance. We will in the following chapters come back to these initial questions and see how the task force develops them; but here are the initial five questions as posed in the *beställning* (order), with some comments on how they relate back to research on tax compliance.

1. Are the regulations and the legal framework unclear? Here we can draw upon compliance work looking at the law itself and how the Agency has interpreted the law and developed it into regulations and information to be followed.
2. Studying how common obvious faulty deductions are is an attempt to quantify the existence of such faults among the Swedish population at large. These quantifications could for example become part of the tax gap calculations.
3. The question of how other taxable entities are affected directs attention towards the legitimacy of the Agency. If taxpayers believe that

other citizens pay their dues, they will continue to comply with what they owe.
4. What are the consequences resulting from the rapid expansion of COENs? This question builds on the replies to the previous questions and thus prepares for the more encompassing and final question.
5. How to identify the risks (to the Agency) from these deductions?

We can see from initial discussions how different insights and knowledge on compliance overlap. Lars said that it would be interesting to see why people deduct costs this way. Is it because everybody else does or do people think the law is wrong? What should the Agency do? Should it change the rules or should it provide stricter controls and audit more COENs? These deductions probably concern small amounts in comparison, but perhaps they are very common? If so, it would be very difficult to use controls and audits as preventive effects. As Wera, a seasoned analyst who took part in the initial preparations, said: 'We can never defend such a project in response to resources used'. Implicit in their discussion is thus their deep knowledge of the research and strategies the Agency has applied over the years. The analysts started to direct their gaze towards finding explanations for why people comply, or do not, and whether compliance depends on perceptions either of other taxpayers' willingness to comply or whether the law is fair. The task force posed suggestions as to what the Agency could do as a response. The analysts looked for various numerical estimates – how many, how much – but especially used these numbers to find relations to other types of issues that make up the tax gap. They also acknowledged their view on the role of control at the Agency. Finally, they are cost-conscious, as they, along with the rest of the Agency, work within budgetary limits and had actually been subject to cutbacks during the last few years.

How the task force would approach the problem of defining these cost deductions was also a subject for discussion. As we will see in the following chapters, discussion sidetracked so that what a deduction meant could be explained to different actors. In the upcoming survey, how should they be described so that respondents would understand what they were actually responding to (see more in Chapter 2)? The task force carefully tiptoed around finding an explicit definition to avoid the possibility of accusing an innocent taxpayer of wrongdoing. For the Random Audit Control department, the task was easier, as it meant auditing specific input (e.g., boxes) on the tax return form, yet taxpayer practices came to accentuate a dividing line between private and public (Chapter 3). We will also see in internal discussions throughout the Agency how the definition took on different guises. Spelling out the results was perhaps the most challenging task, as both managers, and especially the Director General, saw flaws with the definitions they had worked with and compared to the numerical results (Chapter 4).

The Workings of the Agency

In this chapter I have, through references to research on tax compliance and the development of strategies and practices introduced by the Agency, created a context from where we can move on to understand in more detail the knowledge the Agency works with.

The organization of the Swedish tax collecting agencies has changed over the years as a response on the one hand to its fiscal and other duties as stated by the government, and on the other hand to a society that is continuously changing. We have, for example, read about organizational changes as a response to new tax laws and new responsibilities, public discontentment, and especially the technical development of IT solutions and the availability of the Internet to the population at large. As has been hinted, the organization of taxation is also influenced by internal and academic research on tax compliance, by other countries' experiences, as well as by insights into the Agency's own errors in practice.

About forty years ago, we could see the start of national standardization of taxation practices. The aim was to ensure that tax laws were homogeneously interpreted; that all taxpayers received the same message to ensure equal treatment of all taxpayers. This work has paid off. It has been a work aimed at increasing compliance yet not necessarily maximizing the fiscal income. Decisions influencing the organization have been made to a certain extent as responses to what society thinks about the Agency and its work. Simultaneous to the reorganization, ideas of other ways of working – of collecting tax and controlling tax returns – influenced citizens' views on taxation practices.

The flow of different ideas on how compliance is increased can be illustrated by the simultaneous location and relocation of taxation practices. Buildings and workplaces influence peoples' working practices. The Agency's new HQ is designed as a modern office landscape where groups of people sit out in the open. As a visitor to the current office I pass by employees' desks but also pass many meeting rooms of various sorts and sizes. The smallest rooms have one table with two chairs on each side. These rooms are where discussions or smaller meetings between employees are supposed to take place or phone calls taken. Needless to say, everybody has a mobile phone and the physical phone lines are no more. If we go by the new architecture, the Agency is now more withdrawn and impersonal, yet inside there is more warmth. The carpeting has shades for different departments and these colours are reflected in the names of the meeting rooms; the blue shades are accompanied by marine themes such as the 'Lighthouse' and 'Cabin', and in the red carpeted areas the rooms 'Poppy', 'Sweat-pea' or 'Cowslip' and others with similar flowery connotations are found. This is perhaps a sign of the times? The Agency was on the list of the most popular employers for young business professionals in 2014. The interior colours are warm, whereas the facade is of bricks with the modern addition of glass and natural anodized aluminium.[38] The facade reminds us that the Agency has adapted to contemporary modern society. The friendly and helpful service is substantiated by increased control, as the Agency now reverts to conducting more audits and makes these through computer sampling (Skatteverket 2014b). Although the contemporary audit is very detailed and goes into almost intimate detail of the taxpayer, it is no longer based on any personal knowledge, as was the case during the reign of the Tax Board peopled by responsible citizens fifty years ago.

This is not a reductionist explanation but a playful attempt to illustrate the many different facets of work shaped by compliance in an organization such as the Agency. It is helpful to think about those different aspects in terms of socio-technical agencements that in different set-ups consist of technology, knowledge, wordings, research, numbers and people; in all a history or hinterland, in reference to John Law (2009), but a hinterland that is continuously challenged by societal changes. There are new technologies and programmes that enable different controls and communication as well as information initiatives for citizens that aim to simplify their lives. New tax laws or court decisions prompt adaptations to Agency work praxis: amended controls and audit procedures, and updated information and ways of working. The Director General introduces new ways to think about tax compliance that encompass established as well as contested notions of CSR. New research, polls and surveys provide estimates about various taxation statistics. The media alters public discourse on who pays, and creates headlines about those who avoid paying.

There is obviously much, much more to the Agency's work; but the reader will hopefully now have a better picture of what types of knowledge about tax compliance are current and have been used and sometimes rejected. As John Law proposes 'sustainable knowledge rests in and reproduces more or less stable networks or hinterlands of relevant instruments, representations – and the realities that these describe. And this is why realities – together with the techniques and representations that enact these – generally feel solid and reliable' (Law 2009: 242).

We have also seen, in the mottos and descriptions of the taxpayers used by the Agency, how it mirrors its own role in Swedish society and how it regards the creation of compliance. The first attempts to campaign for increased compliance focused on taxes, making the state responsible for the benefit of its citizens. Then followed a more introspective view of the Agency's own work and how it could be legitimized in society. Currently, emphasis has moved to educating and morally shaping the taxpayer. It is up to the individual to pay in order to improve society generally, with the Agency most recently extending these educational and training messages to corporations and organizations by aiming to make tax compliance part of CSR. Even the buildings that host the Agency can perhaps illustrate this development, from the tax-scraper towering over 'all' economic activities to the anonymous and solid HQs in the red-brick buildings underscoring the importance of fiscal work in Swedish society. The red-brick facade is, however, 'reinforced' with steel and glass structures and hides a very modern interior where employees adapt to the modish 'activity-based' ways of working and where computer programmes increasingly choose taxpayer subjects for a more thorough audit.

The Agency has grown in terms of numbers of employees but has also consolidated into one large nationwide organization. While its usage of technology has increased, personal knowledge about taxpayers has decreased. Its employees seldom 'know' the people they tax and therefore different socio-technical set-ups are increasingly used. This has allowed the Agency to change from adopting personal control to embracing a more compassionate treatment of taxpayers in order to encourage them to comply. However, the Agency seems to have retracted from the somewhat quite naive stance that 'everybody wants to do their fair share' to a more realistic approach recognizing that controls and audits are also needed. This does not mean that the motto has changed though. Control is part of the compassion, as other taxpayers will not believe that others pay up unless they themselves are subject to occasional, and very unpredictable, control. The lingering feeling when going beyond the public strategies and smooth talk is that the Agency leans on control, and thus the threat of sanctions and penalties, as the main tool that makes taxpayers comply. Clearly, the Agency pays attention to what taxpayers say and do. It has thus been a shaper of taxpayers, but has also very much taken on board what practices are seen as acceptable among those same taxpayers. The Agency in its practices and thus in the values it expresses walks a fine line between shaping and being shaped by Swedish taxpayers. Maintaining this balance is of the upmost importance in the Agency's continuous efforts to be seen as legitimate in its practices. And it is from this hinterland we depart to see how this cost deduction project was performed.

Notes

1. The Swedish Tax Agency was ranked fifteenth among the most attractive employers, as seen by young business professionals. The list was topped by Google, followed by IKEA. http://universumglobal.com/se/karriarbarometern-2014. Retrieved 10 October 2015.
2. This was partly due to the fact that Gustav Vasa could sell the items collected. Kings at the time were not only rulers, but also merchants, seeing their country as a factory and store house. The other part of the explanation was that the taxes levied were to finance provisions for soldiers at war. At the frontier money was quite useless, as there prices rocketed (Odén 2008: 8).
3. Sweden was far from the first country to institute this reform but followed initiatives taken in Great Britain, Denmark, Italy, some German states as well as Austria (Ekman 2003a: 10).
4. For most of last century, the head of the tax board was appointed by the regional boards *(länsstyrelsen)* and the remaining members by the municipal council.
5. As a result of the centennial tax reform, the former tax law of 1956 was replaced with two new laws. One was the new taxation law, the other addressed tax return and was a statement of earnings and reductions.
6. http://skönstaxering.com. Retrieved 5 September 2016.
7. These agencies were Riksskattenämnden, which was responsible for direct taxes; Kontrollstyrelsen, which handled excise taxes; the population registry at Centrala folkbokförings- och uppbördsnämnden; and the magistrate's office, Exekutionsväsendets organisationsnämnd.
8. This can be seen in the number of reports produced on organization work during the 1980s as well as in the introduction of diverse automated systems.
9. http://skrapan.se/om-skrapan. Retrieved 15 January 2015.
10. http://www.hydrophobe.org/pdf/bruxelles/V_33.pdf. Retrieved 15 January 2015.
11. I am grateful for this story told to me by the former Director of Information Björn Thärnström.
12. Nöterian is named after the city block 'The Nut' where the building is situated.
13. On the Swedish Tax Agency website there is a motto prominently displayed: *Vår vision är ett samhälle där alla vill göra rätt för sig.*
14. Everyone living and residing in Sweden ought to be registered regardless of nationality. All residents have a unique 10-digit code consisting of year-month-date of birth followed by four digits, the third digit indicating gender. The code was introduced in 1947 and was probably the first of its kind covering all residents in a country.
15. An estate inventory is a document detailing the assets and liabilities of a deceased person.
16. *De eftersträvade skatte- och avgiftsintäkterna ska säkerställas rättssäkert och på ett för samhället ekonomiskt effektivt sätt samt på ett sätt som är kostnadseffektivt och enkelt för medborgare och företag. Brottslighet inom skatteområdet ska förebyggas och bekämpas. Medborgare och företag ska ha förtroende för Skatteverkets verksamhet.*
17. For example, the current Director General Ingemar Hansson was prior to his appointment in 2010 responsible for taxes in his position as second in command to the Minister of Finance. His title was Undersecretary of State at the finance department. The Deputy Director Helena Dyrssen came from a similar position at the Cabinet

Offices. Former Deputy Director Magdalena Andersson is currently the Finance Minister (since autumn 2014).

18. Presentation Lennart Wittberg, Almedalen 30 June 2014.
19. *Statens Offentliga Utredningar* (Swedish Government Official Reports).
20. RRV – The Swedish National Audit Office.
21. Brå – Brottsförebyggande Rådet (Swedish Crime Prevention Council).
22. Although the Agency is often consulted before laws are passed in the Riksdag and can also suggest changes in the law.
23. *Förvaltningslagen* SFS 1986: 223.
24. ROT (*reparationer, ombyggnad, tillbyggnad* – repairs, refurbishing, attachments) subsidies have been used now and then to boost the building industry in times of a slack economy. These subsidies could be used for certain types of reconstruction work in private homes with tax deductions up to a given amount, but also as a way to lessen the propensity for undocumented work. ROT is almost unanimously supported by both politicians and citizens. RUT stands for *renhållning, underhåll, tvätt* (cleaning, maintenance, laundry). RUT is also a play on words with earlier established ROT deductions as Rut is also a female name and women traditionally perform the cleaning in Sweden.
25. Provided that a bank account has been registered to which this money can be transferred.
26. Based on an interview with former Director of Information Björn Thärnström.
27. The other aim for the Agency is to retain high legitimacy within Swedish society.
28. The Swedish parliament consisted then of two chambers.
29. *Svenska akademins ordbok* (the Dictionary of the Swedish Academy).
30. *Vi är en modern och och effektiv förvaltning som arbetar utifrån ett kund och processorienterat synsätt. Mebodrgarna och företagen kan ta del av vår service när de själva vill och på det sätt som passar dem.*
31. Mona Sahlin in an interview on Swedish Television 8 September 1994.
32. *Att bidra till det gemensamma är rätt och ansvarsfullt, och att inte vara solidarisk är ofräscht.*
33. Article by Ingemar Hansson in *Dagens Industri*, 18 May 2011.
34. The respondent was asked the question: 'Which issue(s) or societal problem(s) do you think is/are the most important in Sweden today? Please provide a maximum of three issues/societal problems'. The percentages presented are based on all respondents.
35. http://www.ekonomifakta.se/sv/Fakta/Foretagande/Naringslivet/Antal-foretag-i-Sverige/. Retrieved 15 January 2015.
36. *Baggrundsrapport Samfundsøkonomiske konsekvenser af hjemmeserviceordningen*. No date available.
37. I use COEN as an autonym for a variety of commercial entities. I promised from the very start not to disclose any details about the project until finished and published, but as the report was buried I stay with COEN. For the purpose and argument of this book, the legal identity is not important.
38. As noted by the architects behind the refurbishing. http://reflexark.se/projekt/kontor/skatteverket-huvudkontor-och-stockholmskontor/. Retrieved 15 January 2015.

Chapter 2

Talking with People

What Can We Learn from an Attitudinal Survey?

From the very start of the project, the task force discussed a survey – a survey that would provide insights as to why these cost deductions are claimed. Yet Lars also knew that 'these type of questions are both difficult to pronounce and also difficult to answer in a survey'. This was an insight that all task force members expanded on throughout the construction and performance of the survey(s) – as finally two surveys were conducted. Within the aims of the book I am, perhaps, not so much interested in the actual results of the survey questions but instead on the premises of a survey, the assumptions inherent in the questions posed and how they relate to what came out of it. I wanted to know what types of knowledge are produced by a survey and also the type of knowledge it creates in a broader sense. To achieve these insights, I address three main issues in this chapter.

First, I question, with the help of the very few critical studies of surveys made, what a survey actually is and what limitations such an analysis tool is seen to have. Thus we are able to better understand why the survey as a knowledge-creating method was questioned in the deliberations among the task force members. On what assumptions was the survey made and why were its results contested? We will see that historical traditions of managing knowledge are not easily erased, even if these traditions are questioned. This brings us to the second point; there are also other participants/stakeholders who can be affected by surveys. If possible do these actors take an active role in the survey's production and execution while along the way disputing various parts of the knowledge it creates? The task force's questioning of surveys as a knowledge-creating method also indicates its shaping aspects, the third aim of this chapter. Conducting the survey brings to the fore some of the political issues that are part of taxation practices. On a societal level there is a perception that the Agency handles the question of who is seen to pay and who is seen to cheat and that it cares for its legitimacy in Swedish society. Thus, it is not only the knowledge and insights that emerge as a result of a survey that shape the taxpayer. By looking at the process of designing and executing a survey we will see how participants, who in some instances take on more of the role of stakeholders, are continuously trying to impact surveys in society, in the role of a commercial entity, to create a societal image of COENs as taxpayers and to retain surveys as *the* knowledge method to use.

This chapter takes the reader on a chronological journey and follows the conducting of two surveys. I will especially focus on the creation of the second survey – from the initial posing of questions through the task force's elaboration of which methods to use, how the methods were applied and external stakeholders' opinions on the survey, to the analysis of data and the place for its results in the final report. All involved in this survey thought that it was well-planned and executed with a valid number of respondents. However, with the help of the task force, we can question what surveys as a method can say about a societal phenomenon such as these faulty deductions and see why the outcome of the survey in the end was considered if not useless at least greatly constrained. Thus we will learn why attitudinal surveys should be used with caution, 'not just because it is something that we usually do'. More importantly for the aim of this book, we will see what the survey says about how the Agency views the taxpayer, how its practices are shaped by such views and thus, in the end, how it shapes the taxpayer.

The Social Life of Surveys

Survey and surveillance come from the same etymological root. The origin is in the Medieval Latin *supervidere*, *super* meaning over, and *videre* that translates to see; to oversee something (cf. with the French *surveiller*). The contemporary meaning reveals a tension between the noun and the verb. The former means acquiring 'a general view based on an inspection of the opinions or experience of a group of people' and the latter to 'look carefully and thoroughly at', as proposed by Oxford Dictionary, 10th edition. Thus, the English meaning of the verb survey is to simultaneously take a view of the 'whole' but to do so in great detail, to really get to know what is going on. The aim of a survey is therefore to find out what is happening by looking very closely at a selected excerpt of this whole. This tension between the noun and the verb comes to the fore in the survey we follow.

So a survey is conducted to enable us to understand something a group of people do or think; it is a secret that is to be revealed (Didier 2005: 638). And this revelation does not lie in an individual response, but in the mass of answers to one or several questions about people's doings or thinkings, most often referred to as attitudes (surveys are often called attitudinal surveys). The new insight lies in the totality of answers – which due to anonymity is still a secret. So we are never interested in who is saying something about what in a survey, but rather what a particular set of traits the respondents have in common when they select one particular answer over another to a particular question.

Approaching surveys as having social lives of their own (Law, Ruppert and Savage 2011; Savage 2013) can highlight how such types of methods are used within social sciences and why these methods persist. The researchers within this vein draw attention to the critical stance towards quantitative methods especially, and notably their often positivist assumptions. But instead of declining them as 'bad', they instead focus on 'the affordances and capacities that [sic] are mobilized in and through methods themselves' (Savage 2013: 5). Savage argues that although questioning the social scientific quantitative methods is not something new (cf. Porter 1995; Sjöström 2002), this movement is made possible by a dual challenge to the quantifications and their resulting insights. On one hand there is an increased reliance and belief in ethnographic methods and verbal depictions of societal issues, but on the other hand there is also a proliferation of digital analysis with the introduction of big data and diverse types of data-mining methods.

Taking this critical stance on the survey as a method means that we can better understand the qualms the task force members express throughout the conducting and execution of the survey, without abandoning the idea of performing it. Surveys have a life at the Agency, as it continually carries out surveys, but as we will see it is a questionable life following how the task force question the knowledge produced by the survey. As Savage summarizes: 'the question of method as raising fundamental theoretical questions about the limits of knowledge itself, and to reflect on new ways of understanding the relationship between the cultural, social and material' (Savage 2013: 18).

John Law draws attention to the performative aspects of surveys and survey research in his article 'Seeing like a survey' (2009), paraphrasing James Scott's famous book (1999). Looking at this survey through Savage's agenda of 'Social Life of Methods' (2013) helps us to understand how results of such surveys do not only describe reality; they also enact it into being (Law 2009: 239). Thus, what do such methods and the insights they provide actually do to our understanding of society?

Law approaches a survey as an 'archaeologist' in order to reveal different aspects of what a survey can say about society; he reveals layers. The example he uses is the result of the Eurobarometer regarding peoples' views on farm animal welfare. Within the idea of Europe as one society, he unveils how this survey shows: (1) the individual as a consumer; (2) politics revealing what issues are currently at stake and who has access to the political decisions; (3) political subjectivities regarding individuals and issues; (4) a group of individuals carrying certain opinions and possibly thus enacting them; (5) romanticism, as the 'collectivity [is] being naturalized as a population of individuals' (Law 2009: 248).

In the following section I will borrow from Law's insights above to see how the surveys initiated by the task force contribute to the making and shaping of the Swedish taxpayer. As we will see, exploring the views of the various stakeholders reveals their concerns about how a survey can affect various societal aspects – and on various grounds. With Law's help, it is also easier to understand the failure of this survey. Yet, applying his analytical tools is carried out with a certain number of caveats.

First of all, I do not concentrate on the individual as a consumer, but rather as a taxpayer. A taxpayer pays money and does not know what s/he gets for it, whereas a consumer mostly has a choice as to whether spending money or not and knows what s/he is getting for it. However, once in a while the consumer aspect creeps in but not as posing as the COEN, as a protagonist of neoliberal society (Law 2009: 246), but rather that this survey is made emphasizing costs. And costs occur as a result of consumption. We will thus see both how the idea of a taxpayer – and even a tax cheater – is shaped working through this survey.

Second, with the ethnographic material at hand I can expand on Law's discussion. What is conducted here is not an archaeological survey but one of ethnography; I do not only have the results of the survey, but have been with it from its initiation. I have followed the construction and execution of the survey – from the 'hinterland', to speak with Law. We proceed from the Agency's inherent idea of surveys, through the task force members' deliberations of what such surveys do, to finally seeing what knowledge these answers could provide and what use they were in the final report. It is thus not the results of the survey, but the making and execution of it that makes certain insights from it prominent and put others in the background in this risk assessment project.

This brings us to Law's third point; the participants'/stakeholders' role in the creation and execution of such a survey and how they can impact such a survey and the knowledge it creates. We will see how, by fulfilling the aims with the project, they also hold various views on the survey and thus keep them alive (Law, Ruppert and Savage 2011). There is the commercial aspect of a research consultancy that has a customer in the Agency, but there is also the restrictive, disciplining views of the Näringslivets nämnd för regelförenkling (NNR, an acquaintance we will make below) – views that are mediated by SCB (Statistics Sweden). The stakeholders interfere in differing ways with all three of this chapter's aims. We can thus also see the emerging shape of the political aspects of Swedish taxation.

But here we will concentrate on the transformation of knowledge and the performative aspects of such knowledge throughout the construction and execution of surveys. However, I use the notion of performativity, and its linguistic relatives, cautiously. As Daniel Neyland has pointed out, there are limitations to the notion of performativity (Neyland 2013, see also in the Introduction). He argues that when a performative idea, such as a survey, is applied in practice by different actors in different contexts, the basic idea will mutate. It does not 'perform' in its original sense throughout the chain of events. Instead it takes on a slightly new form. Second, although the participants/stakeholders pronounce their concerns with a survey's performative aspects, I find it important to emphasize that they do not know exactly how the survey impacts citizens' opinions; how certain sentences and questions within the survey will be received and interpreted.

Surveys Are What We Usually Do

Already at the very first meeting, Lars had said that they considered a survey of sorts because they wanted to distinguish whether there were differences in opinions between categories of taxpayers (e.g., employees and entrepreneurs of various sorts). The task force thus wanted to know about attitudes the public at large held on such cost deductions, and on the other hand the attitudes held by the COENs – the group of taxpayers in focus here. The task force thus constructs a distinction between a 'general public' and 'stakeholders', where the latter are thought to express predefined views based on interest (Lezaun and Soneryd 2007: 292–93).

It turns out that attitudes held by the public can be established by getting them to answer a few questions of interest for another larger survey, an omnibus. This strategy is often used at the Agency. Questions from several analysis projects are grouped together in one survey in order to save on costs. This larger survey recurs annually and addresses citizens' views on the tax system and on the Agency; the omnibus was due shortly, and the task force decided fairly quickly on three questions to put to the public. Two of the questions in focus here were if the perception of the public is that (1) entrepreneurs (such as COENs) commonly deduct costs for private consumption; and (2) if the public think these deductions are consciously made. The citizens could choose between agree, neither/nor, do not agree, or no response.

Responses to this survey were returned quickly. Noteworthy is that the response percentages for each type of answer was almost the same for both questions. Thus, according to the general public's view almost half think entrepreneurs deduct such costs and that they do it on purpose. Second, when taken together, these answers implicitly include the view that the COENs also enact their opinions (Law 2009: 244–45), which makes for a special view on causality. These answers provide somewhat negative news for the Agency in its ambition to operate in a society 'where everybody contributes their fair share'. This is what the general public (*allmänheten*) thinks but it does not necessarily reflect the views of a taxpayer, but presumably so (as most adult Swedes earn some income and therefore pay taxes).

The second survey was intended for the COENs themselves. The majority of the meetings throughout the autumn involved the construction of this survey. The two regional analysts, Gunilla and Svenne, were mainly responsible for drafting this survey. There were seven versions in all, which were up for discussion during autumn, and the survey went through one internal and two external reviews before finally being approved – without any major changes, to the obvious delight of the task force.

At the outset there were many things the task force wanted to know about the COENs and therefore had many questions to pose. As Julia said: 'it [the survey] ought to provide questions that address a mix of the COENs' values, what costs they think the Agency can find and what they think is *comme il faut* in society. The [completed] survey should show what they think.' To start with, how is information about COENs personal experiences with the phenomenon and their views on it obtained at the societal level? The questions obviously circled around the aims of the entire risk assessment project and put the experiences of individual COENs at the heart of it. The individual aspect was deemed the easiest, as shown by these direct questions: Who are you? What do you think? What do you do? How do you do it? Questioning why someone is doing something (e.g., why they are claiming deductions) is slightly more difficult. The question in the background that alas cannot be directly posed is whether the COENs are intentionally cheating.

The task force discussed issues such as whether it is too difficult to do the right thing. Are the rules fuzzy? Should the Agency work to provide more information so that more taxpayers can deduct the 'right' costs? Should the Agency try to simplify the procedure; make it easier by changing the technology and the reporting requirements? Or is it the law in itself that makes it difficult to make the right deductions? If so, how can the Agency propose changes? In the wider perspective, what consequences does a change in the law have? The Agency is very reluctant to ask such questions, as it would require them to propose legal changes to the government (as we will see in Chapter 4).

Finally, perceptions of others' behaviour were deemed important. The more the social aspect was included in the reasoning of WHY people do certain things, the more perceptions played a role. The task force kept returning to the point that taxpayers do what other taxpayers do (cf. Braithwaite 2002; Kornhauser 2007) and so do tax cheaters (cf. Björklund Larsen 2010). If this is so, we must ask who the 'others' are; other COENs, the general public, or some other group of people taxpayers feel they belong to – family, neighbourhood/geographical location, ethnicity, work, class, political belonging, profession? Here we start coming closer to the idea of stereotyping or categorizing the public.

The task force's discussions surged back and forth in meetings and in emails concerning the type of knowledge that should be used, in which order the questions should appear in order to elicit the most replies, and the perceived ease of analytically penetrating the results. I want to present the task force's very careful considerations by looking into the nitpicky details of how they constructed this survey, so bear with the following detailed account of their work. The task force knows that the way questions are posed impacts the answers they get and thus the opinion respondents might have of the Agency as a result of such a survey.

Making and Framing the Survey Structure

A first concern was to lead respondents into and through the survey. The final order of questions went from general ones to the very explicit questions about the COEN's own cost deductions. The survey was divided into five parts – A, B, C, D and E – a structure that was maintained throughout the entire process. But the content of the sections differed depending on concerns for representability and objectivity in the answers. Section F asking for other opinions on the subject was already removed at the second review.

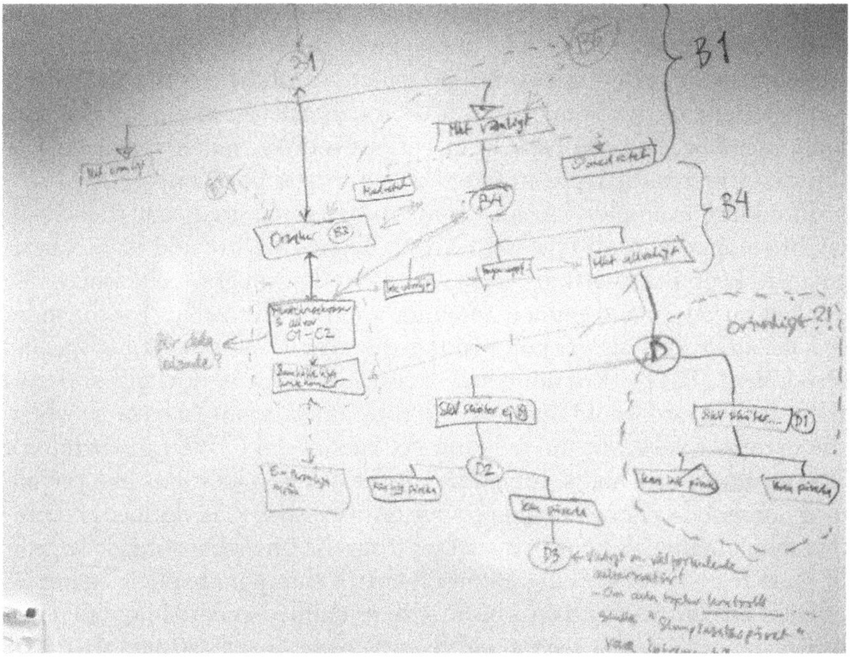

Illustration 2.1 Analysts making surveys. Photo by the author.

Section A considered the respondent's background information: gender, age, education, annual income, present professional attachment, and industrial sector to which the COEN belongs, turnover of COEN, number of employees and who does the bookkeeping. A third of these questions could be answered from the registers from which the respondents were selected and so these questions were eventually removed. The initial question regarding a respondent's geographical origins was also scratched, as it could be perceived as negative and influence the response rate.

Section B underwent many changes and finally addressed the WHYs. Initially, this section's blunt and explicit questions about the respondent's view on cost deductions were shuffled around and were eventually moved to section C. The first framing regarded 'your view on cost deductions for COENs', offering four alternative answers; from 'definitely subject to tax' to 'absolutely not subject to tax' and a final fifth one 'I do not know/ have no opinion'. In the end, section B did pose 'questions regarding scope, causes and consequences of cost deductions for the COEN', as these questions were deemed to contextualize the issue at hand. Section B contained a number of questions about perceptions and/or knowledge of casual explanations on why such deductions are made.

Section C ended with questions that addressed WHAT type of cost deductions ought to be subject to tax. Here the reply options were more straightforward, offering yes, no, or somewhat and then the usual final opt-out reply of 'no opinion'. In a thorough discussion among the task force members and feedback from various sources, much attention was directed towards the type of examples that should be given.

Providing examples was important. Julia emphasized that the survey ought to appeal to all types of COEN. Therefore 'it could be advantageous to keep the questions vague. A respondent might feel cornered by explicit questions and explicit amounts'. Gunilla chimed in that the more specific questions also risked making them more abstract for a specific respondent. They risked not being of concern to the respondent and thus the response rate would diminish. So they aimed to find a balance where the extremes were not too obvious. As Svenne said, 'We cannot have a Boeing at one end and a Toblerone[1] at the other'. Questions like private usage of mobile phones would provide answers that were deemed too predictable. Finally, an array of questions from the one addressing deduction of costs for a good working environment to the more explicit examples of costs for journeys and refurbishing that mainly benefited private usage were opted for. Both Gunilla and Svenne were finally satisfied that they had managed to provide many different examples.

Section D concerned how the respondent saw the Agency fulfilling its task. Initially, questions with many explicit examples concerned the risk of detection if a COEN made faulty deductions. In the final version there were only two questions left: an estimate of how many resources the respondent thought the Agency used to find faulty deductions and how many the respondent thought the Agency ought to use. The final section, E, began by explicitly asking why the respondent thought there were cases of tax cheating. But to mention the word 'cheating' leads the respondent to think in extremes. As Julia said: 'I do not think we should talk about cheating at all. We should look for the reasons why these types of deductions exist'. So 'cheating' was quickly scrapped in favour of a focus on the respondent's own treatment of taxes, framed as 'What do you do with your own cost deductions?' 'If we get an honest answer', Lars said, 'then it could be interesting to compare it to how they see others' behaviour'.

As they had a range of questions, they also discussed the type of answers the respondents would choose. In a survey, answers are provided, but what type of choices should be offered to the respondent? Instead of verbal explanations, the replies were quantitative evaluations of reasons. Would the scale expressing agreement or disagreement with a statement consist of three, four or five choices? As an example from their discussions: Would it be a scale from 1 to 4, where 1 refers to not agreeing at all and 4 is equivalent to full agreement? Alternatives 2 and 3 would be undefined but give a sense of what people value. Svenne said that the numbering should be the other way around. It is strange to start with 'not agreeing' therefore 1 ought to be full agreement. 'We must have copied from old surveys', Gunilla excused. In the end they opted for a range of answers in order to make the respondent more proactive: from 1 for no causal connection to 5 for complete agreement with a given statement. For causal propositions there was a final 'no opinion'. For responses to more quantitative statements, the same scale was used but now 1 was 'very unlikely' and 5 'very likely'. There were also yes and no questions, with the occasional addition of 'do not want to respond' or 'perhaps'.

So the survey started and ended with explicit individual questions about *whom* the respondent was and HOW s/he makes cost deductions. The mid sections, B and C, considered opinions and perceptions on them as a societal phenomenon – what the respondent's views were on WHY these deductions are claimed and WHAT they consist of.

All these questions make the survey an evaluation of the work done by the Agency, said Svenne. Implicit in most answers was how well the Agency fulfils its work – not least from the questions in section D, where the task force could not resist asking a specific question on the Agency's performance concerning cost deductions. While aiming to survey what people do and think, this survey also became a meta-level appreciation of the Agency's surveillance of taxpayers; whether it does the right thing when making sure taxpayers do the right thing.

While conducting the survey, the task force pondered which execution method would ensure most feedback. Would it be a mailed enquiry, a telephone survey, or even coming from focus group interviews? The idea of focus groups was quickly abandoned, as it was deemed too difficult to analyse the answers. The focus group method was now and then brought up again as some wishful thinking of engaging directly with people but was repeatedly rejected because of analytical constraints; it was too costly and time-consuming. For the main, they talked about a phone survey where the most important argument was the better reply rate given by previous phone surveys. An additional argument was that the interviewer can explain complex questions and help the respondent. But as Julia pointed out: 'If the survey is performed on the telephone, it has to be short and with a flow built into it'. On the other hand, the advantage of a survey in letter form is the increased feeling of anonymity, which Svenne argued could result in 'truer' answers. But Lars intervened that if coming across a sensitive question in a letter, it would be easier then to discard the whole thing. And thus they would have no response at all.

The discussion about the 'best' survey method went back and forth during several meetings, yet there was an underlying feeling that these deliberations served only to confirm the choice of a phone survey. It was as if the phone method was decided upon by tacit mutual consent, yet other options had to be explored due to budgetary restrictions. Although a letter would be substantially cheaper, the task force finally settled on telephone interviews as it was deemed less likely for a respondent to hang up instead of throwing a written questionnaire in the bin. Lars vented their concerns with the RC with whom the Agency has a business agreement. RC could execute both telephone and letter surveys so the final choice of the former was, in addition to the above arguments, also influenced by ease of execution.

While working on the content of the survey, Lars simultaneously thought about respondents. How easy would it be to find respondents? How would they be selected? How many were needed? And foremost – would they be willing to participate? The task force needed to make it clear that no one partaking in the survey risked being identified. Therefore the framing and anonymity came next into focus. COENs, yes, but there are different types of legal entities that can be referred to as COENs. So the corporations that were finally selected had diverse types of legal status, but no corporation employed more than four people. It was important that the registers that provided information about corporations contained the correct information. How these cost deductions are accounted for is the responsibility of the owner, therefore it was important not only to find the COEN from a statistical registry, but also to be able to locate the owner.

So where would they find appropriate data? Would it be from the governmental authority Statistics Sweden (SCB) or where? It turned out that selecting respondents was a service RC provided, simply made via a commercial address register (PAR). It is privately owned and is according to its website 'the leading Swedish company regarding commercial information, CRM (commercial relationship management) and direct marketing'. However, the information originates at SCB, said Lars.

So, a survey is meticulously created, respondents are identified and the mode of execution is chosen. Yet there are still some issues to address. Once the phone as a method was decided upon, the question was how the initial representation would be worded. A missive to be sent out prior to the telephone survey was discussed. However, as Julia pointed out: 'If we send a letter beforehand, we might only get replies from those that are positive towards us. It will not be a random selection then, but a stratified one'. Gunilla agreed, stating that 'one usually does not have much patience with phone surveys'. Lars forwarded the question to RC and its manager acquiesced. A missive was quickly decided upon and they quickly agreed to inform on: confidentiality; what the results of the survey should be used for; who would be responsible for performing the survey; and how the selection of respondents was decided on while underlining the randomness of the selection.

A letter originating from this controlling governmental agency needs much work to establish the right tone. Much time was spent on articulating the assurance of anonymity and on how to explain the intentions of the survey. For example, Gunilla said: 'Perhaps we should write that the Agency aims for a better understanding [of these issues]? [By participating in this survey] you contribute to *our* understanding of COENs challenges and problems. But at the same time we get very close'. 'However already stating that it is a problem, may influence their answers', Lars chimed in. There was a big fuss regarding the very first sentence, with Julia adding: 'We should write something very positive for [the respondent]'. Lars agreed and suggested that 'Perhaps we should include the fact that wrong cost deductions lead to unfair competition. This is something our Director General talks about a lot. Or perhaps we should state that the purpose of this survey is to understand better the borderland between the COENs and the private economies?'

Apart from contextualising the survey, the letter also needed to pronounce clearly what the subject of the survey was; it needed to provide everyday examples of what such deductions are all about. The definition of these within the survey proved yet another time-consuming issue. How to make comprehensible what seemed like a simple issue in legal terms, but that in practice became quite messy? How to characterize it? As Julia said: 'Cost deductions are like the concept of black work (svart arbete). It is a notion that encompasses more than one thing' – both in the legal sense and with reference to where such deductions should feature on annual tax returns.

Because of the complexity of explaining cost deductions, Lars was adamant that examples were needed in the survey. Such examples should include acquisitions paid for by the COEN but used in private, using 'current assets' from one's COEN such as items on sale in a store, but also include inventories owned by the COEN, but used privately. Could these deductions be referred to as 'private acquisition' (*privat inköp*)? This definition does not make the picture complete, as the costs also include when you take home some food you sell from your store or ingredients if you have a restaurant. Neither would a private acquisition include usage of the (in)famous snowplough. It was Svenne who initially introduced the idea, being from the north with its long, snowy winters. A farm (most are registered as a COEN) needs a snowplough to clear out the courtyard so that, for example, the forestry machines can get out. An assumption, reinforced by anecdote, is that most snowploughs are paid for by the COEN. However, following the law to the letter would make usage of such a snowplough in front of a private house income and thus taxable. Who makes such an economic estimate and more explicitly puts such income in the books? Although the snowplough did not make it into the survey, it kept appearing throughout the project as a silly and extreme example of what interpreting the law to the letter would mean.

Gunilla knew that COENs are not usually so up to date with more intricate accounting and bookkeeping terms. Lars proposed to follow Gunilla's suggestion: 'With this deduction we refer to [private] usage of COENs' assets, to "take out" assets from the COEN, or that the COEN acquire assets for private use'. This sounded reasonable to the others. In the final version the emphasis was more precise, reflecting the fact that taxation is made through accurate and precise bookkeeping practices in the corporation.

Finally, they agreed on three definitions for the cost deductions in the missive: (1) A deduction made by the COEN that is entirely or partly used privately; (2) An owner's private usage of a COEN's assets without being taxed for the amount; (3) Owners' consumption of a COEN's acquired or produced products without being taxed for the amount.

Caveats in Theory, but Not in Practice

As has already been hinted, despite all the work put into the survey, the results were not of much use. This was not because of sloppy work by the task force or by other participants, but rather because of the inherent problem with the survey itself. From the ethnographic snippets above about devising questions and answers, we get a hint of all the work that went into the creation of this survey. The task force had many opinions on the shortcomings of surveys as a data-collecting method, opinions that will be elaborated on in the next section. So a survey certainly has a social life at the Agency – surveys are what they usually do – and although the task force did perform one, it was not carried out without their questioning what type of information they could get out of it. There were a number of such musings. However, these were often asides or uttered late in the meeting when general fatigue had set in.

Before continuing with this story and seeing how other stakeholders participated in the making of the survey, we will stop and see how the task force is in different ways aware of the impact such surveys can have. Borrowing insights from Law's 'archaeology', we will see that it is not only the various ways that questions are posed that might shape the 'objective' knowledge they should collect, but also the respondents' view of the Agency's intentions by the very wording used in these questions.

So paraphrasing from Law's five points, the task force's concerns about this survey could be articulated as follows:

1. How the COEN is made into a taxpayer (and not a tax cheater).
2. How the Agency comes to be seen as legitimate in its actions regarding the political issues that are currently at stake. And who has the power to influence these issues.
3. How political subjectivities are decided with regards to who is seen to contribute and who cheats with taxes. Which carries over to:
4. How a group of individuals who carry certain opinions and possibly enact those is constructed.
5. How the romantic idea of 'collectivity as a population of individuals' surfaces (cf. Law 2009: 239) – a collectivity that ought to help reveal the secret about these faulty deductions.

As will be seen below, it is not always easy to disentangle one point from the other in the task force's reasoning. 'If we are not careful when we pose the questions, we might seem like we make some taxpayers look like cheaters. Instead of asking about, we might confirm prejudices', said Gunilla. Thus are Law's first three layers exposed, and her comment also brings the hinterland to the surface. On one hand, Gunilla was taking account of the reasons and causes for what historically had publicly been said about COENs and their entrepreneurial colleagues as a collectivity of (potential) tax cheaters, and on the other hand acknowledging the risk in missing out on information that could be obtained when posing 'new' questions. Gunilla's comment also highlights tensions between the noun and the verb 'survey'. The task force wanted to understand what a group of specific taxpayers (COENs) do, by looking in detail at each specific type of deduction, yet in so doing they would simultaneously reinforce the views of what these taxpayers are perceived to be doing (wrong). The political issues might risk exploding within the use of the grammar.

Demonization became a political issue. Swedish entrepreneurs often complain that reports and information from the Agency makes them a scapegoat for tax cheating (cf. Skatteverket 2006b; see also below). The task force knew that they had to tread carefully, as COENs are one of the groups that in the media and in the public conscience are depicted as potential cheaters. This view is something the Agency did not want to reinforce. Just posing such questions turns the respondents into a homogenous container of COENs (cf. Law 2009: 247), as opposed to other taxpayers. The latter would come across as more compliant just by the very questioning of cost deductions among the COENs.

The task force wanted to get as many truthful replies as possible; they aimed to create a collectivity that spoke with if not one voice, at least the number of voices that would be seen as statistically secure. Framing these questions was thus an issue of statistical representability. We will see when we come to RC how the task force were helped with this. By applying statistical methodology a category that has validity is created and thus the views of respondents can be taken seriously. But would it be the 'truth'? The task force questioned how respondents would answer in relation to their actions. 'If the respondent does not need to mind about the consequences of their actions, it might make their answers more truthful', proposed Svenne. Paraphrasing Law, they know that the 'taxpayer is not an individual rational-ethical subject' (cf. Law 2009: 249). Or perhaps it was as Julia said: 'If you are prone to cheating, perhaps you do not want to call attention to this fact by saying that others cheat'. So rather than telling the 'truth' about what a COEN thinks about others' cost deductions, COENs' answers might show how they want to be perceived in light of others' practices. It becomes a political question of positioning oneself, and other COENs, as more compliant than their perceptions of reality really were. But this view was turned on its head when Gunilla added: 'On the other hand, you might want to appear less problematic by saying that you do what everybody else does'. Regardless of whether the respondent is more or less prone to deduct these costs, s/he responds according to the perception of what everybody else does – or should do.

An answer to such a question can thus either reflect actual practices, which are to be objective, or align with the idea of what others do, where answers are subjective. Regardless, the problem with such questions is underscored. What is the aim of a respondent: to be seen as part of the perceived views of the collectivity or to respond truthfully to what s/he thinks and does? The task force was well aware of this dilemma for the respondents. 'Perhaps they do not want to reinforce this view regardless of how they look at the issue themselves', proposed Svenne. He continued 'It is often like this. [If you get a question on] what do you think about your boss? Everybody answers 3; otherwise it becomes a tough situation' and smirked. Yet Svenne's reflection was again only an expression of what other members of the task force found difficult to say out loud; in this case that the Agency is really perceived as knowing about Swedish taxpayers' most intricate income details and has the power, like a boss, to use it every which way it likes. So the suspicion can linger among respondents that any survey, although said to be anonymous, can have some secret code identifying the respondent. Thus, if s/he does not provide the 'right' answer, s/he is in trouble.

The task force also recognized the political consequences such a survey can have. Thinking with Law, we can through the task force members' reasonings get a hint of how a collective is thought about through questions about views and behaviours; that respondents recreate what Law proposes is a romantic idea of such collectivity – 'one' voice – instead of the messy and non-coherent voices of the many respondents. But which 'one'? Law points out that there are always alternative ways to enact collectivities (Law 2009: 249); as for example when Svenne wondered if respondents refer to the behaviour of other COENs when they speak of them as colleagues or as competitors.

Finally, the task force was concerned about how the Agency as survey provider was perceived. We have seen that they knew they had to pay attention to how respondents related to examples in the questions and they repeatedly returned to this issue. As Gunilla said: 'If they scoff at the questions, it would be bad for our legitimacy.' Scoffing could be interpreted in many ways. On the issue of anonymity in the survey ('does the Agency *really* think I would be so stupid to reveal what I do as they obviously could be able to trace who I am'), on the type of questions ('these are really silly examples. I am a serious entrepreneur who has always paid my taxes. Who do they think I am?') or ('Bah! These examples are ridiculous. The Agency does not have a clue about what I am really doing').

Thus, we have seen through the creation of the survey that the Agency does not only shape the taxpayer, but is also quite sensitive about what taxpayers think about it. Does the Agency understand the reality of being a COEN? The task force thus recognized the survey's performative (or, perhaps more appropriately, counterperformative) aspects (MacKenzie 2008), which might undermine the Agency's quest to treat all taxpayers equally. The Agency's legitimacy could be at stake. 'Perhaps it would be easier to compile a survey on things we do not know', pondered Gunilla late one afternoon. 'This one is based on preconceptions'. 'And all the answers risk being concentrated in the middle', added Svenne, bringing back the task force's concerns for representability together with the survey's performative aspects.

We do not have to go the critical studies of surveys to see their limitations regarding tax faults. In the 1980s, a huge research project was undertaken (1,200 respondents were interviewed for about 45 minutes each) regarding Swedish taxpayers' views on taxes and the usage of them. Axel Hadenius notes:

> Strictly speaking, the replies given are inconsistent. Comparing the response to questions about tax levels and whether the subject's personal income tax is reasonable in view of the benefit derived from society reveals that 46 per cent gave contradictory replies: they think that the tax level is too high but at the same time consider the tax reasonable in relation to the benefit. (Hadenius 1985: 353)

This study points out that given answers depend very much on the context of questions posed.

The task force's reaction to the replies in the surveys did not explicitly pronounce itself until the result of the random audit control came in (see Chapter 3). Here attitudes were compared to realities; to the actual numbers COENs account for in their bookkeeping and thus try to deduct. Despite all these insights on the limitations of surveys – the knowledge they create and the possibility of 'counterperformativity' of the Agency's aims (cf. MacKenzie 2008) – the work with the survey continued. Because otherwise, how would the task force gain the input of COENs on these deductions?

Disciplining the Survey

From the start Lars knew that the survey needed to be approved by the NNR, Näringslivets nämnd för regelförenkling (Board of Swedish Industry and Commerce for Better Regulation). Lars was slightly worried about this process – 'what do we do if NNR say no?' – yet he expected the survey to receive pro forma approval. But Lars wanted this approval in good time, before the survey was finalized and executed by the RC. He had reason to be concerned, as the entire issue with the NNR became rather drawn out and in turn quite expensive. In the end, no major changes were made to the survey. Irritation with this process was illustrated by the task force member's comments at a later stage when they considered doing focus groups. Svenne pointed out that it might be necessary to contact the NNR again. 'I think we can forget it this time', Lars remarked, provoking laughter among all.

The NNR is a non-profit body and has fifteen business organizations as members, to which 300,000 companies that represent virtually all sizes, legal standings and industrial sectors belong. Yet, only five people work for NNR, handling about 300 cases per year; the organization leads a fairly quiet existence and is seldom heard about in Swedish society. The aim of the NNR is to work towards fewer and simpler business regulations and to minimize the extent to which companies are required to report information. The NNR says its principal tasks are: 'To consult with public agencies before they impose new reporting obligations on business and to coordinate the business sector's scrutiny of the Government's public agencies and government committees' impact assessments'.[2] Furthermore, the NNR is said to be assisting in bringing about an improved legislative process in the EU. Its motto is 'Cutting red tape for business'.

Lars had been in contact with the NNR several times previously and was somewhat sympathetic to their aim to make sure that corporations are not overrun by *uppgiftslämnarbördan* – the duty by organizations and corporations to provide information for the government's official statistics. Thus all governmental institutions that address corporations ought to coordinate their activities with the NNR – 'Even a very small survey like ours with only 2,000 respondents', said Lars.

The Agency had previously never had problems. 'Perhaps it is the issue at hand that is sensitive', mused Lars as the process went on. 'You know, I can suspect that they think the Agency is out to demonize the entrepreneurs as a group – which is definitely not our aim. We just want additional knowledge in order to improve our [the Agency's] mission'. So Lars sent the fifth version of the survey to the NNR. After looking at it, a representative of the NNR expressed their concerns on the phone; s/he saw the survey as an unnecessary intrusion into their members' activities, underscoring Law's critique of surveys representing one group of individuals as holding certain views. Lars replied in a letter.[3] The introductions are of interest here, as Lars really tried to put his foot down on behalf of the Agency, pronouncing that its aim is not to pester corporations. Thus, Lars emphasized that:

> In order for the Agency to pursue its mission, it needs to have as much insight as possible into how the tax system functions [in practice] and into how taxpayers, both individuals and corporations, perceive its function. A current area of analysis is the borderland between corporations and their owners' economy. The Agency perceive this to be a difficult area for several reasons; for one, a strict interpretation/application of the tax rules may make many corporations err, either explicitly or unconsciously. The existence of unconscious faults may point to a legitimacy problem between what the rules say and what is considered reasonable. Explicit wrongdoings might point out that the tax system is used for private economic benefits with the results of a tainted competition, an eroded tax base, etc.

After this introduction a description of the survey followed, responding to two concerns of the NNR as interpreted by the Agency. First, they thought the questions were sensitive and perhaps leading. The NNR does not think it is possible to ask someone about their perception of 'legal offences' due to their sensitive nature and to the fact that any answer would be difficult to interpret. We would not know how honestly the respondent was replying. Second, a corporation should not be asked questions about its perception of other corporations' behaviour. A corporation should only receive questions about their own corporation, as this is only what they can know about.

The NNR was thus highly sceptical about 'perception' questions, but for different reasons than the task force. The latter had an assumption that a person's behaviour is influenced by what others are perceived to do, whereas the NNR proposed an essentialist approach. An objective answer to these questions was not possible, it argued, instead only subjectivities were possible. Perhaps the real concern was that the NNR did not want to risk disloyal opinions about colleagues (or competitors, as Gunilla suggested) flooding in from respondents. The director at the RC, who was now involved in the process, was quite surprised by the NNR's objections. He stated that the NNR probably never sees 99 per cent of public authorities' surveys carried out within the private sector.

As a response to Lars's letter, the NNR wanted SCB to evaluate the survey, looking especially into the technicalities of the questions and their validity. Following the suggestion by the NNR, SCB was contacted and took on the task of looking through the survey and the missive (the accompanying letter that framed the survey to the respondents). Lars had attached both a long and short version of the missive. This evaluation was a costly exercise, but resulted in a sixteen-page report produced by SCB's unit for measurement techniques[4] (*Enheten for mätteknik*). The report was very thorough, with comments on the structure of the missive and its contents, and included practical advice on whom to contact, etc. SCB's unit for measurement techniques had also gone through the structure of the survey and commented on each specific question. The report specifically pointed out attitudinal questions as problematic; the difficulties in formulating them so that the respondent would interpret them as intended and not find them a challenge to respond to. Most attention was given to section C where the questions were regarded as both difficult to answer and also having a somewhat leading character. The task force reformulated these questions into statements.

The NNR seemed somewhat appeased by SCB's report. One of its representatives visited the Agency and he and Lars spoke about the purpose of the survey for about an hour.

Following this meeting, Lars sent a formal email replying to some of the stated concerns and attached a new version of the survey, for which the task force had taken into consideration the opinions of both SCB and the NNR. Lars duly spelled out that the task force recognized the risks in asking for opinions on what other corporations do and that therefore they would be careful in their analysis of the survey. Lars also mentioned that in the missive he wanted to state that the survey had been prepared in cooperation with NNR and therefore asked for examples of such supporting statements.

So, in the email, Lars acknowledged the NNR's views and admitted to some changes. However, he underlined the importance for the Agency of getting information about these issues and went on to explain and advocate the proposed questions. Regarding the first demur (which was really directed to two different sections in the survey), Lars emphasized the need for the Agency to understand any legitimacy gap, between tax law and taxpayer practice, and referred to internationally published research on entrepreneurial behaviour.[5] The best way, according to this research, was simply to pose direct and up-front questions. The NNR's second concern was dismissed, as these questions were not aimed at understanding reality but the views on the reality in which corporations worked. In essence it was a question of diverse epistemologies. The letter finished by stating that the survey was a tool to fulfil the Agency's mission statement. It was spelled out in a few sentences, but the content was the same. 'The Swedish Tax Agency's mission is to determine and collect democratically decided tax in the simplest and most efficient manner for the taxpayers and to share, in a fair manner, the tax burden'.

On 19 January Lars finally received an email from the NNR, written in the truly Swedish bureaucratic prose of mutual consensus (cf. Graham 2002; Rosenberg 2002).

> We hereby assert that NNR and Skatteverket have carried out a consultation according to SFS 1982: 668. The issue discussed concerns over a proposed survey by the Agency in order to identify the presence of and attitude to faulty cost deductions as part of business activities. The survey will be conducted in the form of a telephone interview. The Agency will contact about 2,000 corporations and participation in the survey is optional. NNR has during the consultation expressed concerns that corporations are expected to report their subjective perceptions on what they think other corporations do regarding unauthorized cost charges. It is difficult for NNR to see any empirical value of this type of information. NNR and Skatteverket agreed upon, given the differing opinions on this matter, to send the survey to SCB's *uppgiftslämnarlaboratorium* [literally a laboratory for informants] so that the survey and questions asked within it could be examined. SCB believes that these types of question can be asked, although it stressed that "you should be aware that the answers you

> get are not accurate responses, but only what business owners think they know about other corporations".[6] NNR has great respect for the SCB's experience with survey techniques and the design of studies, so we conclude that Skatteverket can carry out the proposed survey. However, in light of our concerns put forward in this consultation on the values of such empirical data obtained on these kinds of issues and what SCB emphasizes, NNR presumes that Skatteverket is very thorough and very clear that any future reports will properly account for how this information is retrieved and that there may exist methodological problems related to the interpretation of results.

Interesting to note is that there is no such place as *uppgiftslämnarlaboratorium*. A more specific translation than the one given above would be a laboratory for informants or whistle-blowers, as suggested by Google translate. The wording directs one's thoughts to a scientific place where diverse strategies for disclosures of secrets are tried out. On Statistics Sweden's website, this seemingly murky place is more objectively referred to as the unit for measurement techniques (*enheten for mätteknik*).[7]

Besides gaining an insight into the intricacies of Swedish bureaucracy and corporate associations, getting in contact with the NNR put into focus the societal perception of the Agency as an organization that mainly pursues corporations. As Svenne said: 'There is a view out there that the aim of the Agency is to demonize any owner of a corporation/all entrepreneurs. If the Agency aims to affect norms and attitudes, an effect of such a survey could be an increase in prejudice that society has towards us, instead of the influence of norms in a positive way'.[8]

That the Agency is seen to pursue businesses like COENs has several explanations. There are several reports that point to SMEs[9] as more vulnerable to making mistakes than other taxpayers, which as we know could indicate cheating (e.g., Skatteverket 2006b, 2009b), but could also be accidental, as an individual assessment of income for tax returns is more likely to incur faults (Daunton 2001). The cheating is not always easy to define, as there is a grey zone between planning/avoidance and evasion (cf. Gracia and Oats 2012; Hasseldine, Holland and van der Rijt 2011). After all, one of a corporation's purposes is to make a profit. There is also a political dimension; for example, in 1975, based on a Riksdag decision, the RS (rationalization of tax administration) reform started to be implemented. One of the aims of the reform was to increasingly control and audit entrepreneurs and other more complicated returns, instead of, as had previously been the case, the more easily controlled ones from individual taxpayers (Malmer 2003: 44). The RS reform was probably also a sign of the times, as Swedish politics became more radical in the aftermath of 1968, and measures perceived as hostile against private businesses, especially SMEs, were introduced. A fourth reason is that the yearly tax return has been made easier for employees, whereas the SMEs have largely been left out of this process (Ekman 2003b: 78).

Regardless, the task force noted in the collocation of the survey results that the NNR questioned the value of entrepreneurs 'subjective' views on other corporations' views regarding faulty cost deductions within businesses. The NNR's intervention in the survey shows its concern for agencement between what they see as diverse types of knowledge, somewhat aptly voiced by Svenne above. The NNR sees differences between facts and opinions. Facts are what COENs say they do, whereas what they think other COENs do 'are not accurate responses' – opinions. In addition would such 'thoughts' be pronounced actively. Changing the most 'challenging' questions to statements in the survey was deemed acceptable. Responding to statements would make the COENs more reactive to what the Agency proposed. According to the NNR, and supported by SCB, the survey could ask COENs if certain costs ought to be taxable or not, but it cannot ask what COENs think about others' behaviour regarding such costs. The possible correlation between what I think others do and my own behaviour is just too strong. Just posing such a question to a COEN means that it becomes a political subject within a group that has the same dubious opinions about cost deductions. The anxiety the task force had about pinpointing COENs as tax cheaters would be reinforced. Agencement here lies in the careful pronunciation of survey questions; statistics as a method is never doubted.

The NNR is very careful about how survey questions are formulated, but there is never a questioning of relying on this method as such. This is yet another example of the uncritical stance of contemporary Swedish statistics. This has not always been the case (Sjöström 2002), and several of Sjöström's arguments for this lost stance resonate with the above account. First, statistics has over the twentieth century increasingly been applied as a practical profession for knowledge production within public administration. And professions tend to hold dear their own expertise (e.g., Abbott 1988). Second, Sjöström proposes that statistics' transformation from a critical discipline is also an example of marketization; SCB produce statistics for consumption, as ordered by clients (Sjöström 2002: 211, 215). In the above example SCB shouldered the role of expert and paid 'judge'. A final point is the administrative language as 'data'. The computerization of society has made the 'production of statistics' (ibid.: 216) enticing for decision makers where 'databases' can be created for mass storage and comparative purposes.

Executing the Survey

A ready-made survey approved by the NNR for the Agency with an accompanying missive was finally sent to the chosen RC with a provisional contract. Lars had been in contact with the RC early on in the survey-making work. A fairly decent version of the survey, the third version, had already been forwarded to the RC. As Lars mused: 'They probably have opinions on it, especially on the language. It is difficult to get rid of one's bureaucratic role'. However, the project manager at the RC praised the task force, judging the survey to be more elaborated on than most other surveys that they receive from clients.

The NNR was not the only problem. Another hiccup occurred in relation to the missive sent out to the 2,000 intended respondents. For the RC's pilot project with 100 respondents, Lars had prepared the letter on the Agency's letterhead, converted it to a pdf and emailed it to the RC, who posted it to the respondents. This was followed up with the phone calls, and the pilot was executed and evaluated with very minor procedural corrections. Then came the real survey and the RC posted the missive to the sample of 2,000 respondents. As previously, the RC had forwarded the letter to a mail distributing company; yet somewhere along the line, the Agency logo in the letterhead was lost and replaced with an asterisk (*). The following day the phone on Lars's desk rang constantly. Most callers accepted his apology but a handful were really upset – 'you cannot continue like this, I cannot respond to such questions, you are not credible, is this a joke?' The RC was immediately contacted and corrected the problem by posting a new apologetic missive, this time with the correct logo (see Illustration 0.1).

Minimizing the time between posting the missive and following it up is crucial. The RC's call centre is located in a medium-sized city and has about twenty employees and fifty temporarily employed interviewers. In addition there is a smaller outfit in Stockholm, employing eight to ten people. The RC was started by two former SCB employees and had at the time of the survey been recently taken over by two younger colleagues, in their forties. The Agency sees the RC as 'not totally inexperienced'; it has, for example, an agreement with SCB, and 'they care about us as a client', Lars said. 'Their main clientele are public organizations. You know, sometimes when you speak with these types of companies, they are mostly concerned with the private sector – PR and business surveys. Those types of research companies do not understand what we say'.

Obviously the RC wanted to perform the survey. They had helped Lars through the NNR dealings and had now got the contract for performing the more expensive survey method offered; a telephone survey with an accompanying letter.

I spent a few days at the RC's call centre listening in to the calls and interviewing a few employees, the project manager and the partner who had negotiated the deal with the Agency. About ten people, mostly students but also a few others, worked on this project, which was completed within ten working days.

They all have friendly voices, wear headsets and are seated in front of screens where the phone numbers for respondents randomly appear. The questionnaire and the log of who has called whom and at what time is all computerized. After the initial questions regarding information about the business, the actual survey begins. The questions address what the respondent thinks about the subject: about scope, causes and consequences of the types of costs that are in focus. There are about five choices, plus the choice of "I do not know/no opinion". The woman I first sit with, Stina, never voices the last option. It is something the respondents have to say themselves.

Stina wears slippers and on the back of her chair hangs a slightly worn sky-blue fleece jacket. A tube of hand cream, some lip gloss and a few other personal gadgets lie in a little basket at her side. She fiddles with these now and then while talking into the headset. She has many years of experience at the RC and says this survey is a talk-intensive one. In front of her is a large teacup filled with water from which she now and then takes a sip.

One call starts with a young girl responding that the contact person named on the screen whom Stina asks for is never on site. The young girl offers a mobile number. When this number is called, a man responds and Stina introduces the purpose of the survey in an alert voice while leaning back into the chair, relaxing and folding her hands. The man responds quite reluctantly when he learns about its purpose. He has a distinct dialect from the north of Sweden and gives an impression of ineptitude and ignorance; "it is the girls at the office who know". He responds passively and slowly, starting each answer with "I think …" From his initial almost dumb response, he sharpens his answers and seems increasingly on guard as the questionnaire comes to an end. He really ponders on his final replies. Stina is not surprised. She initially pointed out the anonymity of the survey and repeats it towards the end when the time comes to answer the "porn question", as she calls it: "Have you made any of these deductions yourself?" The notion of porn comes from an earlier survey the RC had made regarding whether people watched porn on the Internet. Hardly anyone did according to the responses and she says the relation between positive answers and actual practice is probably the same with these deductions.[10]

Another call with an elderly woman is quick and efficient. She is an accounting expert and never hesitates, providing answers without ever expressing a doubt. She knows her subject well. Many calls Stina makes are, however, unanswered or end in voice mail. In such cases, Stina clicks on another screen to make a note of the unanswered call. These phone numbers will be repeated on the screen for a recall. Stina says that the interviews take from four minutes to more than half an hour. She thinks the response rate for the survey will be very good, probably due to the missive sent out in advance.

There is a sense of urgency at the RC. The callers talk quite fast, click impatiently on the mouse to call up the next number to phone on the screen, and they seem to reel off the questions without having to reflect on what to say. They are supposed to make four calls an hour; the manager says 0.7 to 2 an hour – it is a company making profits after all – but Stina completes at least five interviews in an hour while I am there. She has a professional and friendly tone to her voice, and the interviews proceed efficiently and calmly. Although her voice says otherwise, her expression shows a complete lack of interest while she completes the form on the screen with the answers.

At the RC, the collectivity of respondents comes to the fore. The RC employees' friendly but automated questioning style, as well as their statistically secure handling of all respondents, makes for the COENs to be presented as a collective. Once the RC had finished contacting the randomly selected 2,000 COENs, the results were assembled into an SPSS file[11] and sent to Lars for analysis. A total of 1,084 interviews were completed out of the 2,000 called; 52 per cent – a fairly okay result according to the RC's manager.

The replies were discussed among the task force in terms of COEN categories: age, type of legal status, education level, etc. Noteworthy in the final report was that the survey presented explicit caveats. First, regarding the definition of cost deduction, it was thought there might be a discrepancy in what the respondents actually considered it to be. It was pointed out that these deductions might be thought of as concerning only acquisitions paid for by the COEN but intended for private use. A second concern was the warning that had been put forward by the NNR on how to interpret subjective questions, such as how COENs perceive other COENs' behaviour. A final concern regarded whether the COENs had responded out of personal belief or from what they considered was the right answer given existing laws/rules or the Agency's perception. The latter questions the entire validity of such attitudinal surveys.

The task force summarized that while a large majority of the COENs view cost deductions for private use as not acceptable, there is a small majority who think it is common practice. The conclusion drawn was that there is no permissive attitude towards such deductions, neither among society at large nor among the COENs. In the final report the answers were summarized on one page (of a total of sixty), but the survey in its entirety was presented and accounted for completely in an appendix. After all, tax money and employee resources were spent on this exercise. Despite all the caveats from this survey, there is now yet another one to relate to in future analysis work – and the life of surveys can continue.

And the Results Are ...

In this chapter we have followed the construction of two surveys conducted by the task force. The first survey consisted of two questions, which were included in the Agency's yearly omnibus survey. The second survey was specific to this project. With the help of John Law's archaeology I have drawn attention to the different stages of this survey where ideas about the individual taxpayer are performed in different ways; but also to instances where the task force is concerned about the legitimacy of the Agency within which its members work.

However, rather than archaeologists, we have been observers/ethnographers, as we have been able to follow this survey from its initiation. We have viewed the creation of questions and the deliberations when structuring and framing them into a survey. We have seen how tradition plays a role – surveys are, after all, what the Agency usually do – and followed the wishes of diverse stakeholders outside the Agency, who wanted a say in the process. The survey has been disciplined by the NNR into trying to protect COENs, as commercial entrepreneurs, from being depicted as tax cheaters. The RC obviously wanted the survey to be performed, as it earned them revenue and reinforced the provider relationship it has with the Agency. The RC helped the task force both throughout the construction of the survey and in its negotiations with the NNR, but as a commercial provider of survey executions it also directed its resources towards winning the contract. It won in many ways – in performing the more expensive telephone survey, including posting a missive, which cost more than planned, and in making more calls an hour than were budgeted and paid for. SCB also reproduced its status and gained commercially in its role as expert mediator, providing feedback on the proposed survey and its accompanying missive. We thus followed the survey and came full circle back to the task force in the form of an SPSS file. So from confirmed or rejected ideas about cost deductions among COENs there was now an array of digital data with which Lars performed some 'trial and error' runs, as he called them, in order to say something about the results.

Surveys are what we usually do, said the analysts. They know how to create them and they thoroughly discuss the construction of questions, the framing of the surveys and the sampling of respondents. They also critically question the reliability of answers and what the results can be used for. The Agency's previous experience of performing such surveys as well as the task force members' own insights and knowledge about these deductions governed their deliberations and decisions.

Although many caveats about surveys have been voiced throughout this chapter, no one seriously questions the ability to survey/measure attitudes and what the results say about actual practices; at least not until the end, when survey results proved difficult to make use of. So the larger insight from this chapter is that methods have a social life, and although acknowledged as having many flaws, such a life is not easy to kill. We can paraphrase Law in that applied methods have a 'hinterland' of their own and it is powerful, although common sense perhaps says otherwise. The actors involved here now and then express the limits of what a survey can say. Still surveys are performed and perhaps reproduce statistics and survey research as reliable tools (Law 2009: 249).[12]

I will conclude this chapter by bringing back Law's five points, which we can relate to the concerns of the task force in conducting this survey: (1) how the COEN is made into a taxpayer (and not a tax cheater); (2) how the Agency comes to be seen as legitimate in its actions regarding what political issues are currently at stake; (3) how political subjectivities are made regarding who is seen to contribute and who cheats with taxes; (4) how a group of individuals who carry certain opinions and possibly thus enact those is constructed; and the final point, (5) how the romantic idea of 'Collectivity as a population of individuals' surfaces (cf. Law 2009: 239).

In the first survey, a group of randomly selected individuals become a homogenous general public (Law 2009: 249) by voicing their concerns over how a particular group of taxpayers, COENs, deduct costs falsely. The two questions posed differed only in respect of the intentionality of this particular action. Although the responses differed, the answers were presented as the *views of Swedes*. Almost half of this public perceive COENs as tax cheaters; COENs thus become tax cheaters, although not even half of the respondents answered affirmatively to these questions. We thus see what political issues are at stake; does the public think COENs cheat with taxes?

The second survey, because of both its scope and work effort by the task force, has been given larger treatment in this chapter, although its role in the final report was small if not insignificant. The COENs are consumers here, as the task force looks for costs.[13] This is a given, so our focus is on the other roles these entities acquire; they are taxpayers, as it is the correct payment of taxes that the Agency is after; but COENs are also (potential) tax cheaters however carefully the survey questions are framed. Taxpayer and tax cheater are the very opposite of each other, and although tax cheaters also pay taxes (perhaps they only cheat with one or two items), there risks emerging a view of COENs as tax cheaters, this time from within. As a group (of taxpayers/cheaters) they both carry certain opinions and possibly also enact those that emphasize Law's fourth point. It also brings to our attention that merely by asking such questions, political subjectivities are at large.

This depiction is what the NNR was afraid of. The NNR has the hinterland view of the Agency, noting how in different reports and surveys it has drawn attention to corporations' tax planning, avoidance and also evasion – thus depicting them as cheaters. Here there is an example of a political struggle between the Agency as a democratic institution that enacts its aim to collect the right tax and the NNR, a representative body for a group of taxpayers that is fighting the portrayal of this group as cheaters. This struggle is mediated by SCB, an organization that emerges as an arbiter that knows how to perform such a survey objectively. When SCB had its say concerning the questions and the framing of the survey, the NNR was appeased. Via its intervention, the resulting potential subjectivities of the survey were made objective. Also, providing examples of deductions meant treading a fine line between being too explicit and risking offending respondents, as repeatedly discussed while making and framing the survey. Yet, examples were deemed absolutely essential to make clear what the survey was all about.

The NNR's reactions can be attributed to several of Law's points regarding what surveys do. First, the NNR's position is political in the sense of always taking the side of corporations. The NNR objected to even asking about perceptions of illegal behaviour among COENs, knowing that these questions reinforce the idea of corporations as tax cheaters. Thus the NNR also underpins Law's fourth point; that certain opinions on a matter are possibly enacted in the same way. The difference here is that perceptions about others' behaviour easily become depictions about others' practices. And if COENs think in this way about others, this COEN inadvertently becomes part of this container. Thus are corporations depicted as tax cheaters.

Depending on who you are – part of the general public or part of a COEN – such a survey can shape you, the taxpayer. The behaviour and views of COENs as taxpayers are depicted in the coming report, and have been added to internal understanding throughout the Agency. Not only the task force understands this, but also the NNR and SCB in contesting survey versions five and six. Instead, such a survey could be said to be counterperformative (MacKenzie 2008), as it undermines the Agency's quest to treat all taxpayers equally and thereby weakens its legitimacy. The missive with the asterisk did not help this, as the Agency was seen to avoid taking responsibility for actually asking these questions.

Seeing the survey as, if not performative, at least mutative (Neyland 2013) brings us back to the etymology. The purpose of the survey was to acquire more knowledge about certain types of cost deductions among COENs; it emphasizes Law's point about how certain individuals acquire certain properties. The survey simultaneously risked undermining its legitimacy when the Agency pointed to certain taxpayers as tax cheaters. The Agency is then seen to *surveiller*, to survey in the sense of pursuing. 'The way in which information is disclosed participates both in the production of the information itself as well as in the constitution of the public that receives that information' (Didier 2005: 639).

Conducting a survey draws attention, in different ways, to the Agency's legitimacy work. The very construction of such surveys (and even worse, publishing the results) risks portraying the Agency as a demonizer of corporate behaviour. We have thus seen how a contemporary taxation issue is at stake and to what extent the Agency is aware of its own position in such discussions.

Although the survey tries to make us understand why COENs deduct certain costs, the answers to these types of questions will struggle to make it into the audit sampling programmes. The numerical results from this survey neither help the Agency to understand the world, nor even provide a way to administer it (Porter 1995: 21). In the aftermath of this survey, a discussion about the right context in which to perform surveys has intensified. The problem is what methods will be applied instead when the Agency wants to know what the public think about certain issues? Focus groups, interviews – or what?

While this survey grew and travelled through different contexts, the knowledge inherent in it also changed form. Ideas about who does what and how, where and why changed from verbal deliberations among the task force to questions composed of letters and digits in an Excel spreadsheet (in a number of versions following discussions among stakeholders). The content of this spreadsheet was thoroughly discussed with sceptics (the NNR) as to what the Agency said was the purpose of the survey and then analysed by experts at SCB. The slightly rearranged spreadsheet was then manually keyed into a call centre programme and read out loud to more or less hesitant respondents whose answers once again were keyed in as digits. Finally these digits were collated into the SPSS file that was delivered electronically to Lars's mailbox – a container of numbers representing a particular group of Swedes, their (voiced) opinions on the practice of certain consumptions and bookkeeping of such purchases. A survey is thus an example of socio-technical agencement; humans, technical devices and knowledge that together can change perceptions about, in this case, the Agency's legitimacy. Queries have to be very carefully articulated so that no misinterpretation of the results is possible.

This type of survey is such a common and often-repeated story of modern society that we often forget what it does and what it most represents; this survey has a double social life (Law, Ruppert and Savage 2011). Although the stakeholders had various aims and disputed part of the survey, they advocated for it as presenting a view of the world (ibid.: 6), or rather their concerns with the world. We have also seen the survey's 'other' social life; that with the historical insights and knowledge of what was the state of the world, the survey needed to reproduce itself to know what had become of the world it once depicted.

Notes

1. Svenne referred to politician Mona Sahlin's once fatal mistake of paying for such a chocolate bar with her work credit card. In 1995 she was Labour Market Minister and the urge to buy a sweet using the wrong credit card forced her resignation after a debacle in the newspapers.
2. www.nnr.se/inenglish.html. Retrieved 15 January 2015.
3. NNR.doc dated 9 November 2010.
4. Report CD project. Version made 1 December 2010.
5. Email 17 January 2011 where Lars refers to Williams (see Williams 2007).
6. p. 10 in the SCB report
7. http://www.scb.se/sv_/Vara-tjanster/Insamling-och-undersokning/Datainsamling/. Retrieved 29 April 2014.
8. The task force members could not agree on what it was possible to make an impact on. Lars for one was quite reluctant to agree to the Agency's attempt to impinge on norms. He thought it was only possible to influence the legitimacy the Agency has in society.
9. Small and medium-sized enterprises.
10. It is interesting to note that this employee performing a relatively simple task was quite adamant about what people in general do with their tax returns. Stina seemed to confirm what the Agency was accused of by the NNR: judging entrepreneurs as inherent tax cheaters. Compare Stina's comment with the discussion held among the managers at HQ (Chapter 4).
11. SPSS (Statistical Package for the Social Sciences) is a common file format for predictive statistical analysis.

12. Although they discussed focus groups and/or performing interviews both at the very start of the project and a year later, questioning the assumptions of the survey, the focus group option was eventually ruled out due to time and money constraints. The focus group route as a method has its own performative problems (cf. Lezaun and Soneryd 2007), but, at least in the minds of the analysts, involves freer discussion and a more accurate representation of what people think and do.
13. Given the definition for these CDs, the COENs can alternatively be seen as users of someone else's appliances. Then they would consume a service.

Chapter 3

X Per Cent

The Birth of a Number at the Random Audit Control Department

A random control (*slumpkontroll*) is a seeming contradiction in terms. To control, steer and discipline the haphazard and irregular appears a daunting if almost impossible task. It is making the irregular regular. For a statistician, a random sample is an everyday tool, perhaps comparable to the anthropologist's participant observation, where all entities making up a whole have the same chance of being chosen. There are a number of random sample methods, but always with the assumption of addressing a larger question by studying a smaller group of entities. At the Swedish Tax Agency it is a direct surveillance method, as it checks numbers and relates them to the taxpayers' reality.

A random audit control (RAC), as it is properly known, is a commonly used method at the Agency. The purpose is to 'fill identified lacunas of knowledge', 'create an unpredictable audit mechanism' or 'perhaps set an example'. The method thus concerns audit and control, which are the core activities for a tax collecting authority. Random controls have a dual purpose; they are used as a knowledge creation tool and are part of the daily work at the Agency when it verifies that people pay the tax they ought to pay and perhaps finds precedents to form praxis (Björklund Larsen 2015).

The randomness in this method involves an unpredictable component, as an arbitrary sample of taxpayer data is chosen. From this selected information about economic activities, results are calculated and often publicly communicated as numbers, sums and percentages. A RAC can have a huge impact on taxpayers' willingness to comply. Results from such audits thus cry out for illustration. How is more knowledge acquired about certain perceived problems, how are the results used in practice, and what is seen as impacting people taxed by the Agency?

In this chapter we leave the HQs in the Stockholm suburbs for the city of Örebro and follow one such RAC at one of the Agency's regional offices. In this chapter, I want to highlight the following. First, how are taxpaying entities selected and how does this sample impact the resulting numbers? Second, what do auditors look for in this random control and how do they go about it? What type of knowledge do they apply in interpreting the law? Third, how are the quantitative results interpreted and what conclusions are drawn? Attending to these three considerations will tell us what is at stake for the Agency when in direct contact with taxpayers; while following the work of the Random Audit Control department[1] we will see the values steering its work surge in its contact with, and audit of, taxpayers. Values are said to be part and parcel of the Agency's work, yet here we will see that some of this department's practices create support for those values, but others work against the Agency in its quest for legitimacy among the Swedish population.

As a result of performing all this work and applying these values we will see how a number is born – the X per cent of taxpayers deducting faulty costs. As a final point, I ask if this is this yet another example of the old, and very valid, anthropological claim that people do not do what they say they do; there is quite a difference between the results of attitudinal surveys and the interpretation of tax laws in practice (of which this audit is an example). The analysts were interested in the percentage of COENs that were claiming faulty costs and had a certain set of expectations. X per cent was the order of magnitude beyond those expectations.

'Strict quantification, through measurement, counting and calculation, is among the most credible strategies for rendering nature or society objective' (Porter 1995: 74). This statement seems to illustrate what is going on at the Agency when it performs a RAC of cost deductions among a certain type of commercial entity (COEN). As the Agency is very anxious to maintain its reputation as legitimate and trustworthy in its actions in order to uphold tax compliance among the Swedish population, we will in this chapter take a closer look at how a statistically secured number is in fact also the result of very careful nurturing and socialization.

Bringing the calculation of a percentage to the fore here is not a direct illustration of an increasing quantification of the world (cf. Guyer, Khan and Obarrio 2010) – an illustration of the 'market turn' (cf. Asdal 2011;

Çalışkan and Callon 2009; MacKenzie 2009) – but rather a discussion of the persuasiveness of numbers that will overrule any verbal deliberations when/if delivered to the public. Any calculation practice ought to be understood in context (cf. Asdal 2011: 1) and we will see that the percentage is not just a cold number (Seabra Lopes 2011: 464) but the added result of audited numbers that are given attention in diverse circumstances. Paradoxically, or perhaps not, we will also see how careful consideration of the circumstances results in an increase in the wielding of power over the audited subjects.

Random Audit Controls: Core Practices at the Agency

RACs are reoccurring activities at the Agency and have two specific aims. On the one hand, they should measure the effect of certain achievements and are thus used to follow up and evaluate measures previously introduced; on the other hand, they are used to estimate risk within the Agency's aim of collecting the right tax, thus contributing to the yearly Tax Fault estimates. A random control is often used to highlight and understand specific problems with the tax returns. Problems could be the extent of employee compliance rates within a specific business sector, if certain questions on the yearly tax return form are difficult to understand and therefore comply with – or compliance rates more broadly, in which case the entire Swedish tax system may be at fault. In addition, a random control often addresses specific research questions from the Analysis Unit – such as this one.

Certain results from a RAC can be addressed within the Agency, so as to improve the information for the taxpaying public or to simplify the forms used (there is even a 'form' day for all governmental authorities where participants can learn about the latest developments in form-making), but results can also impact established strategies and thus legitimacy, as with this audit. Regardless, random controls can shape tax compliance and in a broader sense exchanges between Swedish taxpayers.[2]

A RAC can be performed in several ways. The usual distinction is between a 'desk' and an 'audit'. The desk control[3] only takes place at the regional offices and the aim is to compare the information in the tax return with the actual bookkeeping. In these controls, additional information is demanded by written communication. The taxpayer ought to 'supply information, show ledgers and receipts or send in copies of the same'. Even commodity samples may be demanded. The desk control staff will rarely pay a visit to the taxpayer and only if the information supplied cannot be verified other than by a face-to-face meeting. However, an agreement for the visit is always made first. An audit control is a larger intervention and is used to check more thoroughly that the correct information has been filed. The Tax Law section (*Taxeringslagen*), one of several legal sections that address taxes within the Swedish constitution, states three purposes of an audit. First, to verify that tax filing and other required information is complete and performed according to the rules and regulations for a specific year; second, to ensure that the same information can be provided for ensuing years; and third to acquire, if necessary, information from a third party (e.g., business associates).

Any audit has to be verified and signed off by the office director before it can be started, in addition to the number of supporting forms already completed and signed. The Agency publicly states that an audit includes a visit to the taxpayer, and demands that the bookkeeping ledgers be made available, but also states that daily business should be disrupted as little as possible by the audit. A task as demanding and costly as a RAC has to be ordered and approved. The order has to originate from a manager whose budget pays for it and it entails a detailed plan as well as work procedures. The order thus specifies the aim, questions to be posed, background and motives, scope and limitations, any subanalysis, costs, participants and the named recipient for the results. It is deemed very important to remind everybody about the activity's aim; in this case that it is part of a larger risk assessment project. To repeat: one goal within this project was to obtain more knowledge about the reasons for faulty cost deductions and to estimate the scope of them, and the second goal was to develop better accuracy in the samples selected in future audits.

A random control is something we usually do, said Gunilla. This one was decided even before the order of the risk assessment project was finalized. A random audit is the backbone, the core, the spine of the project we are following. This particular random control had two aims; first to discover how big the problem was with these deductions – how many people were involved, how much money did the costs amount to, and how much money was being lost in uncollected tax. Second: to discover what type of transactions made up the faulty deductions; in which commercial sectors were they most frequent, and among which categories of COENs were they most prominent. The biggest challenge for the analysts was to find out if there had been a change over time. The number of commercial entities in Sweden has increased substantially and so has the Agency's need to control and audit, as there is much more scope for mistakes within a business tax return compared to the largely pre-filled one of an employee. The commonsensical assumption within this project was that, given the number of mistakes made by COENs, the phenomenon would continue to rise with an increased number of registered entities;

both with regard to the monetary amount and to the number of misbehaving COENs.

The previous year's random controls investigated many different aspects of income. This year's focus was on costs. According to the relevant section of tax law, these costs consist of five types of faulty categories in bookkeeping. Two are direct: non-business related expenses[4] and non-business related turnover assets on the balance sheet.[5] In addition there are three types of withdrawals that are errors if not subject to tax: withdrawal of turnover assets,[6] personal use of business-owned cars,[7] and personal use of other types of fixed assets.[8] In common parlance it is to buy goods and services with the COEN's money for private use; or to enjoy private use of things owned by the COEN without paying tax on this usage.

The analysts are very much aware that whatever the result, it cannot be used without further elaboration. A RAC is so easy, said Wera, a senior analyst, who shared her experience at one of the initial planning meetings. When random controls were used in previous projects, the result had too big an impact in the media, she said. There is also a danger of acquiring too much data. The U.S. IRS audited 50,000 entities and did neither know how to, nor have the resources to follow up this enormous amount of generated data. The methodological shortcomings of an audit were thoroughly deliberated on by the analysts as they know that certain types of hidden cost deductions are more or less impossible to find within the legal definitions. Already during the planning phase of the RAC they discussed its weaknesses and they agreed on the need for an analysis of the results from the Random Audit Control office compared to 'reality'.

The Random Method: Planning, Organizing and Sampling

The Random Audit Control office is located within a regional office in Örebro, and according to Petra, the coordinating manager of this particular project, has a great deal of experience with these audits. This office has carried out the RACs at the Agency at least since Petra joined five years ago. The working method is very standardized and Petra proudly introduced it as '*The* Random Method':

> We know how to organize the control, how to design it to ensure a statistically secured result and also how to follow it up. We usually demand more information than at a regular audit. If you simultaneously work with different tasks, you risk letting go of focus, which impacts the result. If you concentrate on these issues [e.g., one particular random control] and

> the discussions surrounding them, we obtain a better result. Therefore, we only work with this task. The most important issue for me is uniformity. Before we concentrated these activities to Örebro, we had experimented with analyses conducted here and there throughout Sweden. When you analysed those results and compared them to those of a more disciplined and pointed survey, we saw a tremendous difference in results. The entire design [of a random control] is important; for my part, how we select the entities, what we control and how we do it and also the follow-up.

She turned to her colleague, Ulla, adding: 'But also your part, how you implement it. It is the uniformity that is most important for the result'. One challenge was to 'secure' the project by adapting their proven random method. Thus, they created specific checklists and diligently worked to take away any auditor's special interests. 'There are those who might think certain items are more important to audit than others', said Ulla.

A random control applied at the Agency entails sampling taxpayers for audit. The selection is decided by the target and does not necessarily mean a complete audit, but only a control of specific information in the annual tax returns. 'We usually steer the sample, as we know where to find the mistakes', said Petra. 'It is the principles of sampling that are important, not the control itself. If we use a stratified sample, we will not know the scope. It is very dangerous. We are therefore very careful to note that with this sample and from this target population, we might be able say something about the magnitude and involvement. We want to state the sampling criteria very explicitly'. A result from a stratified population (e.g., a business sector) returns a higher frequency of revised actions, perhaps 70–80 per cent, compared to the result from an arbitrarily selected group. Choosing the right parameters is thus very important.

Here, the focus was on certain types of deductions among COENs; how much, what sorts of errors and in which business sectors these appear. In addition, the Agency aimed to intervene as little as possible in the audited subjects' daily work. Petra therefore aimed to select, with enough certainty, a large enough sample that consisted of taxpayers with non-negligible declared costs. This requirement was fulfilled by identifying three codes from the tax filing that in total amounted to a minimum of 50,000 krona (approximately €8,000 or U.S.$7,500 at the time), regardless of turnover. Another parameter was geographic dispersion. The sample had to cover a large part of Sweden as well as represent large and small municipalities in urban as well as rural areas. She looked at postcodes, even if the registration locality did not always correspond with the place of business activity. Perhaps you live in Stockholm and own a farm in Norrland, the northernmost part of Sweden, she explained. The consideration to include the VAT registry was rejected, as the COENs offering healthcare would not be part of the sample. Business prerequisites included a widely distributed turnover, a broad sample of business sectors (identified by SNI – Swedish Standard Industrial Classification codes) and no defaulted or out of business COENs. An important criterion was to avoid entities that had recently been in contact with the Agency, as they might feel persecuted and harassed. A final budgetary constraint was the geographic representation in order to minimize travel costs and working time for those auditors who were to pay visits. Statistical representability and internal budget constraints thus go hand in hand when choosing commercial entities to be checked for these cost deductions.

A third of the national population of COENs was found in the four selected regions, in total 100,000. When analysts do not know the extent of wrongdoing, 50 per cent is automatically assumed. With a statistical confidence interval of 10 per cent, 45–55 per cent of the COENs were assumed to deduct incorrect costs, resulting in a minimum of 383 entities to audit. This number was adjusted upwards to 400, but as it was also assumed that there would be some COENs found without any business activity as well as some unable to be reached, a final list of 450 was randomly selected. The sample made this project the largest random control ever performed at the Agency, totalling 4,000 working days and conducted during 2011. The Örebro office had previously handled these audits themselves, but could not cope with this very large one. In addition, some of the COENs were located just too far away and thus help was requested from three other regional offices. On the day the project kicked off, all forty auditors and eight to ten process leaders participated from the four offices. The coordinators Petra and Ulla informed them about the aims and emphasized success factors such as concentration on work tasks as well as uniformity in the actual audits, decisions and in follow-ups. The checklists created for this particular random control were introduced and participants were shown how the template for results, an Excel spreadsheet, should be completed.

One of the original aims with this project was to acquire knowledge about the type of costs that are falsely deduced. It was thus knowledge in the making, which could not be covered by ready-made checklists. Each auditor was therefore allotted a specific business sector (decided by the SNI codes)[9] even if certain costs they were looking for applied to all sorts of business sectors. Each participating office selected a contact person who would be familiar with all the issues that surfaced and would share that knowledge between and within offices, in larger and smaller and official and ad hoc meetings and also with the coordinators in their weekly online meetings. In addition these issues were to be registered in an intranet cooperation forum. This was also where an Excel file with the results of each audit was to be registered. This was a critical point, according to Ulla: 'regardless of how well an audit is performed, if you cannot register the result consistently there is no way we can draw conclusions'. Except for entering the numerical results from the audits, everything in the spreadsheet consisted of pre-programmed choices to ensure compatibility. The spreadsheet was divided into three parts depending on the type of corrections made; yellow for revised changes if not business-related costs; blue for revised changes according to filing codes; and green for revised changes according to type of cost, e.g. car, telephone etc. 'If there is the slightest hesitation, I should be contacted' said Ulla. Ulla and Petra thus set the frame for this audit. In the following section, while visiting the Random Audit Control department, we will see how such an audit is performed in practice.

At the Random Audit Control Department

Örebro is a midsize city that is situated a two-hour train ride west of Stockholm. Located a short distance from the train station is its L-shaped modernist and ordinary office building. When approaching the entrance found in the corner of the L, the feeling is welcoming, as the building seems to embrace the visitor. However, locked entrance doors and a small sign informing me that the reception has been moved interrupt this feeling. No phone number is listed, nor is there a doorbell. Earlier I had received a mobile phone number from my assigned contact, Alice, which I now duly call and she comes down to fetch me. Her personal warmth makes me feel quite welcome after all – although I feel as if I am under scrutiny when I sit down with the department for the regular Monday morning coffee at nine o'clock. But people are pleasant enough and I chit-chat with Ulla, the project manager I had interviewed a few months prior. I nod and exchange a few words with some of the other twenty or so department members.

After the morning coffee, the weekly department meeting starts. Ulla informs us about the status of audits; at the time of this visit there are eighty-two that have been completed while another forty-nine are under way in the Örebro office, of the total sample of 400 statistically secured from the database. The meeting participants pose a few general questions for discussion, mainly of a procedural nature which shows that they are in the midst of the RAC: should it be logged in the registry if COENs do not sign for a document sent by registered mail? This formality creates a lively

Illustration 3.1 Skatteverket Örebro office. Photo provided by Castellum.

discussion with a positive decision. It is decided that if the COEN has not signed for the delivery, it is to be registered as 'not received public document'. When the SIE[10] file is deleted, an employee will make a note of it in their diary, but should this also be registered? When should an employee debit his or her over-time in each audit? Should it be part of their own working time or be debited against the project? This issue creates a lot of laughs and is probably a sensitive but recurring subject. As there is nothing more to discuss, everybody returns to his or her office 'to work'.

An Audit

I follow Alice to her office, one of many adjoining one of the two long corridors that run parallel throughout the department. The walls are painted in yellow and the position of her desk at the end of the narrow office allows her to see out of the window. Two large screens on her desk catch my gaze. On both sides of the room are bookshelves containing an array of the Agency's handbooks and reports, ordered chronologically. These are bi-coloured, with the top part in white and the bottom part in a different colour for each publication year. I can see that they are placed in order; first the bright blue ones from 2007, followed by a few lime green (2008), then some orange (2009), the pinky ones (2010) and finally the current ones for 2011, in a dark green shade. Binders occupy most shelves and some of them curiously have their back towards the wall. I get it; she has prepared for my visit and turned them round so I would not see *who* the subject is to audit.

She takes me through all the steps in the audit procedure; the queries and memos she makes in different data systems, how she creates a binder with the physical documentation, the logbook to record each step of the audit, the diary registrations procedure she has to go through at each step of official contact with the audited entity and the different letter templates that she uses in written communication. There are in total seventeen checklists, procedures, information materials and questionnaires to follow during phone contacts and visits. Ten working days are allocated to each audit; two-thirds of the time involves administrative tasks and one-third concerns the actual audit. The overall head of the department does the signing-off and thus actively participates in four instances; when the letter stating 'decision for audit' is sent out to the selected entity;[11] when the audit plan is approved; when a decision on the audit is made; and when the final memorandum giving the decision on changes in taxation is distributed. Alice views the involvement of the various managers, as well as the diary registration, as quality assurance; it inhibits faulty procedures, hasty decisions and wrongdoings.

Even if checklists are adapted for each particular project, they are far from uniform and/or updated and display a variety of fonts and forms with the occasional handwritten addition. Alice, for example, works in her own way using her extensive experience. She tells me she increasingly uses her computer, and happily acknowledges her two screens that allow for double the amount of information to be retrieved from many different sources. In addition, for each audited taxpayer she has created a binder that will fill up with material as the audit proceeds; after a visit she will return with the COEN's invoices and receipts, perhaps accompanied by a data file with the ledger (in SIE format). Importantly, she will also gather knowledge about the audited subject during the telephone call(s) and from visual impressions at a visit. At every instance she will be taking notes (*tjänsteanteckningar*) in her diary, and in most instances will transfer information to the registry (*diarie*).

A procedural aim of this audit is to negotiate as much as possible by phone. The initial call is regarded as crucial as an indication of how the entire audit will proceed as the auditor aims to create a cooperative relation. One of the seventeen documents addresses this first telephone contact. The list is thorough with many explanatory points: what is meant by an audit, time allocation, the need for cooperation and full secrecy, and the procedural steps. There are questions about the business activities of the audited entity and more specifically about the bookkeeping procedures. Finally, the COEN should be informed about the upcoming visit, what it entails and what material the auditors wish to take back with them to the office. A visit is seen as an intrusion into their private life, as it often takes place at their home. Alice says that the following procedures reflect the Agency's aim for cooperation:

> We should always pose the question "how do you use this thing?" This means that we listen to the taxpayer. We aim to create an understanding for the work we do, but also that we try to understand how they work. If we get off on the wrong foot, the audit might be unnecessarily long and cumbersome and we might irritate them. You know, we aim to interfere as little as possible so that they think we do our job well and with quality.

Alice thus acknowledges that different types of work among COENs also generate different costs. She tries to understand the everyday business reality of the people she audits and aims to be reasonable.

Her reasonableness commences with the first phone call and continues at the actual visit. Even if the auditors emphasize that they only want to see what concerns business activities, they often pass through the home, Alice says. They can then see what can be considered assets. Are there paintings on the walls? How separate is the 'office' from the rest of the home? If any computers or cars are present, they can ask if these are also used for private use. If they see other things that are not needed for the business they audit, they can ask about them. By understanding as much as possible about the taxpayers' business activities, the auditors can claim to be reasonable in their control.

Glancing into a taxpayer's private life, Alice expects the audited subject to behave in a cooperative and reasonable way, commensurate with his/her business role – especially with regard to what costs he/she deducts. Any issues that the auditors do not know how to handle are to be taken up with Ulla, the project implementation coordinator. What about the sports pants for a spinning instructor, are they deductible? How about working from home; how should costs for Internet and mobile phone(s) be allocated? As many answers as possible should come from the systems, Ulla says. If she does not know the answer, Alice will look in the Q&A section of the intranet cooperation forum where large and small issues are addressed and specialists provide answers, or she will discuss the matter with the department's legal specialist. When a decision is reached, Ulla will be informed and the answer logged on the forum.

Alice tells me that the director for the Örebro office has read most of the decisions. At one point he drew up conclusions and presented them for all participants in the random audit. His points specifically addressed the administrative issues; for example, what his colleagues did well, what they can ameliorate and what they missed. For example, there were Post-it notes left in the material. He also talked about efficiency and reminded them about the importance of getting the SIE file quickly; not writing too much; correct handling of receipts and ledgers when revising tax decisions; checking that claims are appropriately supported, adding that even if receipts are lacking it is perhaps reasonable to conclude that some costs, or part of them, are business related. Alice says: 'Often we try to come to an agreement with the audited subject. You always have to impose the decisions, especially when they seem unfair despite what the law says; for example, that COENs do not have the right to deduct wellness services whereas an employee has the right to do so'.

Reasonable Decisions

Standardization at the Random Audit Control department also manifests itself in recurring meetings with regards to what deductions are allowed. I sit in on one of the many discussions between a tax administrator, who needs to deliberate on a few items, and Alice, who is the ordained tax auditor and higher in rank. The discussion takes place on sofas at the informal meeting place in the corridor and my presence is prearranged so as to avoid any possibility of them disclosing the audited subject. Alice has brought two filing binders, again with their backs very consciously kept away from me. The first subject for discussion is an ongoing audit of a PR consultant located in Uppsala.[12] She has a few questionable expenses; among them are travelling receipts of 3,331 krona in[13] public transport ticket slips and 5,053 krona in taxi fares.[14] None of these can be directly linked to the consultant's business assignments and she cannot remember whom she has visited using the ticket slips she saved. They are certainly not for commuting to work, as she bikes the short distance from her home (500m). Sometimes there has been a need for a taxi, she says, when she transports her large computer or the occasional poster screens that she makes for clients. Events, like celebrations and anniversaries for shops and businesses, take place at night, which might explain the taxi receipts from evening journeys.

Although the burden of proof lies with the taxpayer and receipts or similar documentation in support of any claimed deductions, it is underscored that the Agency needs to be reasonable (*skälig*) in its decisions. An often-repeated word, it is probably at this point also intended for my ears. We do not want to appear petty they say, and they allow for deductions that could be crucial for the PR consultant's work activities. It is thus reasonable to assume that some of these travel expenses have occurred while she was working, but the question is how many? They decide to take it up with the departments legal specialist moreover SNO (chairman of the tax board).[15]

The next day they meet the SNO, a bearded man in a checked flannel shirt, who has a relaxed yet imposing presence. We sit on the same sofas as yesterday, he on the same side as me. The case is presented and the SNO asks some questions about the consultant's business – her office, turnover, if she has any employees, etc. The SNO also asks for supporting documentation. The tax administrator and Alice show what they have and add that they have pointed out to the consultant the need to provide proper receipts and correct travel expenditure reports. The SNO also insists on being reasonable, and suggests calculating 'a ballpark figure' that allows for costs pertaining to mobile phone and computer usage, and some travel costs, even if they take place at night. The consultant has a decent turnover, which supports the claim that she actually does business. A subscription fee for a historical magazine is rejected; so are expenses for a trip to Lvov, Poland, as these do not include hotel costs and per diems. She alleges she went there to take pictures for an online shop; but why Lvov they ask – is there a Russian connection?[16] They discuss and reject some other demands for deductions and then the SNO returns to the local travel receipts concluding that the consultant either needs to provide supporting documentation or 'you have to "slap on" some amount – perhaps half?' There is an eerie feeling of power wielding in their discussion, perhaps best described as a type of soft power (e.g., Keohane and Nye 1998; cf. Hannerz 2011: Ch. 12). The auditors insist on finding a reasonable decision while discussing the entity who is the subject of the audit and who in reality does not have much room for manoeuvre. 'It [soft power] coopts rather than coerces' (Hannerz 2015: 802).

This 'reasonable' number will then be proposed to the consultant and if agreed upon, it becomes part of the consultant's tax return. To secure it, it has to be added to the growing amount of erroneous deductions on the RAC spreadsheet. Instead of the sum of 3,331 and 5,053 krona added, there will be half of the total amount – 4,192 entered, thus diminishing the percentage from what a black-letter reading of the law would have yielded.

As another example of reasonableness I overheard a discussion that took place in the corridor outside the office I had been given. It concerned a forest farmer's electricity bills. He had divided the cost 60:40 between his COEN and his private work and was claiming to be heating the place with wood when there. Even so, the bills were much larger in wintertime. The auditors talked back and forth about costs for heating versus lighting. The farmer walks badly; he is therefore not at the farm as often as he used to be. The discussion then turned to how much he could possibly work if he could walk without problems, and if he has not been there much his bills ought to be quite low. He lives alone, as his wife died last year. 'What is reasonable?', asked a voice.

Deliberations can become very detailed in meetings between the auditors. It is difficult for them to draw the line, both regarding reasonable amounts but also on what is actually a faulty cost deduction compared to an appropriate one. The most intimate private details of health and private relations are drawn into the discussions – information that adds to the taxpayer's proclaimed ability to work and deduct costs thereof. Although the auditors' deliberations almost seem like prying, they humanize the cold facts of filed digits.

The auditors repeatedly talk about being responsible and reasonable in their decisions. If the queried figure is less than 4 per cent of the total cost, only a missive (*påpekande*) is sent. However, it also depends on what type of costs the figure is made up of. Sometimes decisions are made to make an example and become part of the auditors' specific knowledge, yet taxed amounts cannot be revised in absurdum. Being reasonable is nurtured in a perception and estimation of a COEN's life in private and at work. Item by item, these costs are divided between the two and translated into *kronor*.

The SNO gratefully acknowledged that 'we are fortunate at the Agency as we, for example, compared to the Immigration Agency for one, can interpret the law and establish praxis'. Praxis refers to interpretation of the law in everyday practice and was often mentioned in the deliberations about being reasonable.[17] Although much of what the auditors do is documented, there are issues that are treated differently in reality to what the law specifically states. The Random Audit Control department thus takes on a somewhat more human face, although at the same time risks decreasing its legitimacy. 'In our contact with the taxpayers, we must be empathic and considerate' said the SNO. He continued:

> These amounts are usually fairly small. We want to show that we think of our relationship with the taxpayers as long term; we have to show empathy. This has not always been the case and it is difficult to change our approach [within the Agency]. We have worked a lot on our service attitude over the last 5–10 years, which has taken on an increasingly distinct form. We want to create confidence, as taxpayers then are more prone to comply.

Alice said that she always aims to find an agreement with the COEN when a revised tax decision is proposed so that it does not need to be forced; her behaviour in every contact with the audited subject is of importance.

It is fairly easy to find a cost deduction, but it can also raise a lot of questions and the issue can quickly turn personal. Most of the auditors seemed aware of and sensitive about these practices, as people's private behaviour is questioned in the process.[18] One auditor was blunt however. 'When a cost for private usage is booked to the COEN, well, it is not private anymore. No doubt about it. It is only talked about as such'. However, Alice tries to agree with the taxpayer over what is deductible and what is not. It is the happiest solution, she said. The Agency actually is reasonable in its decisions, although the law states that any cost deduction should be supported by evidence. Being reasonable can seem far away from the reading of the law, however, as Max Gluckman pointed out, 'reasonableness and the like [does] exist in every legal book' (1963: 179). In Gluckman's depiction of Barotse/Lozi Law in Zambia (what was then Northern Rhodesia), a reasonable man is described as an integrated character in society, although the notion can have different qualities in diverse professional settings. Reasonableness is contextual. A Barotse judge looks at the evidence and an accused person's practices in relation to how a 'reasonable man' would behave in general but also how this man would behave in the role he acted. It is thus a universal persona that is identified by a society's norms for certain behaviour.

As the legal specialist gratefully acknowledged, the Agency can interpret the law and establish praxis and thus be reasonable as long as they do not breach explicit laws, court rulings or precedent decisions taken by the Agency (cf. Epstein 1973: 650; Gluckman 1963). Furthering a critique of a reasonable man but also expanding on the concept, Bill Maurer provides examples from due diligence procedures in tax havens. These procedures aim to establish someone's identity; a 100 per cent secured identity is never possible, but instead it is the process that is in focus. It 'gathers material for a process of judgment that will allow one to be reasonably certain that one has taken reasonable care and reasonable steps ethically to warrant a regulated person's identity' (Maurer 2005a: 490). The auditors at the Agency aim to maintain that cost deductions have been tried in the same manner, regardless of the type of business the taxpayer is involved in. All audited subjects should be treated equitably. But being reasonable as a human subject is partially out of sheer humanness (Maurer 2005a). An auditor can ask when s/he has to make a decision given overwhelming evidence, evidence that is so opaque that it cannot be understood and deciphered – especially given the time s/he has been allocated to complete a tax audit at this Agency. These auditors are subject to time constraints. Although there are ten days allocated to each audit, getting to the bottom of a complicated one might be very time consuming. A visit to a COEN must not take more than two hours – and as Alice acknowledged: 'We only scratch the surface'. They might miss out on important information, which could inform on false deductions.

Reasonableness among the auditors is negotiated in terms of knowledge about the audited taxpayers' business and in relation to the audited person's private life. In this random control it is thus a very processual take on understanding taxpayers' business activities in relation to what the praxis says; it is not a case of acknowledging each auditor's assumptions about what should be controlled, but about establishing a sort of collective take on what business activities imply – as costs. We cannot know what a reasonable auditor is 'because it cannot be grasped as a whole or in terms of its grounds, it compels an aesthetic of the "Reasonable Man", seeking not certainty but rather engaging in the embodied activity of scrutiny' (Maurer 2005a: 498). Being reasonable is a messy practice and cannot be otherwise, as reality changes – as do the business and tax practices of COENs, the praxis at this Agency and society at large. But by being reasonable, the auditors also insist that the audited subject has behaved reasonably. So it gives the Agency a human face – can anyone be against reasonableness?

Being reasonable thus points in many directions and to nail down exactly what a reasonable audit implies is not possible; despite all the lists and procedure checks that Alice is provided with there is always the tacit knowledge, the contextual fact findings, verbal deliberations with colleagues and, not least, contact with the audited COEN; and a dose of Swedishness in the sense of deducing a lagom amount. It is an 'art' (Maurer 2005a: 491).

So a reasonable and secured figure is delivered to the analysts, who have very much looked forward to the result from the Random Audit Control. Lars receives an email with an attached Excel file on 11 January. The overall number creates quite a stir among them. X per cent have claimed a faulty cost deduction. This is a markedly different percentage from other studies and from the survey results (Chapter 2) in this risk assessment project, and at their next meeting it provokes a long discussion with almost 'random' comments. The analysts had a certain set of expectations and it takes a while until their opinions on the percentage convene into a proper discussion. Lars, who is usually no man of big words, says:

> It [the result] gives you a hiccup. It is distinctly different from what we expected, given the other field studies. We have to think hard about what to make of those we have not been able to make contact with. Did the auditors contact another [i.e., a replacement]? Perhaps then it would make the number even larger? This number is really quite shocking.

The percentages the RAC yielded makes for a number of political and material reflections (cf. Ballestero 2014). The analysts turn and twist the results. Per insists that each faulty cost deducted is actually quite small so that perhaps the X per cent is not so bad anyway. Gunilla has calculated that the mean of erroneous deductions found is 28,000 krona for each COEN; only Y per cent of the faulty ones amount to more than 50,000 and of those only Z per cent are larger than 100,000. No one questions her percentages. Svenne wonders how to communicate this number publicly; what the reaction will be and how COENs in general will respond to the Agency after this disclosure. Julia makes a number of assumptions to be able to add this number to the tax gap calculation, a number that is of the utmost importance for the government's assessment of Agency performance (Skatteverket 2008b, 2014d). A final disappointment for the analysts is that they are not able to address the most difficult initial question – whether the phenomenon has changed over time. There is not anything to compare the result with.

The task force's initial consideration about looking more closely into the number is brought to the fore. How have the Örebro office arrived at this number? The secured result is questioned by its sheer size. X per cent. The analysts decide to hold interviews with a handful of participating auditors, and these confirm what they suspect. You can find these deductions among most COENs and perhaps they are more common the smaller the outfit is. The reason for why they are claimed is probably a combination of not knowing and, as some auditors suspect, a certain level of chance-taking. It is not what it is possible to deduct that is questioned, it is rather the extent of what can be deducted compared to what is used in private. These boundary problems are mainly due to a nitpicky law that is seen as virtually impossible to follow in practice, thus creating a legitimacy problem for the tax system, including the Agency that enforces such a law. Some of the deductions are easy to detect; others more complicated, and some, as in the usage of current assets, are virtually impossible to find. Yet, most auditors are not at all surprised at the result. Every COEN has incorrect cost deductions, says one auditor who took part in the RAC. There are many that are illicit, yet do not create consequences for tax and control purposes and do not even get a remark from the Agency, such as the usage of a COEN inventory for purposes other than its business activities.

A Secured Result?

An effectual RAC at the Agency is one that reaches a secure result (*ett säkert resultat*). We have, in the not easily digestible ethnography above, seen how the Agency's largest random control ever was designed and conducted, and resulted in a secured but still rather questionable number. 'Statistically, it is very good material we have', said the manager of the office in Örebro proudly, a fact that Lars also acknowledged despite his demurrals above. However, there is neither precision nor accuracy in the secured result (Wise 1995). Norton Wise exemplifies these concepts with the metaphor of shooting. Precision means that many shots hit the same spot, although it is not the same as hitting the target, whereas accuracy means striking it (Wise 1995: 7–8). We will see how this result is questioned when presented among the Agency's management (in Chapter 4). But a RAC is the best method the Agency can apply given an all-encompassing law, where everything that can be used or consumed privately is under suspicion of being taxable. However, in this (for the Agency) depressing mood, a couple of practices emerge that highlight the values held and practiced by it in its quest for legitimacy – values that both nurture and discipline this number.

Selecting the COENs for audit is not only performed according to a random, statistical method prior to the audit, but is a continuous practice throughout. Sampling demands a detailed knowledge of audit procedures, how various expenses and incomes are filed, how different types of commercial entities are registered and which code each represents. There is a demand especially for a more experienced-based knowledge of relations between those codes. What should be the association between codes for turnover, VAT payments, deductions, expenses and incomes, balance and result activities to identify an auditable COEN? Always mindful of the quest for legitimacy, the auditors' work is a balancing act between on the one hand not disturbing taxpayers too frequently or with too minor issues and on the other hand conducting themselves professionally but with empathy. The precision can be questioned because of unforeseen changes in the sample, such as COENs that cannot be reached and cost consciousness at the Agency. We can only imagine whether if other types of deductions could have been found and had become part of the audit these costs would have differed from the mean results.

Both in sampling and in actual contact, the Agency tries to be empathetic by aiming to understand the everyday commercial reality for each COEN and not bother them more than necessary. The auditors are dedicated to such projects and no other work tasks are supposed to interfere. The majority of tasks during the ten days each audit is allocated are interactions between various technical devices. This allows the auditor to gather most of the information needed about the COEN. However, the personal contact via phone is seen as crucial, especially the initial call. A good relationship established by a polite yet pleasant phone call prepares for the actual visit, the most sensitive part of the audit, acknowledged in the auditors' refusal to let me accompany them. *Cooperation* is another value that emerges, although perhaps it is only on the Agency's terms. As Alice noted, 'The happiest solution is if we can agree on the revised tax'.

The Örebro analysts pride themselves on a random method that is *uniform* and produces *secure* results. Planning is essential and the aim is that all employees will perform their audit in the same manner, will look for the same things, evaluate discrepancies in a similar way and report them in an orderly and consistent fashion. Each auditor's experience is applied but also streamlined with that of their colleagues so that personal preferences and views on specific issues to audit are removed. It is a standardization of working, thinking and talking. Specific expenses that arise during the audit are addressed in different meetings between the RAC participants, and decisions are disseminated horizontally and vertically, within and between the offices, and posted in the electronic intranet cooperation forum, (*samarbetsrummet*). This is one way to establish and adjust praxis.

Although X per cent is a quantification of human practices, it is carefully calculated. The random audit is an example of 'how technicality is constituted by ethical, cultural, and mathematical sets of relations in a constant state of becoming' (Ballestero 2015: 275). Both analysts and auditors embody the values of the Agency, while paying attention to praxis. A RAC is conducted with the aim of acquiring knowledge. It is done with uniformity but also with the aim of increasing uniformity in the overall treatment of taxpayers. A RAC is a process where small alterations change conventions very slowly. The audits accumulate and so does the increased knowledge about costs to be allowed or rejected. We have seen how each audit consists of many different steps with retractions and (re)control; how it applies new facts and is continuously negotiated between auditors, supervisors and the COEN. The head of the Örebro department pointed out to his colleagues that although the audit might be seen as addressing petty sums, this project is probably the closest the department will ever get to making an impact on practices in society – or the Agency's forms for that matter.[19] The Agency applies the law to reality and draws conclusions from it. But the law is too encompassing and makes it impossible to detect all incorrectly claimed costs. It thus stands in the way of obtaining an accurate number. To make praxis more legitimate, they want to lobby for changes in the law – a challenge for the Agency (as we will see more of in Chapter 4). They seem to aim for *fairness* in all their decisions.

Audits are at the very heart of the Agency's practices and each random audit has a distinct focus and follows a strict procedural protocol. But the auditors do not follow it to the letter (e.g., when documentation is missing). Recurrent meetings and discussions between auditor, tax auditor, the SNO and the head of the department aim to propose and reach a verbal agreement with the commercial entity subject to tax. They want to understand the specific business in which the COEN is involved, in order to allow for cost deductions even if proof (receipts, invoices, etc.) is lacking. Although some costs might be mistaken, small amounts should not be concerned with – unless there are many of them. Thus, case-by-case decisions apply and auditors morph out a *reasonable* interpretation, even if the law and established praxis do not always explicitly allow it. They recognize that rules can be complicated to understand, and even if straightforward they are cumbersome to follow in practice, such as those addressing usage of private cars for business purposes or vice versa.

However, all these warm, human values would have been difficult to apply on their own were it not for the technical help the auditors have at hand. The secured and uniform results are made possible by both soft- and hardware: computers, Alice's two screens, access to databases, the (in context) old-fashioned phone in combination with the non-material intraoffice communication channels on screen and via email, various software programs, SNI codes, SIE files, the intranet forum and seventeen checklists. An audit is a true socio-technical feat that can have an impact on the Agency's legitimacy. It has agencement – a capacity to act (Çalışkan and Callon 2010). As the message an audit carries consists of straight cold facts – computerized selection criteria and a law – the auditors in their interpretation of it wrap them in soft, human values.

This chapter has aimed to contribute knowledge on how statistical analysis is not the only creator of a secure number. The number is certainly made, but with legal background and with human/social considerations and much care. There are tax faults out there. Those are found through eager and persistent comparisons of filed numbers in a database with actual receipts and documents – comparisons that always lean towards the support of established praxis. This is where we see the law, perhaps compared to a mould, however rough the edges. In the rich prose of Bruno Latour: 'Law is formal, but its reality is to precede any enunciator, any speaking human, for whom it accompanies all the overwhelming disengagements, all the fabulous fiction, all the audacious organizations, with work that, as far as possible, is not overwhelming, fabulous or audacious, and that reconnects, preserves, links up, assigns, retraces' (2010: 277). There cannot be any incorrect cost deductions, or any deductions for that matter, without considering the law.

And auditors, humans after all, step in where issues in taxpayers' private and public life overlap. They want to be reasonable and cooperative, for instance when they arrive at this 'secured result'. The rough outcome of this application of law and statistical methods has to be honed and carefully nourished through empathy in the relationship with its originator, the taxpayer. The casualness when making revised estimates directs attention to how common such changes are. Legal praxis and audit work procedures have to make room for more empathetic values, as there are just too many ineligible cost deductions.

Following the calculation of this percentage has teased out some values the Agency works with, yet translating various RAC praxis into a number also 'offers new ways to rethink the role that numbers, as a peculiar genre of communication, play in political and legal life' (Ballestero 2014: 52). We have seen analysts' concern with how this percentage can be used when let loose in society, as X per cent makes apparent the will, or perhaps rather unwillingness, to comply with taxes. And this is a threat to established Agency strategies. Obtaining numerical results while simultaneously emphasizing uniformity, cooperation and fairness in contact with the audited subject shows how delicate the accuracy is. Thus it is possible to impact an audit – even an audit as uniform and statistically secured as this one – raised by the experienced Random Audit Control department within the Agency. It is aware of the risks in communicating uncomfortable numbers to society at large and is especially cautious when a result contradicts other/previous results. The implications of communicating this number are discussed in Chapter 4 as we leave the RAC and see how the number is further nurtured and cultured in the analysts' care – and somewhat curbed by the Director General. But as we will see, even in a dense and well-argued report, X per cent would stand out and the verbal explanations contextualizing the number and drawing attention to its precariousness would be lost (cf. Crump 1978).

Notes

1. At the Agency, the name for the physical office space where the work is performed is the same as the name for the methodology (*slumpkontrollen*). In the following I distinguish the methodology by using upper-case initials for the term Random Audit Control – RAC – when discussing the methodology; when talking about the office/department we are at the Random Audit Control.
2. However, for the most part the Agency is frustrated at its inability to impact legal issues that make compliance difficult for the majority of the population. A prominent example is home sales where some information is almost always filed incorrectly. Another problem is business-owned cars used for private purposes. It is an

onerous task to keep track of when and for what purpose the car is used; this is like a red rag to a bull for many small businessmen.

3. The IRS refers to this type of audit as an office or correspondence audit or examination. What the Swedish Tax Agency refers to as an 'audit' is a more precise report of whether numbers correspond to actual bookkeeping procedures and is an evaluation of reality/actual practices.
4. *näringsfrämmande utgifter i resultaträkningen*.
5. *näringsfrämmande omsättningstillgång i balansräkningen*.
6. *uttag av omsättningstillgång utan att man beskattas för detta*.
7. *användning av bil utan att detta uttagsbeskattas*.
8. *användning av annan anläggningstillgång*.
9. SNI is the Swedish industrial sector classification that is primarily used when calculating the national accounts, but is also used in a variety of other ways when categorizing industrial sectors. The classification builds upon the EU standard NACE (Nomenclature statistique des activités économiques dans la Communauté européenne).
10. SIE is an open standard format data file containing the bookkeeping ledger.
11. The Agency does not want to audit entities recently contacted, therefore an extra verification of the chosen taxpayers previous audit history is made.
12. Although the name of the audited was not disclosed to me, they discussed the details. These have been slightly altered in order to ensure this COENs anonymity. The same treatment applies for all other tax return details in this book.
13. The krona is the Swedish currency.
14. All taxi receipts are printed from a fare meter indicating driver and car, start and end time, the distance covered, price and total price, VAT and the type of payment execution.
15. SNO is an abbreviation for *Skattenämndsordförande*. The Tax Board are the people who declare decisions concerning changes to the tax statements as final before a memorandum is sent out to the audited person/entity.
16. They mean if the consultant does business in Russia (misplacing the Polish city). However, their question is uttered with a smirk. The auditors think the consultant took a chance registering a vacation as a business expense, which is alleged to be quite a common practice among COENs.
17. When asked how praxis is established, the SNO seemed a bit uncomfortable but also intrigued by the question. 'It is difficult to describe', he said, 'legal praxis is one thing – there we have court cases. For other issues there is documentation such as those on the Web' (writs, consultative responses, handbooks, standpoints, etc. – a patchwork of rules and regulations) (Påhlsson 2006). Then there are problems that really ought to be forwarded to the legal department, he said, but in general praxis concerns convention and consistency nationwide.
18. This is different from auditing larger companies where all people are viewed only as employees and not as private persons.
19. Forms are an important subject at The Agency. According to the law (2001: 1227, 1 Chapter, 1, 3 and 4 §§) the Agency has the responsibility to devise forms for various legal entities on which to declare their income.

Chapter 4

To Publish or Not?

Communicating and Legitimizing Concerns Regarding the Project's Result

The task force is aware of the risks of communicating uncomfortable numbers to society at large and is especially cautious when a result contradicts other/previous results. Regardless, even in a solid and well-argued report, the results from the RAC will stand out. After much deliberation, various presentations for managers, discussions with Gunnar and many rewrites, a version of the report is finally to be presented to the Agency's *generaldirektör* (the Director General). Julia, who is back from parental leave, and Lars are smartly dressed in black for the occasion – 'we look like we are going to a funeral', Julia says with a smirk when taking the elevator up to the top floor. And in some ways, they are.

When attending this, and other, meetings we will see the tensions between the facts the Agency can communicate given its strategies, and how this new knowledge is used internally. Studying the questions the Director General raises about this project, we are able to see on a more general level what is at stake for the Agency working with compliance. We will see how decision makers talk about applying control measures, here discussed in terms of *controllability*, versus information initiatives educating the taxpayer, which will be discussed as *communicability*.

In this chapter, the emphasis is not on the actual results of the report – they are not important to the aims of this book – but rather on the questions and reactions these results create within the Agency. You will follow me to a number of meetings where interim and final results of the report were presented. What are of interest here are the implications the new knowledge is seen to have. Which of the proposed suggestions is it possible to implement; which ones cannot be implemented and why not? What knowledge has to be kept hidden and for what reason? One of the pertinent issues the Director General raises is what conclusions the Agency can make about relations and causalities between people's intentions and practices. Can we ever know why people make errors in their tax returns?

We will see, again, how the values the Agency emphasizes as important connect to certain societal practices and thus stand in the way of wording certain strategies, for implementing specific practices and also for publishing the report. We will also get a hint of where information from the report is actually implemented and applied internally. But let us start at the end this time and visit the Director General's office to see his reaction to the first version (he has read) of the report.

The Director General had been given the report prior to the meeting and, as we will see, he did read it thoroughly. This was not the pro forma meeting that Gunnar, Lars and Julia had expected but they were nevertheless encouraged by the Director General's comments and went back to their desks to discuss and incorporate his proposed changes. However, additional lengthy meetings to which I was not invited followed on from this one. As the refusal to include me indicates the sensitivity of the issues discussed within the report and ultimately therefore affects the aims of this book, the exclusion needs to be mentioned.

We take the elevator up to the top floor and are greeted by the *överdirektör* (the second in command at the Agency). There is some small talk on the sofas outside his office for 5–10 minutes; a discussion concerning authorship within the Agency's reports. Should the Agency claim authorship or should it be the employees who actually write the report? The discussion sways back and forth pinpointing questions of agency from within the Agency when outsiders read its reports. The Director General appears and we walk briskly to a nearby meeting room enclosed in glass walls. After introductions and a short brief about my own work (that Gunnar had asked me to prepare), the Director General goes straight to the point of today's meeting. He invites Gunnar to explain the starting points for and the conclusions from the risk assessment project about cost deductions.

The first issue questioned by the Director General is the number of COENs with seemingly correct tax returns. 'We know that we cannot find all errors', he says, referring to usage of fixed assets. 'Maybe everybody files errors?', he asks, indicating that the X per cent could be 100 per cent. 'What about the greengrocers that eat the fruit they sell?', he says with a grin. His comments question which of the COENs charge these deductions and whether the Agency can be sure that those identified are the only ones.

The Director General also notes the difference between intentional false deductions, compared to 'forgetting', or not knowing how to include benefits subject to tax. 'We have to be wary of saying that many cheat', he says. One of the contemporary strategies for the Agency is not to distinguish between deliberate cheating and making errors, as it cannot know for sure. The fiscal result is the same – less tax collected – but the intentionality behind it points to very different views on tax compliance. Yet the *why* resurges again and again in discussions about tax compliance and especially in light of the Agency's standing in Swedish society.

A third issue the Director General brings up is whether all audit decisions emerging from the RAC will hold up in court. Knowing that a cost deduction in theory is incorrect in practice is difficult, as we saw from the discussions at the Random Audit Control department, both among the tax auditors and even when the SNO (the tax board chairman and legal specialist) took part (Chapter 3). Are there decisions about rejected cost claims or other issues falling under the definition of these deductions that if challenged will not hold in court? On the other hand, maybe the total amounts will be increased if it includes cost deductions that are not detected?[1] The X per cent could be a very shaky number, according to the Director General. Ultimately, do the auditors interpret the law 'correctly' regarding these deductions?

The fourth issue is what they spend most of the time discussing. It addresses the inconsistency in the law, which highlights two problems: one regarding taxpayers' receiving different treatment and one regarding items treated inconsistently by different tax laws. And inconsistencies are dangerous, as they make a tax system seem illegitimate (cf. Lodin 2007). According to the law, some deductions are disallowed for COENs, but allowed for employees. This distinction does not apply to all COENs, but depends on their legal status (please recall that there are several business types grouped into what are known here as COENs). It is a catch-22 situation for the Agency, as there is no way to deal consistently with this issue. 'We have a problem with legitimacy as it stands now. If we take away the possibility for employees to get fringe benefits like free fruit at work, we will have a political problem. If on the other hand we allow these deductions for COENs as well, we will create an even fuzzier border', says the Director General. So no more free fruit and wellness subsidies for employed Swedes, in the name of legal coherence, if he has his way.

In addition, the law addressing income tax and the law for VAT differs on certain specific issues for what is deductible. For example, if a

COEN's property is privately used it should be subject to income tax according to the property market value, whereas for VAT it is according to the purchase value. Market value obviously differs over time. What is the value of a litre of milk on its expiry date – half compared to the day before? Or the day after – nil? For a grocer it is then seen as a disposable item, whereas from a fiscal perspective all food taken home for private consumption is rated according to market value.[2]

A fifth issue brought up by the Director General is the target population for the RAC. The argument for selecting COENs with reported expenses of more than 50,000 krona was that an audit control is a huge intrusion into a COEN's activities; therefore should COENs with lesser costs be left undisturbed. However, as the task force also aimed to say something about the so-called hobby corporations, 50,000 krona in costs was too large a sum for them to be included. In hindsight, the selected amount should perhaps have been lower. The choice of cost level is yet another issue that exposes the difficult decisions that have to be made regarding the task force's consideration about retaining Agency legitimacy. The particular selection of 50,000 krona therefore prevented the report from being regarded as 'a container' of all COENs (cf. Law, Ruppert and Savage 2011: 10). Thus it is difficult to draw conclusions about COENs' faulty deductions, as a large number of these entities were from the start exempt from the RAC.

So the Director General pointed out both internal analytic problems with the project as well as shortcomings within the law applied by the Agency. Both arguments could be used against the more encompassing aim of the report: to create knowledge about the amount and type of cost deductions claimed by COENs and to suggest countermeasures to decrease them. The internal criticism and the report's problematic insights that could be concluded in different ways were probably the reasons for excluding me from the follow-up meetings.

A few months later I was as before invited by email to the next scheduled meeting, and waited as usual in the reception for Lars to come and collect me. However, this time he was accompanied by his manager, Gunnar. He was quite apologetic as he told me that the very same morning he had received an email stating that the meeting was postponed. First, the Director General wanted more time than the fifteen minutes allocated for what Gunnar and Lars had expected to be a pro forma go ahead with the publication. Second, I would not be invited to the upcoming prolonged meeting. Gunnar said he was surprised as he thought it had gone so well the last time I was present.

We talked about the reasons for the changes in the Director General's attitude regarding the report and why I was no longer welcome. Gunnar speculated that perhaps the Agency might come across as both petty and capricious in spending resources on such cost deductions among COENs when the report was communicated. The press release could make them appear like that, even though the content of the report was much more nuanced. Or perhaps it was the timing of all this? Lars pointed out an op-ed that had been written the previous Saturday in one of the leading newspapers. The Agency was accused by three risk capitalists of interpreting the law beyond praxis (Johnsson, Bergkvist and Schömer 2013), thus reinforcing the view held among some taxpayers that the Agency pursues small businesses (see also Chapter 2).

There were at least two further meetings with the Director General and also a two-hour session where the manager of the unit was apparently frankly told about the flaws of the project, the analysis and the report itself.[3] Gunnar defended the project in an interview afterwards: 'the analysis work got some bruises. But if we, at the Agency, want to know about certain things, we also have to take the consequences of what we find'.[4] The unit learned that it had to be more precise in its analysis, identifying samples that related better to the aims of a project but perhaps also to be more precise with questions posed in risk assessment projects.

Although this break in my following of this project was at first frustrating, the entire sequence of events pinpointed what was at stake for the Agency when shaping the taxpayer – creating tax compliance. The following issues are thus based not only on the Director General's views, but also on presentations for managers, meetings with colleagues, interviews with task force participants, and readings of the differing versions of the report and its conclusions. Which of the issues is the hen and which is the egg is not easily established, but more important is to single out whichever issues are problematic for communication to the public and thus the reasons for not publishing the report. The issues brought up by the Director General were apparently easy to separate out, but in practice they intermingled when it came to how the Agency sees causality between them and how they in turn influence tax compliance.

When the results from the task force's work began to appear, Lars and Julia started to give presentations of their findings for colleagues and managers. The purpose was to get feedback, to prepare the ground for what they saw as somewhat controversial conclusions and to pave the way to start thinking about what to do with these results. The purpose of a risk assessment project is, after all, to provide support for the Agency's managers in making decisions. In the following section we will see how the managers in their discussions wrestle with different ways of handling the report's insights – against a background of increased compliance.

The manager presentations were held in various meeting rooms and always started with a number of PowerPoint slides. I will point out various opinions, reactions and comments uttered by the participants of these meetings that illustrate in more detail the Director General's criticisms and his reluctance to publish the report. His views will be reinforced, but also sometimes contradicted – by managers at various levels of the Agency, who will be using the report's conclusions; by other employees working with control; also by the task force's fellow analysts and how the latter relate to the new knowledge that comes out of this project and what was finally included in the report.

Overall, managers throughout the Agency were quite surprised about the result, especially those who adhere to the strategy that taxation should be 'right from the start'. Strategists and visionaries do not have the view of reality the report presents, explained Gunnar, whereas employees working directly with taxpayers were on the other hand not surprised at all. 'We know what the neighbour does', as someone said.

The presentations of the report and its results repeated previous discussions about how the Agency sees taxpayers' behaviour. Why do taxpayers make errors; who are these taxpayers and what types of measures are possible to reinforce in order to minimize the problem? Many of the following discussions, provoked by the presentation of this project, are thus old issues dressed in new clothes. 'It is an interesting subject as it pinpoints many issues that are at stake [for the Agency]', said one manager. The issues raised are not exceptional reactions to a specific risk assessment project. Instead, this project is a good illustration of many issues discussed at the Agency; it is helpful for our understanding of issues that the Agency considers in its daily work creating compliance.

The Problem of the Who …

What in hindsight surged as the biggest issue for holding back the report once the Director General had thought the entire project over was the risk for the Agency, once again, in pinpointing certain groups/categories of taxpayers as more prone to avoid paying taxes; entrepreneurs and corporations would once again be in the Agency's sights. Or in the words of Gunnar: 'The entrepreneurs will not like our conclusion, neither will Svenskt Näringsliv, The Confederation of Swedish Enterprises'.

In several discussions concerning the report the Agency's official standpoint was restated; the willingness to pay tax should not be seen as a tension between different types of taxpayer, in this case between employees and self-employed. This is one strategy the Agency communicates in order to avoid demonization of various types of entrepreneurs and self-employed, who manually complete tax return forms and therefore file more errors than employees. It thus brings back the Agency's aim of not targeting certain categories of taxpayers as having separate morals (i.e., possible reluctance to pay tax). Taxpayers cannot be categorized as more or less good, ethical or moral, as the Agency does not know the intentions behind mistakes. We can compare this with employees, where some have been found to be working extra hours on an informal basis, getting paid 'cash in hand' or 'under the table' (Björklund Larsen 2010; Skatteverket 2006a, 2006b) and thus leaving behind no record of his/her activities.

'Can we say anything about these categories of taxpayers', asked someone. 'Are certain types of business activities more prone to claim cost deductions than others?' And subsequently, in which types of commercial sectors is it easier to find errors? Another participant asked if it is the consultant or the grocer who errs most. The fact that some occupations seem less predisposed to claim deductions is manifested in this project. 'Seem' is the keyword here. Fewer cost deductions are found in sectors like restaurants and agriculture, yet previous research has shown that owners use current assets privately; in this context farmers should sell food either as meals in restaurants or as a produce and not eat it themselves without paying tax on its value. The control mechanisms available are just not made to detect the usage of these types of assets, which, according to the law, should be accounted for as benefits and taxed accordingly. For example, the audit found fewer errors in grocery shops than among consultants. One could ask whether the former entrepreneurs are more moral; or is it because they have other, easier ways to cheat (such as taking home food on the verge of expiry)? Consultants do not have such opportunities; instead they might try to deduct the occasional inventory used privately. This statement created a longer discussion among the analysts as the reason for claiming faulty deductions; it is a question of intentionality vs opportunity. This was not the first time this frustrating dichotomy of behaviour had appeared and it is something the Agency struggles with, with respect to defining strategies. The dichotomy could not be resolved this time either; but the Agency knows that it can work at reducing opportunity; addressing intentionality is less feasible.

Instead of exposing specific occupations as more prone to cheating, the Agency considers how taxpayers do the actual reporting. The view is that there are different conditions for creating compliance among taxpayers depending on how automated the filing system is (as we saw in Chapter 1), but also to what extent a third stakeholder, such as an accountancy expert or tax consultant, is involved in the completion of annual tax returns. The propensity to make errors, and/or to cheat, is easier if no one else checks the tax return. And COENs have both the opportunity and the duty to file manual returns.

During the last ten years politicians have focused on promoting entrepreneurship with the aim of creating more jobs. Therefore all entrepreneurial applicants are more or less directly accepted into the corporate registry and receive an *F-skatt nummer* (the corporation tax registration number), which is obligatory for issuing invoices. The political reasoning was to reduce unemployment, but the Agency is hesitant about this all-inclusive welcome. All governmental authorities are obliged to simplify entrepreneurship, yet there are quite a substantial number of entrepreneurs who do not fulfil the requirements for registration. What to do with entrepreneurs with non-existent levels of business activity and who are not profit-seeking? The Agency currently struggles with possible ways to curb abuse of such registration without making it difficult for serious entrepreneurs. The entire exercise is concerned with helping and promoting serious entrepreneurs and making sure they pay appropriate tax, while making it difficult for cheaters, criminals and others who are out to abuse the system with tax-planning schemes and evasion activities (Skatteverket 2013a).

Against this background, the findings in the proposed report are disruptive. The analysts are adamant that these new findings should be made known, but showing how it is 'out there' includes an educational element. 'This is the world new COENs have to adapt to', says Wera, implying that new corporations learn about these illegal practices. And as the Agency knows, the prevalent view in society is that if others cheat then why should I not? New COENs are thus at risk of copying bad accounting and reporting habits (e.g., including cost deductions that should not be claimed) and faulty tax return practices.

'Perhaps we have cornered the criminals, but to the extent that we are not able to find them', proposes Ingela. 'It is just so easy to create a new business, and being found out is virtually impossible. By controlling the ordinary – that is, non-criminal – activities, perhaps we contribute to the ease of those with criminal intentions to register as entrepreneurs?' Julia says what everybody is thinking – it will be a problem for several reasons when the report is published, as categories can be read into it of who is seen to cheat (cf. Porter 1995: 42). This is regardless of whether categories of taxpayers are explicitly singled out; it is enough to hint which of the kinds of issues that are up for discussion are deductible or not. Employees are offended when/if they realize the extent of what the self-employed, such as COENs, can do, and do do, privately with business assets. Regardless of how they view fellow COENs, either as colleagues or competitors, they see these actions as a reason for not paying up themselves.

Gunnar's somewhat idealistic idea is collectively refused: 'If we communicate that X per cent file erroneous cost deductions, then will new COENs know that what we do helps to control things and that we do that well?' The reply seems to be made in unison: 'This is not true and COENs know it'.

… and the Why

Regardless of the reasons for these cost deductions, Lars does not worry about the question of intentionality vs. opportunity, but sees it pragmatically from the Agency's viewpoint, repeating that: 'It should be easy to make it right but expensive to err'. In his view, the Agency has to continue to inform on what are the correct practices and try to control the wrongdoers. It is a challenge.

Regarding the grocers for example; everybody realizes that taking home food has a value, but as perishables approach expiration date, their value decreases (cf. Heuts and Mol 2013). These products should therefore not be subject to preferential tax. It is simple in theory but very difficult to enforce as a control practice. Private usage of a COEN's fixed assets is a second matter. According to the law, this usage should also be subject to preferential tax. What the law says and what is done in practice differs, from both the taxpayer's and the Agency's perspective. The intention of the law is obviously to make a sharp division between business and private life and in the end create fairness; all taxpayers, regardless of whether they are employed or self-employed, should be treated according to the law. Recalling Svenne's example of the snowplough in Chapter 2, who would rent a plough to shovel away the snow outside their house if they had one in their business? And second, if the farmer does shovel snow with it in front of his house or in front of his barn where his/her business is should the former be subject to preferential tax, whereas the latter considered a business activity? Enforcing taxation on activities such as snowploughing at home or consuming products on the verge of being waste shows that it is not just controllability that is an issue here; at stake also could be the Agency's reputation as either being too fussy or even ridiculous in its controlling efforts.

Controllability is a property most often used to describe technical devices; control systems that manage or regulate other systems; for example, in the production industry and in IT solutions. I find it a better term than auditability or verifiability, which are more directly connected to economic issues and would perhaps at first be thought more fitting in this context. We are very appropriately described as living in an audit society (Power 1999), but I prefer controllability, as it emphasizes how the Agency performs legitimate audits. In addition, controllability draws our attention to the technologies that makes legitimate audits possible.

Following the seminal works by Michael Power (1999, 2000), an audit has been described as a change in the functioning of contemporary society, where audits, borrowed from the verification of accounting practices, seep into an increasing array of professional activities. Introduced by Thatcherite politics as a way to ensure that public money was being used efficiently, Power describes the consequences when monitoring activities increasingly govern how organizations and corporations do what they do (e.g., Power 2000: 114). Audits, besides their fiscal collecting practices, are, however, the very essence of what a tax authority should do. Although audits shape activities, control is more proactive. It also directs our thoughts to a broader but also more precise function of an audit, which, in its original financial meaning, can verify actual bookkeeping entries. As we have seen in the work to define such deductions, not all of them are able to be verified according to the law. The actual definition of an audit is purposely kept vague (Power 2000: 116). Therefore controllability is more precise.

Perhaps COENs do not know about these specificities in the law? 'A reason for these cost deductions', says an auditor in an interview, 'is the lack of knowledge of what is subject to tax and not'. But he adds: 'As we do not know why these costs are claimed, there is probably an element of chance-taking that ought to be included when considering intentions'. Analysts also discuss the legitimacy of the law. Someone says that some taxpayers think that people ought only to be taxed for work done between eight and five; or more explicitly – on any work performed full time. What you do beyond that, that is what is performed in leisure time, the Agency should not be bothered with it and therefore it should not be subject to tax. Working extra and not paying tax is clearly a breach of the law and an intentional wrongdoing, but it is an opportunity taken, because the law, and the Agency's interpretation of it, is not seen as legitimate (cf. Björklund Larsen 2010, 2011). These types of activities are not aimed at deducting incorrect costs but at earning extra income; but the point is that these together make up 'decompression valves' – in an all-encompassing tax system.

From a historical perspective, are these deductions a growing problem or are they one of many ways to let the steam out that have existed throughout time? Ingela pragmatically adds a cliffhanger: 'If certain practices, like these faulty deductions, were made illicit and we can enforce this, maybe it will be compensated by cheating in other ways? If you feel unfairly treated, perhaps you justify it by compensating yourself on some other issues?'

One auditor, working with the RAC, pointed out that quite a few of the corrections made by the auditor were met with surprise. This especially concerned items that are deductible for employees, another fact that undermines the legitimacy of the system.

Let Lars's comment be the concluding one:

> The actual analysis illustrates reasons for why faulty cost deductions can exist. From these insights we can identify plausible actions. These taxpayers have to do the big job themselves [in comparison to employees] since they should [account for and] pay taxes due. There are many ways for them to easily profit [e.g., by deducting too many costs] and there are other issues that are very complicated and everything [all incomes and costs] must be correctly reported. As a taxpayer, you should actively do things correct. However, in certain areas the rules are [seen as] wrong; they are considered illegitimate.

Interpreting and Applying the Law

The content of the report is also an illustration of the frustrating inability of the Agency to act. 'The law says one thing and practice another', says Lars, a statement that is followed by widespread sniggering around the conference room where the analysts meet. His view, if anything, is nothing new and a well-established fact. Gunnar spells out the reality: 'We will never get a set of regulations that are exact. It will always be our praxis that decides where the actual boundary is drawn'.

Some rules are actually easy to understand for the taxpayer; for example, that these cost deductions are in theory illegal. 'However, our problem looks at how the boundaries are drawn [in practice]', says one manager. A colleague emphasizes the greyness of these areas – the boundaries are not easily identified. He reminds his colleagues that since the centennial tax reform (see also Introduction), Sweden has had a law that encompasses everything that has value as being subject to tax. Previously – that is, prior to 1991 – items that were subject to tax were explicitly specified. Now it includes everything unless documented as specifically exempt (cf. Björklund Larsen 2015).

So what strategy should the Agency apply? Should it employ zero tolerance, as the Swedish government does with regards to traffic exceeding the speed limit? 'If we do, we might no longer be able to say that everybody provides their fair share', muses Gunnar. This comment triggers many similar discussions (cf. Skatteverket 2007a) – that of zero tolerance setting a limit for certain activities. As previously, the discussions lead nowhere. Each time you move the boundary or each time new details are specified and added to existing regulations, new questions often emerge and so do new loopholes within the law – loopholes that must be closed again and again as society around us changes (cf. Jareborg 2008: 156; Picciotto 2007).

The discussion turns to the non-issue of *schablonbeskattning*, a flat rate tax amount. This issue had also been brought up[5] by the Director General, who asked them to write about it in the report and to be explicit both with the advantages and disadvantages. 'Politics apart', says one manager, 'regarding flat rate tax. Would it be possible to find an adequate level?' Why Sweden cannot propose flat rate tax for certain activities, like so many other countries, says something about its societal values.

Flat rate tax is internationally a common way to tax small businesses. It is easy to impose and evades the problem of difficult estimates for and commensuration of specific exchanges of what is taxable or not. For example, do some countries assume that restaurant owners and grocers take home food to consume in private and consume food at work? Why this is an issue is that not all employees have the opportunity to do so; only those working in this sector. It is seen as a fringe benefit.[6] Estimating this might perhaps be difficult: can a flat rate be imposed that eradicates this issue? Prior to the centennial tax reform, any Swedish grocer or restaurant owner was supposed to report an amount for this. If they did not, the tax authority routinely estimated a flat rate tax amount – a calculation based on the size of the household and what they ate for such and such an amount. 'It was called revolver taxation',[7] said Per.

In contemporary Sweden, a flat rate tax law or regulation is virtually impossible to impose despite its efficiency. As Gunnar explained:

> We have tried several times but it always stops short of the risk of being seen as unfair. This is one part of our [the Agency's] puzzle. We have a set of regulations (regarding cost deductions) that do not allow for any exceptions: it is easy in theory but more or less hopeless to apply in practice. We would probably fail if we tried to sort this one out. So at the Agency, what are our options? Are we avoiding the most obvious? How should the auditors work in practice? We, the analysts, have looked under the rug and this is what it looks like. How should we handle this?

This was not the only time that Gunnar voiced these concerns. The denial of a flat rate tax in the discussions is due to its inherent unfairness. According to the law, Swedish taxation is imposed 'according to each and every one's ability'. The content in legal proposals has always been regarded as tax adjustment rules (*jämkningsregler*). 'A flat tax rate is easier to control but more unfair and we do not have this in view in our political climate. We have to tax according to profit. For example, if you think about a restaurant in the countryside compared to one in Stockholm? … I have seen many attempts at this but to no avail' said Gunnar'.

To propose a flat tax rate falls flat on the details. Who should be included in such a flat rate? Restaurant owners and grocers? Farmers? And once the business sectors are decided on, the Agency has to work out the flat tax amounts for each given case. It ought to be fair after all, but then we are back at the never-ending patchwork that Jareborg and Picciotto describe. Flat rate tax is, however, fair in another sense; no one who has the opportunity for such consumption/use of inventories escapes taxation and it is thus fair for all other taxpayers. 'And it would take away the view that we, at the Agency, spend our time on nitpicky issues', says Svenne.

Could flat rates perhaps be more easily adapted for inventories? For COENs working from their homes and investing in items that can be used both for work and in private, there ought to be some sort of flat rate. A flat rate tax seems like a last resort solution, perhaps to be imposed regarding these type of deductions where some costs are virtually impossible to audit, regardless of whether they are plausible deductions or not. As Lars says: 'Basic legal tax principles make it possible to deduct these types of costs. If the Agency concludes that more or less everybody cheats with something, then it is time to discuss a flat rate tax'.

The Role of Analysis

The whos and the whys and a law that is problematic to apply in practice – from both the Agency's and from the COENs' perspectives (which also is making the law increasingly illegitimate) – suggest that the proposed report is dangerous matter. In addition, and perhaps because of these drawbacks, the Director General pointed to the report's analytical flaws. 'After all, he is a scientist', said Gunnar, referring to his background as an economist. For example, the Director General questioned the cost level used for sampling, which was one point of criticism. The cost level used omits COENs from being talked about as *one* collectivity of taxpayers (Law 2009: 248) and more specifically singling out a certain percentage, X per cent, of this collectivity as employing deviant behaviour. There were quite a few other issues as well, and in his view, while not every single issue was itself contentious, taken together they became so, making the report unpublishable.

Perhaps the wrong question was posed from the start? The issue of these cost deductions is just too encompassing. In a presentation Per said: 'When you study such a complicated issue you can conclude almost anything'. He struggled to comprehend the wide array of questions within the project. Perhaps the questions posed should have been narrowed down when the task force realized that the definition of the seemingly simple issue of cost deductions produced a broad spectrum of errors in the tax returns? The project simply addressed too many issues that in the course of events could conclude almost anything'. Gunnar stated his thoughts more generally. 'It might be that if we at the Agency learn new things then we might also create more problems for ourselves. New knowledge creates new questions', such as how to deal with these deductions. Should this project never have been done? Is it knowledge that ought to have been retained and perhaps now recognized within the Agency swept under the rug? Or perhaps a report from the Agency should only propose doable cures for phenomena and problems? The Analysis Unit's task is to provide support for the Agency managers both with analyses and suggestions for changes in information, execution and collection of tax.

Implicit in all this is the question of why the analysts undertook this project at all. One can question the role of analysis at the Agency. The task force, and also the Analysis Unit writ large, seem fairly united in that they would like their conclusions to be publicly available. They have produced knowledge that deserves a wider audience. As Gunnar said:

> We present all our findings in the report, about how we have considered the results from the audit and the surveys. The results are accounted for in detail in the appendices. If we have an Analysis Unit, we should be open about what we find. If we just "bury" it in the Analysis bank, it risks being public anyway, but without us telling the story around it. The Agency has some positive results to communicate, but this area is not one of them. It is not a great problem, but this is how it looks.

Politicians and other decision makers should know about the facts and the issues the Agency has to deal with. With these insights the ensuing political debate can be more multifaceted and informed, as these facts are taken into account. This means that even for the Agency uncomfortable facts ought to be available for a wider audience; that is – the taxpayers at large.

But as this new knowledge goes against established strategies, published as 'other knowledge', the Agency was uncomfortable about how to deal with such contrasting messages. What could the consequences be of going public? It is as Gunnar said 'an existential question', as this risk assessment project also became an evaluation of the Agency's own work. There is a feeling that so long as the results are positive – that is, reinforce the Agency's strategies and compliance – it is OK to publish, and perhaps even to analyse. One analyst critiqued other areas within the Agency;

according to him it uses only facts that support its own standpoints and strategies. This is something different from what the analysis at hand points out. Should the Analysis Unit critically use research to widen knowledge about tax compliance or should it provide informed support for decision makers? How curious should the unit be?

The Agency has a hard-earned reputation to defend. It is seen as legitimate in its actions and ranked among the top contenders in various surveys about citizens' views on governmental authorities they trust. This trust makes the Agency less susceptible to changes with regards to the knowledge it communicates; it does not want to rock the boat [*sic*]. At one presentation of the report's conclusions an analyst mentioned Simon Singh's book, *Trick or Treatment*, about so-called alternative medicine and its doubtful healing effects; does the Agency perhaps draw foregone conclusions about which strategies work and which do not in relation to increasing tax compliance.

We thus see how difficult it is to navigate through the grey zones of an all-encompassing law. Should all matters of interest be brought to light, or in Gunnar's words – all stones be turned over – or is it better to let such issues lie? As the conclusions from such a project lie in the eye of the beholder, can diverse stakeholders in the public tax arena use them to serve their (manifold) purposes? There are many throughout the Agency who are very much aware of this risk.

Measures: What Can the Agency do?

This risk assessment project was indeed an interesting one, as it addressed many contemporary issues that are at stake for the Agency. But what to do with this new knowledge? We know that the report was deemed too controversial to publish, yet measures were taken. These are, however, clouded over because of the secrecy of the internal doings at the Agency. Although the Agency is quite open with information on many issues, there are certain things that need to be kept secret in order to address those taxpayers who intentionally make erroneous claims – although it is not possible to say publicly what properties they have or 'who' they are. But we will know what the managers discuss and thus hear how they see connections between the various countermeasures that they regard as being possible to implement.

When talking about how to counter the prevalence of these cost deductions, it is as we have seen not always easy to keep the analytical distinctions apart from what is being proposed. Reality is messier than clear distinctions and categorizations propose. As Gunnar concluded in one of the final meetings: 'What we have looked at here is really interesting; it is a complex matter. What have we found? Which stones have been turned over? How have the estimates been made? Regardless of how we pose our questions, the picture is fairly clear – there are X per cent of such deductions'. The X per cent is a fact that was found for the Agency by the Random Audit Control department in its very thorough and meticulous way of working. Yet, as the Director General pointed out, it is a shaky number for several reasons. Most of the audited COENs accepted that they had erred and paid up accordingly. However, the Agency does not know why these cost deductions were claimed. Instead they are making educated guesses, with the task force and managers including the Director General commenting on the report's conclusions. It could be that the COEN does not know the law or that it is deliberately taking a chance on not being reprimanded in order to earn a few extra krona, or perhaps even trying to survive during a bad year. The intentions behind these claims are unknown, but the Agency can work out who has the opportunity to make them.

In the following section, we will remain with the Agency, but take a closer look at managers' internal discussions when they do not have to deal directly with taxpayers. The Agency's more humane and compassionate values that were emphasized in Chapter 3 are replaced with colder concepts of controllability and communicability. Controllability means identifying what it is possible to do with information about taxpayers. What can be verified in practice in an audit? Communicability regards what the Agency can say in order to retain its legitimacy. However, it is not an easy causality between those concepts so that controllable issues can be communicated. We will see that the issues that are controllable – that is, the tax faults that can be contained and addressed – do not necessarily qualify them to be communicated; yet those issues that cannot be controlled ought to remain out of sight of taxpayers in general, left under the rug as it were.

So I am back in one of the glass-walled meeting rooms, coffee cup from Nöterian in hand and seated around a large conference table. A dozen managers with differing responsibilities have gathered to listen to a presentation by Lars. He takes a remote control, logs into his computer and starts off yet another PowerPoint presentation with the latest insights from this project. There is a feeling of relaxed curiosity within the room. Everybody knows their own and others' roles of responsibility, including my own, and once Lars has finished, questions abound. Specific questions mix with jokes and banter, as insights from the project seem to confirm some managers' preconceptions about 'smart' tax-cheating practices.

The most pertinent comment seems to be that – once again – certain taxpayers are worse than others; a message that goes against the Agency's motto in their view of collecting taxes in a society 'where everybody pays their fair share'. As Gunnar says: 'We have a problem when we say that most taxpayers "do the right thing" when in reality they do not'. On a political level, COENs are seen to create growth and employment opportunities, thus their activities ought to be encouraged/endorsed. As has been hinted throughout the book and made explicit by the Director General, it is difficult to communicate the results from this project when the Agency wants to retain its legitimate stance.

The Agency has an economic estimate of faulty cost deductions that is part of the tax gap calculation. All issues making up the tax gap point to flaws in collecting the right tax – the tax collected if all taxpayers paid their fair share (Skatteverket 2014d, cf. Björklund Larsen forthcoming). This amount points to problems both with the legitimacy of the tax system and of the Agency's work. Most of these deductions found in the RAC are small, but as we know, many small brooks make great rivers. And this is what worries decision makers: both with regards to the total monetary result but also especially the number of taxpayers that actually err; the X per cent of all controlled.

Deducting faulty costs is something that distorts competition and if X per cent of COENs do so, it is bad for society as a whole. Economic theory says that if a business is not paying the correct tax, it means that it can provide lower market prices than the competitor that pays the full amount in tax. Such a theory assumes that consumers will choose the cheaper provider, in this case the cheater, who will then have cornered the market against its full taxpaying competitors. Prices can then be raised, as the COEN now has the upper hand on the market. And this is a well-established fact throughout the Agency; a fact that is deemed easy to communicate to the business community and shows the Agency in a better light than as a pursuer of businesses (see Chapter 2).

To communicate such a report with an amount that makes up a substantial part of missing taxes (the tax gap) is thus not easy. The Agency's strategy is to communicate news that goes with the message that 'most [taxpayers] want to provide their fair share', but if they do not? It is a grey area of certain costs the COENs think – by not knowing or by justifying or just taking a chance – they ought to be able to deduct. Although COENs might consider that they do their fair share, they do not provide it in the Agency's view, when compared to employees' contributions. It is a concern that the Agency's motto is not being upheld.

Publishing this report as one in the annual series is deemed too risky. The reports, mainly produced by the Analysis Unit, are available in both print and in pdf form on the website. They are usually accompanied by a press release, but in this case it is not enough. The communication unit tries to find a positive edge; for example, information about the Agency's strategies, but this time the head of the unit was clearly nervous and said 'no, no, no' to the task force and did not want to talk to me about it either. Although the Agency says 'it prioritizes disseminating knowledge and creates a discussion around the most important questions' (Fredriksson and Pallas 2014: 22, my translation), this example shows that trying to tame media reports is an important part of the Agency's communication strategy. With the report at hand, it was difficult to create a public message that would not be controversial.[8]

The results from the report have to be seen against the background of an entanglement of well-established strategies, previous research, communication of such research, political concerns and theory and also how such a report might be made available. These reasons all add up to causal explanations of what creates tax compliance. Regardless of how the report would be presented, the commensuration of the interpretation of law – the X per cent – would stand out. It does not matter how the combination of socio-technical issues is arranged, this number governs what can be said right now; it has agency (Porter 1995).

The managers continue to discuss the report: it is still viewed as something that is going to be published. The production manager, Lena,[9] plans a package of countermeasures. 'We have to be prepared', she says, 'we have known for a long time that this is a problem, but we have to show that we know how to deal with it'. So they discuss how to prepare for the publication of the report. One measure is not enough, that much is clear, and Lena makes a case for preparing for an array of measures: specific audit controls, an information package with the responses, a display of increasing control of the registration of new COENs and especially some sort of monitoring of their activities (are they serious in their business endeavour?) as the COENs develop and mature. These measures have to be made public through the communication department and spread internally so that all units can prepare adequate measures. All have to be on board.

Second, it is proposed that there ought to be better information provided about what COENs are allowed to deduct and what they cannot. This is a cheap measure, especially compared to audit controls. The prime channel for such messages is the Web portal; other outlets are the public meetings the Agency routinely organizes for SMEs (small and medium-sized enterprises). The Web structure is in need of improvement, Anna says, as there are different internal conflicts of interest between the Web production, as such, and the information that appears on it. The information is not always easy to find. A third concern is that when COENs do find it, can they understand it? How to make this problematic issue of cost deductions legible and understandable? Such a message is thus based on selected insights about what types of cost deductions have been claimed incorrectly.

And even if COENs were able to find relevant information about how to deduct certain costs correctly and understand the content of it, the Agency does not know whether this advice would be followed. As someone in the room objects: 'improving the website is one thing; whether the taxpayer cares about this new information is a completely other ballgame'. They recognize the interplay around the communication channel (the Web) and that the content on it should be legible yet refer accurately to the law and be put in a style and a tone that reassures the taxpayer about which costs ought to be deducted and which should not. Yet nothing can be communicated, as the Agency does not know what the intention is behind registering such deductions. There are many things simultaneously at play here, even writing a small, yet informative note on the Web that ought to be easily found and read by all COENs.

Given all the problems in communicating the results externally, there are still many things to be done internally by the Agency. Suggestions of how to eradicate the problem with faulty cost deductions were discussed at all levels. Since not all costs are able to be audited they cannot be controlled; so how to find them, how to tax them and how to eradicate the incorrect ones? One central issue the project pinpointed was one of controllability. What can the current controls detect and what changes in the rules ought to be suggested? Should the Agency perhaps even propose changes to the law?

One proposed solution is to increase the controls. From an internal revenue perspective, the auditors say that the actual audits carried out are very complicated and expensive (recall that each and every audit is allocated ten working days), while they pay off very little in actual fiscal revenue. The Agency has the slogan 'it should be profitable to do right, but expensive to err', a slogan that seems to apply to the Agency as well. As with all governmental bureaucracies, it adheres to budgetary constraints and thus only a fraction/certain amount of all tax returns can be subject to audit. 'With controls like this, we can only scratch the surface', says someone. The project audited 400 COENs, which is obviously a tiny proportion of all registered COENs, and yet it was impossible to find every cost deduction.

The most practical and easily adapted uses of the report are the adaptations to the data-mining models used to identify the taxpayers that appear to be most at risk of making an error. There is a department, XOX (my abbreviation), that works entirely with big data and other quantitative means of identifying risk. With knowledge gained from the report, the representatives from XOX think that the models they apply can now better identify taxpayers with erroneous deductions. Although the sample in the RAC was quite small, there are indications that certain information from the annual returns could be used to find these deductions. For example, they try to take into account such issues as imbalances between costs and revenues, age of the COEN, type of business activity, etc.

This internal usage of insights from the project is not made explicit in the report, but tax returns can be analysed by quantitative analysis and statistics in a different way from the rather qualitative study made within the report. Although there is a lot of information to deal with from the report, one of the XOX managers, Göran, says: 'This is very, very interesting, as I think that we can now detect the slobs from the wrongdoers'. Thus he aims to change, although crudely, taxpayers' intentions, while sorting out the direction in which they are heading. Those in sectors with small incomes, and probably deducting minor costs, will not be included. For example, should not small amounts of costs deducted pass without action? It is the large deductions such as for boats and holidays that are found to be the most problematic. As we have seen previously, the Agency does not want to appear nitpicky in its practices, but nevertheless wants to find the bigger offenders.

The same type of knowledge within the Agency can thus be used both qualitatively, to learn more about certain phenomena, as well as quantitatively for fiscal purposes. The different analysis approaches work in tandem. The XOX aims to identify the 'risky taxpayers' – that is, those who are suspected of not providing much of their fair share. Thus the total amount of tax collected is to be increased.

Although costly, both in finance and in compliance terms, specific result from this project was that the Random Audit Control department conducted a further audit in the subsequent year. The Agency wanted to see the impact of audits; do they change taxpayers' future behaviour? The very same COENs that were audited were once again selected. This was quite an unusual measure, as the Agency are usually not keen to contact the average taxpayer too often in order for them not to feel pursued – it is, after all, called a random control audit (see Chapter 3) – unless the Agency has very good reasons for suspecting incorrect behaviour. But getting additional insights into how controls/audits impact taxpayers' behaviour is just too good an opportunity to pass up, therefore the Agency decided to do it.[10]

Delivering material for an audit is, as we saw in Chapter 3, quite an extra workload for a COEN. Julia jokingly said: 'Can you imagine these COENs once they got the second audit letter? They must have really questioned it. Me? Again? Whyyyyy?' She grinned at her joke. The Agency navigates in a society that is constantly changing and it has to respond to those changes. A way to show this is by nailing some heavy offenders now and then. It is an implicit strategy of the Agency and something that was pointed out by one analyst colleague: 'Society at large becomes more prone to pay taxes while we simultaneously find increasingly advanced tax-cheating. The Agency needs now and then to show some prizes, e.g., find errors and catch cheaters, otherwise it can lose its credibility'.[11] So on one hand, the Agency needs to show that it recognizes the honest taxpayers, those that want to contribute; but also that it has control over even the smallest but widespread faults while being proactive in finding the big, bad wolves. Control and communication make use of each other: providing the message that tax offenders are found and caught increases the Agency's credibility among the population at large.

It is a fact that more incorrect deductions are made by COENs than by employees when it comes to a tax return. As COENs are required to have invoices and receipts for all costs and need to prepare most of their tax return themselves, the risk of error is obviously larger than when done by an accounting department; here, specialists report incomes and costs.[12] So the Agency is convinced that if more than one person is involved with the annual tax returns there are fewer faults. But will help from external accountants diminish these deductions? For example does the Agency communicate with FAR (Branschorganisationen för redovisningskonsulter, revisorer och rådgivare) the Professional Institute for Authorized Public Accountants[13] in Sweden to find ways to increase compliance.[14]

The task force looked into whether external help decreased the number of erratic cost deductions. The way to identify it was basic, as there was a box to tick on some years' tax return forms to indicate if help had been used. Comparing the tax returns containing faulty deductions with those that were filled in correctly did not correlate with using an accountant/external auditor or not. For political reasons, the non-correlation between external actors and correct tax returns was not discussed further, as the Agency needs to continue to promote this external cooperation; it is one of its important strategies.

The work to continue increasing E-services and simplifying annual filing, especially for COENs, was also reinforced by earlier findings. A specific issue was that 'corporations should receive better support in their bookkeeping. The software they use should be able to generate tax returns that can be directly sent to us', said Gunnar. Having followed this project, the Agency now knows more about what type of tax issues can be controlled and those that cannot.

To Control or to Communicate – What?

In this chapter we have seen more explicitly how the Director General and other managers deliberated over how the new knowledge the report created should be used. We have followed if and how insights from this risk assessment project could be disseminated to society at large and what the results of such dissemination are considered to offer for compliance. When new knowledge goes up against established strategies that are deemed successful the latter will succeed. What has followed in these discussions thus reflects on earlier knowledge and strategies teased out in Chapter 1. It has also confirmed how the Agency deals with this all-encompassing law that is virtually impossible to apply in practice.

The results from this risk assessment project were deemed too controversial to disseminate to the public if the Agency were to retain its legitimacy. Although this project's intention was to increase compliance over cost deductions, COENs cannot be said to claim more deductions than other taxpayers for a number of reasons: political, statistical uncertainty, legal inconsistency, philosophical. The proposed report from the project was not therefore published. Perhaps one or two of the issues that were brought up in the above discussion could have been communicated on their own, yet I am interested in issues that are deemed to impact compliance. For analytical purposes, I have discussed knowledge in terms of its communicability and controllability properties. I made this distinction in order to underline that although the Agency historically has increased both its legitimacy and tax compliance in society by showing that it works diligently to ensure that everybody provides their fair share, it cannot divulge all of its work – such as this report. Thus, there is no simple correlation between controllability and communicability; issues that can be controlled are not necessarily the same as those that can be communicated and vice versa.

Taking the uncommunicable issues first; the opportunity for a COEN to err is there, but the Agency can never know for sure *why* an incorrect deduction is made. Much of the literature on tax compliance emphasizes intentional wrongdoing (e.g., Boll 2011: 8). But just as employees at the Danish tax administration were encouraged to see that taxpayers had different reasons to comply (Boll 2011: 82), so too are the Swedish Agency's employees very clear that there are different reasons for claiming these cost deductions. Speculation would abound if a COEN's reason for claiming these is through ignorance, carelessness, or intentional cheating. This is why only parts of the new information in the report can be communicated. There are just too many ways for taxpayers and others to want to challenge the authority and work of the Agency, and words could be at risk of being taken out of context in the report. Unfortunately for the Agency's reputation and that of the tax system itself, people at large can come to other, bad conclusions about the connection between deductions claimed and who has claimed them; what the report states might unintentionally be interpreted as specific categories of people making incorrect claims. In this case, just by investigating if and how a COEN deducts such costs, with the result that X per cent of those investigated do, the implication is that COENs do claim erroneous ones. Although the Agency does not know why they do so, they can be seen as not paying their fair share, and voilà – society at large can conclude that COENs are obviously tax cheaters. The Agency has communicated such information historically and received heavy criticism for it. The Director General does not want to repeat this scenario.

Entrepreneurial activities such as those that take place within COENs are encouraged in Swedish society; these are seen as ways to increase economic growth and address unemployment. To criticize certain COENs' economic behaviour on grounds that can be challenged is thus politically stupid. The Agency sees a range of problems with COENs as a group of taxpayers, yet on a societal level their activities are just too manifold and their behaviour too diverse for the Agency to say something about their propensity to claim such deductions. Instead, the Agency works with ways to avoid offering opportunities for error. One way is to make information easily available and as understandable as possible. This is not an easy task; we saw in Chapter 3 how Agency employees, including one legal expert, struggled to interpret the law in audits. In addition, although X per cent of those audited were seen to have erred, the Agency did not know whether the audit decisions that were changed were challenged and/or upheld in court.

The law the Agency has to apply is imprecise and sometimes inconsistent, and can thus appear illegitimate, which is reflected in the results from this project. But this is another issue that should not be communicated, although it has been pointed out previously in the Agency's reports (e.g., Skatteverket 2006a). COENs do have the legal right to deduct all costs pertaining to the making of income from their business activities.[15] As many COENs do perform work from home, this is an opportunity that can extend to costs that are partly or entirely used in private. It is a grey zone and the Agency has worked diligently, writing in detail about whether specific items are deductible or not (Björklund Larsen 2015), for employees, self-employed and COENs. Presentation of such detail seems awkward, as we saw with employees' plausible ability to deduct wellness costs or to eat free fruit at work – fringe benefits that are not available to COENs. Swedes have confidence in the Agency, whose work rests on the foundation of tax law and thus the system. The Agency thus finds it difficult to communicate contradictions within the law; as such, contradictions are seen to diminish trust in the tax system as a whole. Fairness is one of the guiding principles for the Agency, and unfairness in the law, as already seen, is better kept at bay.

Another way to decrease the number of errors in tax returns is to make a third party responsible for bookkeeping or annual returns. The latter strategy is currently tried in various ways: cooperation with both accounting consultants, their interest organizations and with makers of accounting software so that annual tax returns can be generated and forwarded directly to the Agency. This would be a seamless solution where bookkeeping has to be done only once. The objective is to minimize the number of items that have to be filled in manually on the tax return. The task force tried to evaluate whether help by an accountant resulted in fewer faulty cost deductions, admittedly in a crude way, but the result neither confirmed nor contradicted it. And as the Agency has great expectations for future cooperation from these professionals, it was also problematic to reveal this result.

Finally, the Agency has the troublesome X per cent. Could it ever be communicated to society at large without having an impact on the legitimacy of the tax system and taxation practices? A percentage is always in relation to something, so X per cent on its own is meaningless. We need the who and the what in relation to it, a container to speak alongside it (Law 2009). Stated on its own that X per cent of COENs claim erroneous deductions makes them stand out from the rest of society. Regardless of the reasons for deducting such costs – the whys – the opportunity is there and the COENs profit from making such incorrect deductions. Ordinary employed taxpayers do not have the same opportunities to deduct costs. It is not fair and the message is that not all taxpayers receive the same treatment from the Agency.

That X per cent of COENs claim faulty deductions also sends a message to other COENs and similar corporations that there is leeway to do so. X per cent is seen as setting a bad example, as the Agency knows that taxpayers tend to replicate what other taxpayers do, especially when it is for individual advantage. What can be told, however, is all the specific detail on what is and what is not deductible, which came out as a result of the RAC. So there are many issues that are difficult to communicate to the public. Yet, knowledge from the report is used internally. There are a few questions raised by this risk assessment project that will, perhaps, be looked into in the future. As with any good research project, this one generated questions. How cooperation with the organization of authorized auditors would be implemented is one issue; another is how audits of registered COENs will be followed up in order to ensure they take their business endeavours seriously.

The new knowledge is applied especially when sampling taxpayers. In this way, statistical results can improve the Agency's efforts to find credible tax evaders as subjects for audit. These audits, it is important to underline, are not for any random purpose; we are talking about old-fashioned audits that aim to identify faults and errors in annual tax returns. Statistical results are not at all problematic here. These are now exclusively used for internal purposes in order to select taxpayers automatically for manual audit. Statistical probability is verified when controlling and auditing tax returns in practice (similarly to how Alice performed them in Chapter 3).

An old issue that is brought up again and again as one that is easy to monitor yet illegitimate (cf. van Schendel and Abraham 2005) is driving. It is easy to determine whether a car has been driven for private or business use because of the very explicit rules and regulations (Skatteverket 2009a). A logbook should be used at all times for COENs' cars so that they can show that they have not been used privately. Although it is therefore very easy to monitor such activities, auditors maintain that these rules have very low legitimacy (Björklund Larsen 2015). People get very irritated by the sheer workload involved in logging their driving. Usage of other vehicles that lacks such specific rules is virtually impossible to control, such as the snowplough Svenne repeatedly brought up. Non-controllable issues are thus better left uncommunicable as well.

So what does thinking about communicability and controllability of this new knowledge in terms of a socio-technical agencement add to the discussion? We have seen how technology made this new data available; the point is that humans can never draw these conclusions without all the devices they have to help them. As we saw in Chapter 3 the feat to make X per cent was a great socio-technical achievement on its own, involving: humans, hardware and software, hundreds of years of collective experience of auditing and control, uniformity in performing random controls, lists, folders, papers and mediating knowledge through talking with audited COENs and with colleagues in order to retain legitimacy. But decisions on what knowledge can be communicated are always left to humans, regardless of whether the decision is to publish the report in its entirety or only part of it, hide it, or even leak it to the public at large. Yet, the starting point is the law – always – and that is something the Agency cannot change on its own, neither can technology. Representatives for the Agency (e.g., the Director General) can advocate for changes to be made by the government and Parliament or wait for court decisions. Until then, it is the Agency who has to do all the work interpreting the law into praxis. And as we have seen, it is not easy when the law is as imprecise as it is.

For these reasons, X per cent and the arguments above have to be contained when the law is inconsistent. The Agency cannot communicate this inconsistency publicly, as it would then appear disloyal to its democratic constituent – the government. More importantly, emphasizing that the law is inconsistent would make the tax system appear increasingly illegitimate and no one would gain from this. The Agency has to do the best it can, given the law and specific instructions communicated to it via the *regleringsbrev*, appropriation directives. So what cannot be controlled and/or communicated has to be kept at bay. Such unresolvable issues should be left under the rug, as the Agency cannot do all the work involved in interpreting such an all-encompassing law if it is to retain its legitimacy.

Notes

1. We discussed whether it was possible to check if there were demands for audit decisions to be reconsidered (*omprövningar*) or even appealed (*överklaganden*). The Agency is also interested in this information, but there has not yet been the time to extract this, as the work entails quite extensive database searches.
2. Final version of the CD project report.
3. The Director General declined to be interviewed due to lack of time. Email 18 March 2013.
4. The RAC was used instead as a comparative control. The following year, the very same 400 COENs were contacted and audited once again.
5. A flat rate amount (*schablonbeskattning*) is different from *skönstaxering* (presumptive taxation).
6. Food and meals consumed during work are taxable except under specific circumstances; for example, meals consumed during military operations or by policemen when on duty (special conditions apply). In addition, all meals provided for pedagogic reasons, such as when it is deemed necessary to participate in a meal to provide a good example or to help a disabled individual, are tax free. Thus, school teachers, caregivers and personal assistants can receive a free lunch if it is part of fulfilling their work tasks. If the employer is a restaurant or similar provider of meals, the lunch is not free but taxable at 50 per cent if the value for the provider is less than what the provider sells the meal for. Thus, such meals can be compared with other types of rebate for employees (Handbook, Part 1, 17). The details are very elaborate and then we have not even mentioned the rules about being invited to meals while at work, so-called internal and external representation.
7. *skjutjärnstbeskattning*.
8. I tried several times to get an interview with the head of the communication unit, but to no avail.
9. She has not been available for interview.
10. I discussed the possibility of seeing the outcome of the second audit in order to discern if there had been any changes. There were no resources available to make the data available to me.
11. Excerpts from *Analytikerdagarna* (The analyst days) in Malmö, 24–25 April 2012.

12. Another countermeasure that the Agency has worked hard on to introduce is cash registers, which are required for sectors where cash is the most common way of paying (Sweden being one of the countries with most credit card/electronic payments relative to total payments). There are thus machine-produced receipts that report income, and these are machines that can be controlled.
13. FAR is an organization that consists of approved public accountants, as well as other highly qualified professionals, in the Swedish accountancy sector.
14. www.far.se. Retrieved 15 August 2014.
15. 16 kap. IL prop. 1999/2000: 2 del 2 s. 196–215 prop. 2005/06: 3.

Conclusion

Values in Action

'We know that we [at the Agency] apply a set of laws that we can steer into the ditch with', says Gunnar.

> And – it is so important for us to uphold the legitimacy. The rules do not allow for exceptions, but the reality out there is different. We have to acknowledge that the centennial tax reform of 1991 was a political decision that could be agreed upon only because certain issues were left out. But it is the Agency that has to live with its consequences and carry out the law in practical life; we have to be very careful and consider what is reasonable and realistic in our decisions so that these are deemed legitimate. As a manager at the Agency, I recognize this reality, as there is no set of laws/rules that is 100 per cent applicable by the book.

A black-letter interpretation of the law is not possible – it is not practically possible in the Agency's internal control practice and it would be unacceptable in society. The Agency has to do all the work, like all actors that deal with law, as Latour (2010) reminds us, and they have the many court decisions, rules and regulations to work with that provide specific taxation details. As we have seen, there remain many issues to be addressed and these proliferate as society around us changes. The Agency thus has a substantial amount of work to do with the law at hand.

The centennial tax reform that Gunnar refers to cannot, however, be blamed for all incorrectly deducted costs encountered in the risk assessment project followed in this book; the tax reform actually resolved many earlier legitimacy problems with tax law. Since the 1970s, the Agency has worked diligently to increase its legitimacy among the Swedish population (Stridh and Wittberg 2015). It is a feat to collect what amounts to one of the highest income tax rates in the world, yet be one of the most highly regarded governmental institutions among Swedes; particularly, perhaps, on account of the more than 500 modifications made to this tax system, which has increasingly given it the appearance of Swiss cheese (Bergstrand 2014: 13).

In this concluding chapter we will briefly revisit the contents of this book: the work of changing strategies at the Agency and the risk assessment project and its impact on tax compliance. As this authority continuously works to legitimize its activities, we will see how its interpretation of the law brings out certain values it places on Swedish society. Studying knowledge-making at a tax collecting authority might be seen as a shortcut to gold membership of what Susan Leigh Star called the 'Society of People Interested in Boring Things' (1999). But even if you do not belong to us who are interested in taxation per se, you have hopefully gained some insights into contemporary Swedish society and of a seemingly successful bureaucracy. The story you have just finished reading humbly bows to Schumpeter's appeal (1954) that in order to understand any society and its political life, one of the best starting points is taxation. Taxation plays very different roles in different countries, but the general message to take home for a well-functioning tax authority is that it has to pay careful attention – in its application of law and with the room for manoeuvre it has – to the values held by the society it taxes.

Since the Agency recognized that the way it was treating taxpayers did not have a positive impact on compliance, much has happened. The first attempts back in the 1970s were campaigns that focused on the argument that you pay for what you get: taxes make the welfare state possible, which is of benefit to all citizens. Then followed a more introspective view on the Agency's own work and how it could be legitimized from a societal perspective. The Agency tried to communicate and explain the necessity to audit and control taxpayers for the common good, while simultaneously providing massive amounts of information (cf. Björklund Larsen 2015; Påhlsson 2006). Based on laws and courtroom decisions, the available information has been rewritten in a more accessible language and in many languages, mirroring a Sweden where people ought to be able to account for and pay their taxes themselves and where many who work and pay taxes were born abroad. Currently, emphasis has moved to both educating and morally shaping the taxpayer. To fulfil the very moral motto the Agency nowadays advocates on its website, 'Our vision is a society where everybody wants to do one's fair share', the law has to be applied equitably for all taxpayers – regardless of what a citizen thinks about taxes, what legal entity s/he occupies and what knowledge s/he has. The message is that it is up to the individual to pay in order to contribute to a fair society.

Most recently, the educational and moral messages have been extended to include corporations and organizations; for example by arguing for tax compliance to be part of CSR (corporate social responsibility). This is not only to make corporations pay their fair share; for tax compliance purposes the Agency also aims to show individual taxpayers that *everybody* pays what they ought to according to the law. Yet, tax returns still have to be audited, as taxpayers need to know that they, like anyone else, are at risk of being monitored. Audits are, however, a laborious and very costly feat for the Agency, who relies mostly on a range of persuasive and informative compliance measures.

Noteworthy is that the Agency's progress would not have been possible without technology paving the way for a more comprehensive distribution of information for taxpayers, simplifying and automating annual return procedures and even sampling tax returns for manual control. Information for taxpayers, information about taxpayers and even from taxpayers has increasingly been automated and this work continues. The time of *taxeringsnämnder* (taxation boards) where 'responsible' citizens judged and evaluated whether taxpayers in the vicinity paid the correct tax, and control was based on direct or indirect personal knowledge about people's activities, seems distant; control is increasingly based on statistical samples from a mass of information in huge databases. To encourage people to comply, the Agency has had to succeed in being seen as legitimate in its interpretation of the law. We can thus say that it tries to apply the values that Swedish taxpayers hold, both in the ways it carries out such taxation but also with regards to what is seen as acceptable to tax.

Knowledge Used in this Risk Assessment Project

To understand how the Agency practises these values, I followed one of its risk assessment projects.[1] I was interested in knowledge production at the Agency and more specifically in how this knowledge is used to shape the seemingly compliant Swedish taxpayer. I followed this project from the analysts' initial idea to the finished report – through the survey, the random audit control (RAC) and the internal deliberations that made up the report, which, in the end, was buried. The new insights gained from the project were deemed negative and challenged the notion of the Agency's hard-earned legitimacy among the Swedish population;

the content of the report challenged the values the Agency says it holds and applies to society and could not be publicly communicated.

The buried report was the outcome of one of the largest analysis projects ever performed at the Agency and as such it came to touch upon many contemporary issues that are at stake for the Agency. The analysis project addressed faulty cost deductions among certain types of commercial entities (COENs).[2] Such deductions reduce the income on tax returns and thus decrease the tax that ought to be paid. Up front these deductions looked easy to identify and describe, yet reality proved otherwise. There were numerous discussions among analysts, who took into account the law, the tax return forms, anecdotal examples from friends and colleagues, statistical methods, audit control procedures and previous analyses made at the Agency. In the end the task force settled for a definition that wanted to establish at the outset whether the COEN was a 'real' entrepreneur – that is, profit seeking and showing good levels of business activity. According to the definition of 'real', the costs deducted from the tax return had to be relevant to the COEN's business activities and be used to carry out these activities. Then followed a more specific definition of five different types of costs that were more or less easy to identify: (1) Had the costs been entirely or partly used privately? (2) Did the costs refer to the owner's private usage of COEN assets? (3) Could the costs be regarded as private consumption of COEN products? (4) Or of its acquired products? (5) Was it an acquisition that did not have anything to do with the COEN's activity? Needless to say, these cost deductions had been made without paying taxes for the stated amount.

The project aimed to understand why such errors are made, how common they are and their consequences for tax compliance among other COENs as well as among taxpayers at large and how to determine the risks posed by these types of cost deductions. The answers to these questions were sought in two of the Agency's standard analysis methods: a survey and a random audit control (RAC). IT solutions played a vital and active part in both. The knowledge produced by the survey could hardly have been obtained without using technology: computers, software programs, databases, telephones, the respondent programmes, the SPSS file, etc. A manual survey, even if it had at all been possible, would have taken much more effort and time; it would not have been as efficient and would have been more costly. Although the task force (the analysts who performed this project) recognize that surveys have many flaws, they are not easy to substitute. Surveys are cheaper, for example, compared to focus groups, but they are also a common way to acquire knowledge – 'we usually do surveys', said the analysts. Surveys can thus be said to have a social life, as the analysts know how to do them, work with them and also compare results with earlier ones. The Agency had valuable help, as external stakeholders also have an interest in upholding the use of surveys. RC, the Research Consultancy, helped the task force throughout the construction of the survey and in its negotiations with the NNR, the Board of Swedish Industry and Commerce for Better Regulation. As a commercial provider of survey executions, the RC directed its resources towards winning the contract and perhaps also argued for the most encompassing, and expensive, solution.

The survey also gave a glimpse of how stakeholders see the Agency's legitimacy played out in society. By imposing discipline on the survey, the NNR tried to protect commercial entrepreneurs from being depicted as tax cheaters. In NNR's view, all potentially subjective answers in the survey should be avoided, thus in reality making it impossible to perform. With the intervention and mediation of the supreme Swedish authority and specialist of statistics SCB, Statistics Sweden, a compromise was found and the survey executed. SCB pointed out what it saw as differences between attitudinal views and the objective practices that COENs actually carry out. SCB both reproduced its status, the societal impact of statistics and even earned some income (cf. Sjöström 2002: 215) in its role as expert mediator providing feedback on the proposed survey and its accompanying missive. The survey's etymological roots bring to our attention the fact that statistics is perhaps not so much a subject to aid our understanding of the world (survey it), as it is a way to administer and even rule (*surveiller*) it. 'It should show what they think', said an analyst. However, in the end, the results from this survey did neither; it mainly seemed to confuse the Agency when the task force compared and presented the results of the survey with the numbers from the RAC, which had provided knowledge about what type of costs COENs actually deduct.

The Agency regards a RAC as both a regular form of audit control and also as core knowledge for a risk assessment project. The RAC created numbers for the task force to work with and compare with the survey and to previous analysis, but this random audit also indicated certain values the Agency adopts in its engagement with the taxpayers. A RAC has to be statistically correct, so that the results can be *secure*. Once taxpayers are selected, all audits have to be carried out in a *uniform* way. Seventeen procedural lists ensured uniformity and were meant to exclude individual tax auditors' preferences for controlling certain issues (and not others). Questions about costs falling outside those specified in handbooks, etc. were addressed in meetings between employees with various competences; ensuing decisions were then added to an intranet forum, augmenting specific knowledge about deductible costs.

The Agency recognizes that RACs make for the most sensitive engagement with taxpayers. The strict and rigid internal working values – uniform and secure – were softened by the tax auditors' emphasis on being *reasonable*, for example when estimating what type of expenses should be deductible. '*Empathy* with the taxpayers' situation', said one legal counsellor; and we have seen how these auditors aim to try to understand the challenges COENs face in their daily work. The Agency knows that it is difficult to enter all information correctly on a tax return form, thus acknowledging the possibility of making mistakes. The argument is that this is why taxpayers need help, and having received this help it is perhaps easier to do it correctly next time around. *Cooperation* was aimed for in any direct or phone contact with the audited taxpayer. As Alice, one of the auditors, said: 'The best [scenario] is if we can establish an easy-going yet professional relationship'.

How to Impact Tax Compliance?

These standard analysis methods, the survey and the RAC underline how technology plays a major role in the Agency's transformation; but technology cannot do it on its own. It always draws on human knowledge and it is humans that decide when it is to be used and when not. In the end it is (still) the human eye that audits, defines the frame for a random selection or suspects incorrect tax returns at visits. It is the combination of technology and human action that creates compliance – socio-technical agencement. Yet once in place these technologies, and their supposed objectivity in providing information, are difficult to question.

It was deemed impossible to make the report publicly available due to the new knowledge; it was especially the X per cent that would attract attention, question the Agency's motto and risked having an adverse effect on Swedes' tax compliance. It is a truly contentious number for the Agency, as it cannot say that COENs do not provide their fair share of taxes; it thus questions the overall motto applied by the Agency. So the X per cent cannot be communicated. Many verbal explanations attempted to tease out the context for the X per cent, as the number in itself could be interpreted in devious ways. As Thomas Crump stated: 'numbers succeed because they need no culture-specific support, no culture has an inbuilt defence against numeracy. Numeracy is a sort of Trojan horse, for once it is admitted, the institutions it supports tend to become dominant in every domain, whether it be the local economy, leisure and play, religion or whatever' (Crump 1978). This particular Trojan horse is a percentage; a translator between a part and a whole (cf. Ballestero 2014), as a percentage always connects several facts. As the NNR rightly pointed out – just the very fact of posing questions about a certain practice makes the connection stronger between practitioner and practice and the entire category selected as respondents (cf. Law 2009). Otherwise such questions would not even be posed, right?

Such a percentage has agencement, as it challenged the Agency's legitimacy. This percentage says that the Agency has somewhat failed in its aim to make all taxpayers provide their fair share. The result of the RAC part of the project was initially only secure numbers. Yet, that X per cent of all COENs erred was significant and contradicted findings of previous analysis reports. It was also very different from the results from the survey, and this comparison further undermines the latter method for this type of analysis. Despite extensive deliberations, the task force in the end applied the 'usual' methods and had hoped for their results to agree. Taxpayers, like most other people, do not do what they say they do. In this case this fact is bad news for established tax compliance research.

Statistics is a comrade in arms that can identify potential wrongdoers, but cannot say *why* errors are made. The Agency is meticulous to point out that it does not know why errors are made, but just concludes that they are made. So, although some groups of taxpayers err more than others, and are thus potential tax cheaters, this report wisely reconfirmed that the Agency cannot say for certain why faults are made; furthermore the law does not allow it to draw any conclusions. The Agency avoids talking about taxpayers' intentions and instead focuses on taxpayers' opportunities for error; or, rather, the focus is more explicitly on reducing opportunities for making mistakes. Yet, throughout the Agency, ideas about who cheats/errs still remain. For employed taxpayers the opportunities to err are more or less extinct due to the automated tax return; a third party supplies most of the information. The individual taxpayer has a very simplified job to do: s/he checks the reported numbers against statements received, perhaps adds a few income/expense items and then electronically signs it; over and done with. For the increasing numbers of entrepreneurs and corporations, such as COENs, the Agency tries to remove the individual manual entering of information.

The Agency learnt many things from this risk assessment project and subsequently applied the new knowledge to its automated audit sampling and changed some public information.[3] The measures introduced as a result of the report are thus mostly internal and apply to the sampling of risky taxpayers. The Agency has learnt from this project, although the Director General argued that it analytically lacked rigour and with its result was a misfit in terms of external communication. If the RAC showed us human, softer values in direct communication with taxpayers, the managers and decision makers within the Agency were more technocratically straightforward; communicability with society at large and controllability internally emerged as important properties when the results of the report were discussed. If (new) knowledge about taxation makes an impact on tax compliance, is it adequate to ponder a little what a contribution like this book can do for the perception of this well-liked Agency? Such a discussion can only be speculative, but speculations that follow the theoretical inspiration of agencement used throughout this book. If the risk assessment project had, and has, agencement, so can this book.

First of all it depends on who the audience is. An international readership dealing with less admired and less successful tax authorities than the Swedish one might be inspired by the journey made by the Agency and its usage of various types of things, theories and strategies that increase tax compliance in Sweden. This book has followed only one analysis project; the bulk of the work (briefly described in Chapter 1) has been the long and persistent effort of the Agency and its employees for many years, in order to obtain the seemingly high tax compliance rate among Swedes. However, I have gone into great detail to describe how knowledge is generated and what type of knowledge and what strategies work – and which do not – given the current status of tax compliance in Sweden. Tax compliance is, after all, in motion and subject to change as society around us changes. Such a readership might also feel that they have been somewhat warned of analysis techniques that do not provide valuable insights.

If read domestically, the message from this book will have a different impact. A monograph about a governmental revenue collector is hardly blockbuster material and will not make an effect on its own; it needs 'help' from different translators. Media, commentators, decision makers at different levels and opinion makers in Swedish society need to participate.[4] Such commentators often pick the parts and arguments that fit their agenda. Taxpayers already critical of the Agency might find the book adds fuel to the fire; taken out of context, specific insights from this book can make the Agency an easy target for abuse. I hope that this will not be the case, but that the insights from this book will instead be discussed in their entirety.

Especially salient is, of course, how the Agency reacts to the content of this book. 'Do not rock the boat' seems to be a saying that the Agency live by and obviously critique can change its favourable contemporary standing. The Agency itself states that its prime concern is not to change Swedish taxpayers but rather *its* own practices (Stridh and Wittberg 2015: 145); this includes acknowledging new knowledge and new insights. However, this humble attitude is a partial truth; behind changing ways of working obviously lies a strategy to make citizens more compliant. This move aligns with contemporary research; tax compliance will increase if taxpayers trust that a revenue collecting authority is doing its job to make sure that all taxpayers contribute (e.g., Levi 1988) and that all are receiving fair and equitable treatment according to the law (e.g., Picciotto 2007). At the Agency, a negative reaction towards the book may occur as a result of public critique, but also as a result of the book's description of their internal way of working.

If the Agency reacts, it is an acknowledgement of para-ethnography. The Agency dared to invite an anthropologist to follow such a project, but it also meant that the Agency, as represented by the analysts and their manager, was ready to learn about its own practices. My entry ticket to this fieldwork was my dissertation on how a group of Swedes justified their purchases of black work, which is a form of tax cheating, a book that had been discussed at various levels at the Agency (e.g., Skatteverket 2011b). I cannot pride myself on having educated the analysts in any way, yet I am convinced that at least some of my concerns and questions have remained with them; have been creolized as it were (cf. Hannerz 1997).

A fair and an equitable treatment of taxpayers underlines the para-ethnographic endeavour at the Agency itself, but it is a knowledge that is not always recognized as such. The anecdotes, stories and hunches played an important part throughout this risk assessment project: in the analysts' discussions; in creating and analysing the survey; in the audits around which the law and numbers were interpreted; and in the feedback from managers. Such knowledge informs the Agency's views of those who make cost deductions and those who do not. As one experienced auditor said in an interview the analysts performed as a follow-up to the survey: 'I just have a personal opinion that all COEN perform such cost deductions because "everybody else does them"'. The Agency is adamant that it has to have a para-ethnographic approach to knowledge about tax compliance when it tries to understand values held in Swedish society.

Fair Interpretation, Fair Taxation?

What signifies the seemingly very compliant Swedish taxpayer – is it just a willingness to part with a large chunk of income? The total amount that Swedes pay – quite large by international standards – is made up of many taxes and fees and appears somewhat hidden. It is a very simple affair for an employee to pay Swedish taxes, which is gratefully acknowledged by those who are obliged to make tax returns elsewhere, e.g. in the U.S. Yet, to be honest do most employed taxpayers not have a choice, as most of their income and legal deductions appear as pre-populated information on the annual tax return. And as hiding income and 'creative' deductions are mostly denied them, the practice of paying tax informs on values about tax compliance. As most Swedes (employees) pay, it follows that everybody else should also provide their fair share.

Yet for taxpayers like COENs things are very different. They have cumbersome filing to do. The Agency would like to automate their tax return or pressure them to get help from tax consultants, as analysis has previously shown that both strategies make for better compliance, but it proves a challenge.[5] The Agency tries to accommodate this strenuous task by applying soft values such as reasonableness and being cooperative and empathetic, as well as by providing information on the Web and in public meetings. In this pursuit, it has largely succeeded. As an acquaintance qua consultant said: 'it is impossible to be angry at the Agency as its employees are always so helpful'. The Agency seems to largely succeed in practising its stated values of being 'active, trustworthy and helpful' (Skatteverket 2013a).

In addition, such a governmental authority has to perform according to values that resonate with contemporary society. *Fairness* in the interpretation of the law is an overarching value the Agency tries to express, not only in its contact with audited taxpayers, but taxpayers at large. Taxpayers should be able to trust that the Agency is fair in its work. Although citizens/taxpayers might not like the tax laws, and all citizens pay different amounts in taxes, citizens should at least know that the law is applied in a consistent and equal manner and that the Agency's internal way of working is rigorous. Fairness is the bridge between a secured and uniform way of performing audits and the softer values of cooperation and reasonableness that should govern direct communication with the taxpayer. Fairness means that all taxpayers are treated in the same way and that the law is being applied equitably and correctly to all, not singling out certain taxpayers as more prone to cheat. This is how the Agency sees legitimacy built. Yet, there are not only soft values. The other side of fairness is making sure that everybody complies. In order to be believed, the Agency has to show that it works in a rational and efficient way so that potential free-riders are caught. A bad situation for the Agency is not having control; whether this comes from an inability to identify tax cheaters or to audit income or cost deductions, which was the purpose with the project followed here. Fairness is nothing new in the history of tax compliance; 'taxpayers' have throughout time demanded fairness if they are to part with a share of what they have to the ruler(s); fairness in the way they are treated, in the amount that one parts with relative to another taxpayer but also in the way that revenues are distributed. If all pay, all should also benefit.

It is hard for any revenue collecting authority to create legitimacy on its own. These authorities operate in countries with different tax laws, different values, different governance, and have different tasks to perform. The willingness for citizens to pay up also depends on perceived reciprocity; that the revenue is spent on issues that resonate with values in society. If other bureaucracies in society – that have the task to *spend* what the Agency has collected – apply values that resonate with those held by the public, it will, ceteris paribus, automatically increase the Agency's standing.[6]

Now, interpreting the law in an equitable way could also mean that it should be interpreted for all to the letter. How could it otherwise be equally applied? Not all taxpayers have opportunities to deduct the same costs as COENs have. Back to the task force's snowplough discussions; the plough should be used to shovel away the snow where COEN activities are performed but it could also be used in front of an adjacent private residence or to help a neighbour in exchange for something else having value (cf. Björklund Larsen 2010: 120). In all the latter cases, there should according to the law be an estimate of what this service is worth and this value ought to be added to income and subject to tax assessment. These incomes are seldom found on a tax return. And even if the Agency wanted to, there is no way for the Agency to apply the law and control such presumed costs. How would you, for example, see if a COEN's snowplough had been used in a private context? The possibility exists, in theory at least, that the COEN also has a privately owned snowplough or decided to shovel his private driveway by hand.

And even if the COEN knows that such costs ought to be subject to tax, they are just too cumbersome to evaluate. Besides, why bother to pay tax on something that is not detectable in the first place and probably also viewed as outrageously finicky; such as a cost for using one's own (e.g. the COEN's) snowplough? An employed taxpayer might also have a snowplough, but one that is (supposedly) paid for with taxed income. The mundane yet very apt snowplough example illustrates that all taxpayers are not equal before the law, neither in theory nor in practice, and this is a problem the Agency recognizes.

Values and Valuations

We should, however, not for a moment imagine that Swedes do not avoid taxes. The background for this risk assessment project is just one illustration of the multitude of ways cheating, evading or avoiding taxes can be achieved. To start with, the law does not allow for it, but the Agency knows too well that it cannot apply the law to the letter. Certain income that ought to be subject to tax is just so important for social relations that even just thinking about charging tax on, for example, barter would be a destructive move (Skatteverket 2006a). Barter is often used as a way to make exchanges cheaper, or even when compensated in cash is still referred to as barter (Björklund Larsen 2013a). People are not stupid; if there is a chance to gain something in a legitimate way it is often taken. This is why the Agency tacitly allows for such exchanges. These and the multitude of mundane practices such as the by now (in)famous snowplough usage are seen as a safety valve in a society where income is so very controlled. The clogging up of such valves could push avoidance elsewhere and if the steam is not let out, well …

The Agency could paraphrase Donald Rumsfeld and state that 'as we know, there are known knowns; there are things we know we know. We also know there are known unknowns; that is to say we know there are some things we do not know. But there are also unknown unknowns – the ones we don't know we don't know'.[7] But most importantly the Agency recognizes the unknown known – the disavowed beliefs and suppositions that form the background to our public values. These cannot be publicly acknowledged, as they are in opposition to the Agency's motto. It does not say publicly that it knows about them, yet the underlying feeling is that you know that we (as an Agency) know, but we will not do anything about the issue as long as it is not too obvious and pressing. What is going on in practice with actual tax compliance is a very different matter and the Agency is more or less aware of it. Exchanges that cannot be measured according to established methods are for example difficult to communicate. So things that cannot be controlled cannot be communicated and are thus, wisely, left under the rug. To retain legitimacy it is better to keep quiet and bury such outcomes – just like this report written by the task force.

Throughout this book, the Agency has been shown to balance its actions in a sometimes thought-provoking way between what has been referred to as applying rigid and soft values respectively. Rigid values govern its internal work. Any work has to be done professionally, and in this risk assessment project we have seen it applied in the creation of the survey and most explicitly in the preparation and performance of the RAC. The data from these investigations is created, treated and reported in a secure and uniform way. It is a very rational way of working that creates trust in the numbers produced. Economic valuations that constitute the Agency's core activity are performed with attention to values that are seen to increase legitimacy. The Agency's fiscal duty is, after all, to collect the 'right' amount of tax; and that means assessing and controlling that the right amount – value – has been entered into the annual tax returns and paid accordingly. This activity is very much taken for granted that it is not even mentioned in the introduction to the Agency's *Strategic Direction Document* (e.g., Skatteverket 2013b).

Numbers on a tax return ought to be the result of accurate calculations stating objective facts about economic activity. So in one sense, this activity is seen as separate from the application of moral and social values, yet in this fiscal anthropological approach we have seen that these domains intervene. 'Cost is not a simple fact, but is a very elusive concept' (Walter Wilcox 1941, as quoted in Porter 1995: 94) is an apt reflection of why this project took on so many aspects of tax compliance. We have seen how the Agency pronounces certain values that should govern its work and its contact with taxpayers, those values its employees talk about and emphasize in their work when judging the validity of cost deductions. The Agency both *skattar* (tax) and *uppskattar* (evaluate) citizens' exchanges. Distinguishing between evaluation – assessing, gauging and controlling – and the explicit economic valuation often identified by calculations is another way to see how these valuation practices interact and create ideas about fairness.

In order to say something about the interplay of valuations at different levels of society, let us revisit how different values and valuations are made in the very mundane act of handling costs on a tax return. Already when a COEN adds up the different types of costs that have been incurred during the year as economic values and enters those on the annual tax return form do valuations take place. *Which* costs are selected and for what reason? The Agency views these numbers as a calculation made based on receipts and invoices; but also more suspiciously evaluates whether the tax return has the correct type of costs entered. That is why controls have to take place – the Agency has to make sure that the costs on the tax return relate to COEN activities and that they correspond to actual practices. Obviously it is only a small number of COENs that are subject to such controls; either selected by a random sample, as we saw in Chapter 3, or by selective sampling with the aim of identifying the most susceptible offenders. The emphasis is on evaluating what has been stated on the tax return in an efficient and uniform way – by applying Weberian values. However, when there are doubts over numbers they need to establish another economic value; the auditors need to revalue – that is, redo the economic calculation. An evaluation of costs that are entered differently on the tax return compared to an evaluation of a COEN's practices in reality means that another economic value has to be decided. An 'objective value' is obtained, such as when the regulations explicitly state a number for a specific activity; at other times the purchase price has to be found or a revaluation has to be made according to market values. Then auditors need to find an equivalent item on the market so they can evaluate whether the costs stand for the same thing. If they are unable to find a similar item, they have to try to assess what the market value would be. The cost deduction is then made commensurate or recalculated as a decisive economic value in trying to apply laws and rules to the letter in a standardized way. When in doubt, as the law cannot be applied to the letter, the soft values come into play.

The Agency thus considers many aspects other than the strict economic calculation, including the view on how the Agency will be viewed in the eyes of the taxpayer. In any contact with taxpayers, the Agency will express soft values: empathy, fairness, reasonableness, collaboration. While being reasonable by showing a certain value, the re-valuation of costs often reduces the economic value subject to tax. Being reasonable creates a bridge between the rigid internal values of working and the softer values that ought to govern the Agency's communication and ensuing relation with taxpayers. By simultaneously revaluing and evaluating, the Agency can also show itself as fair (cf. Herskovits 1952). Then the (altered) figures on the tax return are recalculated and compared with the actual payment of taxes made during the income year. This is a straightforward comparison and results in the collection of additional tax or disbursement. The audit work is ended.

The Agency's entire work on legitimacy can be said to be a valuation practice, but one that balances and even creolizes different types of values. Let them, for simplicity's sake, be called economic, social, cultural – the point is that there are *different types of values* that are subject to change as society around us changes. In order to gain and retain legitimacy, any tax collecting authority constantly has to practise values that resonate with those held in the society (it taxes) and be alert to how they change.

Notes

1. These are made to provide decision-making support for management.
2. The exact legal definition of a COEN cannot be revealed here due to the confidentiality I agreed to when invited to follow the project.
3. The risk assessment project I followed was probably the last of its kind, at least for the foreseeable future. The Analysis Unit is now much more integrated in the workings of the Agency and the tasks it gets come from management. The analyses and report it produced addressed larger tax compliance issues and not only specific questions; today the Unit provides more direct decision-making support. This redirection of the

analysis work was inevitable in the long run, but this very long risk assessment project probably hastened the change. Analysts say that the tempo has increased and more, yet shorter, analysis projects are now produced. There is a worry that the narrowing of perspective into very results-directed analysis risks leaving out the larger questions. The analysts have never claimed to do research, yet they liked being able to raise tax compliant questions they saw as relevant in society. This creative reflexivity seems to have been retained or has at least moved up to another level of management, who might have slightly different interests.

4. At the Agency there have been discussions as to whether the Director General should comment on its release pre-emptively, perhaps using the same genre of overall arguments as for the risk assessment report that was not published.
5. Yet no such correlation could be found in this RAC.
6. This comment was uttered by the current manager of the analysis department at a presentation of this manuscript. The bureaucracy par excellence referred to was Försäkringskassan, the Swedish Social Insurance Agency.
7. When Rumsfeld was United States Secretary of Defense, he stated this as a response to a question at a U.S. Department of Defense news briefing on 12 February 2002. The question regarded the lack of evidence linking the Iraqi government with the supply of weapons of mass destruction to terrorist groups. It has been suggested that Rumsfeld was inspired by the argument in Nassim Nicholas Taleb's book *The Black Swan: The Impact of the Highly Improbable* (2007). Taleb had apparently mentioned his ideas to Rumsfeld's aides sometime earlier (Burkeman 2007).

Reference List

Abbott, A.D. 1988. *The System of Professions: An Essay on the Division of Expert Labor*. Chicago: University of Chicago Press.

Agell, J., P. Englund and J. Södersten. 1996. 'Tax Reform of The Century — The Swedish Experiment', *National Tax Journal* 49(4): 643–64.

Aidt, T.S. 2003. 'Economic Analysis of Corruption: A Survey', *The Economic Journal* 113(491): F632–F652.

Allingham, M.G. and A. Sandmo. 1972. 'Income Tax Evasion: A Theoretical Analysis', *Journal of Public Economics* 1: 323–38.

Allvin, M. 2004. 'The Individualization of Labour', in C. Garsten and K. Jacobsson (eds), *Learning to be Employable. New Agendas on Work, Responsibility and Learning in a Globalizing World*. Basingstoke: Palgrave Macmillan, pp. 23–41.

Alm, J. 1991. 'A Perspective on the Experimental Analysis of Taxpayer Reporting', *The Accounting Review* 66(3): 577–93.

Alm, J. and M. McKee. 2004. 'Tax Compliance as a Coordination Game', *Journal of Economic Behavior & Organization* 54: 297–312.

Arkhede, S. and S. Holmberg. 2015. 'Svenska folkets bedömning av offentliga myndigheters verksamhet'. Report 2015: 19. Göteborg: SOM-institutet.

Asad, T. 1994. 'Ethnographic Representation, Statistics and Modern Power', *Social Research* 61(1): 5–88.

Asdal, K. 2011. 'The Office: The Weakness of Numbers and the Production of Non-authority, *Accounting, Organizations and Society* 36(1): 1–9.

Bäck, H. and T. Larsson. 2006. *Den svenska politiken: struktur, processer och resultat*. Stockholm: Liber.

Ballestero, A. 2014. 'What is in a Percentage?: Calculation as the Poetic Translation of Human Rights', *Indiana Journal of Global Legal Studies* 21(1): 27–53.

———. 2015. 'The Ethics of a Formula: Calculating a Financial–Humanitarian Price for Water', *American Ethnologist* 42(2): 262–78.

Barad, K. 2007. *Meeting the Universe Halfway: Quantum Physics and the Entanglement of Matter and Meaning*. Durham: Duke University Press.

Barinaga, E. 1999. *Swedishness through Lagom. Can Words Tell us Anything about a Culture?* Stockholm: Centre for Advanced Studies in Leadership.

Befu, H. 1977. 'Social Exchange', *Annual Reviews in Anthropology* 6(1): 255–81.

Bennich-Björkman, L. 2008. 'Medborgarsamhället. Politisk kultur och politiskt beteende i Sverige', in L. Bennich-Björkman and P. Blomqvist (eds), *Mellan folkhem och Europa*. Stockholm: Liber, pp. 40–62.

Berggren, H. and L. Trägårdh. 2006. *Är svensken människa? Gemenskap och oberoende i det moderna Sverige*. Stockholm: Nordstedt.

Bergman, I. 1987. *Laterna magica*. Stockholm: Norstedt.
Bergstrand, M. 2014. *En Skattereform för 2000-talet - elva röster om hur Sverige får ett bättre skattesystem*. Visby: Politik - Media - Juridik.
Björklund Larsen, L. 2010. *Illegal yet Licit: Justifying Informal Purchases of Work in Contemporary Sweden* ACTA UNIVE. Stockholm: Stockholm Studies in Social Anthropology N.S. 2.
———. 2011. 'Att ge, få och ge igen. Köp av svart arbete som uttryck för medborgarens relation till staten', in K. Jacobsson (ed.), *Känslan för det allmänna: medborgarnas relation till staten och varandra*. Umeå: Borea, pp. 237–66.
———. 2013a. 'Buy or Barter? Illegal yet Licit Purchases of Work in Contemporary Sweden', *Focaal. Journal of Global and Historical Anthropology* 66: 75–87.
———. 2013b. 'The Making of a "Good Deal" Dealing with Conflicting and Complementary Values when Getting the Car Repaired Informally in Sweden', *Journal of Cultural Economy* 6: 419–33.
———. 2013c. 'Molding Knowledge into a Legal Complex: Para-ethnography at the Swedish Tax Agency', *Journal of Business Anthropology* 2: 209–31.
———. 2015. '"Common Sense" at the Swedish Tax Agency. Transactional Boundaries Separating Taxable and Tax-Free Income', *Critical Perspectives on Accounting* 31: 75–89.
———. Forthcoming. 'Mind the (tax) gap: An Ethnography of a number', *Journal of Cultural Economy*.
Björklund Larsen, L., U. Johannesson and K. Thoresson. Forthcoming. 'A thrice-told tale: A collaboration with the Swedish Tax Agency', *JOTA-Journal of Tax Administration*.
Blomberg, J. et al. 1993. 'Ethnographic Field Methods and their Relation to Design', in D. Schuler and A. Namioka (eds), *Participatory Design: Principles and Practices*. Hillsdale, NJ: Erlbaum, pp. 123–56.
Boll, K. 2011. *Taxing Assemblages. Laborious and Meticulous Achievements of Tax Compliance*. IT University of Copenhagen.
———. 2014a. 'Mapping Tax Compliance', *Critical Perspectives on Accounting* 25(4–5): 293–303.
———. 2014b. 'Shady Car Dealings and Taxing Work Practices: An Ethnography of a Tax Audit Process', *Accounting, Organizations and Society* 39(1): 1–19.
Borg, P. 2008. *Historiska perspektiv på skatte-politikens framtida förutsättningar*. Stockholm.
Boyer, D. 2008. 'Thinking through the Anthropology of Experts', *Anthropology in Action* 15(2): 38–46.
Braithwaite, V.A. 2002. *Taxing Democracy: Understanding Tax Avoidance and Evasion*. Aldershot: Ashgate.
Burkeman, O. 2007. 'Days that Shook the World', *The Guardian*, 28 April 2007. Retrieved 18 August 2016 from https://www.theguardian.com/books/2007/apr/28/society.
Çalışkan, K. and M. Callon. 2009. 'Economization, Part 1: Shifting Attention From the Economy towards Processes of Economization', *Economy and Society* 38(3): 369–98.
———. 2010. 'Economization, Part 2: A Research Programme for the Study of Markets', *Economy and Society* 39(1): 1–32.
Callon, M. 1986. 'Some Elements of a Sociology of Translation: Domestication of the Scallops and the Fishermen of St Brieuc Bay', in J. Law (ed.), *Power, Action and Belief: A New Sociology of Knowledge*. Routledge: London and New York, pp. 196–223.
———. 1998. 'Introduction: The Embeddedness of Economic Markets in Economics', in M. Callon (ed.), *The Laws of the Markets*. Oxford: Blackwell, pp. 1–57.
———. 1999. 'Actor-Network Theory: The Market Test', in J. Hassard and J. Law (eds), *Actor Network Theory and After*. Oxford: Blackwell Publishers, pp. 181–95.

———. 2007. 'What Does it Mean to Say that Economics is Performative?', in D. MacKenzie, F. Muniesa and L. Siu (ed.), *Do Economists Make Markets? On the Performativity of Economics*. Princeton, NJ: Princeton University Press, pp. 311–57.
Callon, M. and J. Law. 1997. 'After the Individual in Society: Lessons on Collectivity from Science, Technology and Society', *Journal of Sociology* 22(2): 165–82.
Callon, M., Y. Millo and F. Muniesa. 2007. *Market Devices*. Oxford: Blackwell Publishing.
Campbell, J.L. 1993. 'The State and Fiscal Sociology', *Annual Review of Sociology* 19: 163–85.
Capecchi, V. 1989. 'The Informal Economy and the Development of Flexible Specialization in Emilia-Romagna', in A. Portes, M. Castells and L.A. Benton (eds), *The Informal Economy: Studies in Advanced and Less Developed Countries*. Baltimore: The Johns Hopkins University Press, pp. 189–215.
Cochoy, F. 1998. 'Another Discipline for the Market Economy: Marketing as a Performative Knowledge and Know-how for Capitalism', *The Sociological Review* 46(S1): 194–221.
Cowell, F.1990. *Cheating the Government: The Economics of Evasion*. Cambridge, MA: MIT Press.
Crump, T. 1978. 'Money and Number: The Trojan Horse of Language', *Man* 13(4): 503–18.
———. 1981. *The Phenomenon of Money*. London: Routledge, Kegan & Paul.
Daun, Å. 1989. *Svensk mentalitet: ett jämförande perspektiv*. Stockholm: Nordstedts akademiska förlag.
Daunton, M. 2001. *Trusting Leviathan: The Politics of Taxation in Britain, 1799–1914*. Cambridge: Cambridge University Press.
———. 2002. *Just Taxes: The Politics of Taxation in Britain, 1914–1979*. Cambridge: Cambridge University Press.
Davis, J.1992. *Exchange*. Minneapolis: University of Minnesota Press.
De Swaan, A. 1988. *In Care of the State: Health Care, Education and Welfare in Europe and the USA in the Modern Era*. Cambridge: Polity Press.
Didier, E. 2005. 'Releasing Market Statistics', in B. Latour and P. Weibel (eds), *Making Things Public, Atmospheres of Democracy*. Cambridge, MA: MIT Press, pp. 638–42.
Dussauge, I., C.-F. Helgesson and F. Lee. 2015. *Value Practices in the Life Sciences and Medicine*. Oxford: Oxford University Press.
Ekman, G. 2003a. 'Självdeklarationen 100 år', in *Deklarationen 100 år och andra tillbakablickar*. Solna: Skatteverket, pp. 7–20.
———. 2003b. 'Några drag i den svenska skatteförvaltningens utveckling', in *Deklarationen 100 år och andra tillbakablickar*. Solna: Skatteverket, pp. 71–82.
Ekonomistyrningsverket. 2012. *Medborgares Syn På Myndigheter*. YouGov. Stockholm.
Elyachar, J. 2012. 'Before (and after) Neoliberalism: Tacit Knowledge, Secrets of the Trade, and the Public Sector in Egypt', *Cultural Anthropology* 27(1): 76–96.
Engelbrecht, S. and S. Holmberg. 2012. *Svenskars bedömning av offentliga myndigheters verksamhet*. Report 2012: 10. Göteborg: SOM-institutet.
Engström, P. and B. Holmlund. 2009. 'Tax Evasion and Self-employment in a High-Tax Country: Evidence from Sweden', *Applied Economics* 41(19): 2419–430.
Epstein, A.L. 1973. 'The Reasonable Man Revisited: Some Problems in the Anthropology of Law', *Law & Society Review* 7(4): 643–66.
Esser, I. 2005. *Why Work? Comparative Studies on Welfare Regimes and Individuals' Work Orientations*. Stockholm: Swedish Institute for Social Research.
Falkinger, J. 1995. 'Tax Evasion, Consumption of Public Goods, and Fairness', *Journal of Economic Psychology* 16(1): 63–72.
Falzon, M.-A. 2009. *Multi-sited Ethnography: Theory, Praxis and Locality in Contemporary Research*. Farnham: Ashgate.

Feldman, N.E. and J. Slemrod. 2009. War and Taxation: When does Patriotism Overcome the Free-rider Impulse', in I.W. Martin, A.K. Mehrotra and M. Prasad (eds), *The New Fiscal Sociology: Taxation in Comparative and Historical Perspective*. Cambridge: Cambridge University Press, pp. 138–54.
Finansdepartementet. 2013. *Regleringsbrev för budgetåret 2014 avseende Skatteverket*. Sweden.
Folger, R. 1986. 'Rethinking Equity Theory', in H.W. Bierhoff, R.L. Cohen and J. Greenberg (eds), *Justice in Social Relations. Critical Issues in Social Justice*. New York: Springer, pp. 145–62.
Fredriksson, M. and J. Pallas. 2014. *Den medialiserade myndigheten. En analys av svenska myndigheters anpassningar till medielogiken*. Göteborg.
Friedland, N., S. Maital and A. Rutenberg. 1978. 'A Simulation Study of Income Tax Evasion', *Journal of Public Economics* 10: 107–16.
Frykman, J. and K. Hansen. 2009. *Welfare State, Health and Local Culture*. Stockholm: CarlssonsFörlag.
Garcia-Parpet, M.-F. 2007. 'The Social Construction of a Perfect Market: The Strawberry Auction at Fontaines-en-Sologne', in D. MacKenzie, F. Muniesa and L. Siu (ed.), *Do Economists Make Markets?: On the Performativity of Economics*. Princeton, NJ: Princeton University Press, pp. 20–53.
Gluckman, M. 1963. 'The Reasonable Man in Barotse Law', in M. Gluckman (ed.), *Order and Rebellion in Tribal Africa*. London: Cohen & West, pp. 178–206.
Gracia, L. and L. Oats. 2012. 'Boundary Work and Tax Regulation: A Bourdieusian View', *Accounting, Organizations and Society* 37(5): 304–21.
Graham, M. 2002. 'Emotional Bureaucracies: Emotions Civil Servants, and Immigrants in the Swedish Welfare State', *Ethos* 30(3): 199–26.
Granovetter, M. 1985. 'Economic Action and Social Structure: The Problem of Embeddedness', in M. Granovetter and R. Swedberg (eds), *American Journal of Sociology* 91(3): 481–510.
Guano, E. 2010. 'Taxpayers, Thieves, and the State: Fiscal Citizenship in Contemporary Italy', *Ethnos: Journal of Anthropology* 75(4): 471–95.
Gudeman, S. 2001. *The Anthropology of Economy: Community, Market, and Culture*. Oxford: Blackwell Publishers.
———. 2008. *Economy's Tension: The Dialectics of Community and Market*. New York: Berghahn.
Gupta, A. 2012. *Red Tape: Bureaucracy, Structural Violence, and Poverty in India*. Durham: Duke University Press.
Gupta, A. and J. Ferguson.1997. 'Discipline and Practice', in A. Gupta and J. Ferguson (eds), *Anthropological Locations. Boundaries of a Field Science*. Berkeley, CA: University of California Press, pp. 1–46.
Gusterson, H. 1997. 'Studying up Revisited', *PoLAR Political and Legal Anthropology Review* 20(1): 114–19.
Guyer, J.I., N. Khan and J. Obarrio. 2010. 'Introduction: Number as Inventive Frontier', *Anthropological Theory* 10: 36–61.
Hadenius, A. 1985. 'Citizens Strike a Balance: Discontent with Taxes, Content with Spending', *Journal of Public Policy* 5(3): 349–63.
Hannerz, U. 1997. 'Flows, Boundaries and Hybrids: Keywords in Transnational Anthropology', *Mana* 3(1): 7–39.
———. 2001. 'Introduktion: när fältet blir translokalt', in U. Hannerz (ed.), *Flera fält i ett. Socialantropologer om translokala fältstudier*. Stockholm: Carlssons, pp. 7–35.

———. 2006. 'Studying Down, Up, Sideways, Through, Backwards, Forwards, Away and at Home: Reflections on the Field Worries of an Expansive Discipline', in S. Coleman and P. Collins (eds), *Locating the Field: Space, Place and Context in Anthropology*. Oxford: Berg Publishers, pp. 23–42.

———. 2011. *Café du Monde: platser, vägar och människor i världsvimlet*. Stockholm: Carlsson.

———. 2015. 'Writing Futures', *Current Anthropology* 56(6): 797–818.

Hansson, I. 2011. 'Företagets inställning till skatter är en styrelsefråga', *Dagens industri*.

Haraway, D. 1988. 'Situated Knowledges: The Science Question in Feminism and the Privilege of Partial Perspective', *Feminist studies* 14(3): 575–99.

Hardie, I. and D. MacKenzie. 2007. 'Assembling an Economic Actor: The Agencement of a Hedge Fund', *The Sociological Review* 55(1): 57–80.

Harding, S. 1986. *The Science Question in Feminism*. Ithaca: Cornell University Press.

Hasseldine, J., K. Holland and P. van der Rijt. 2011. 'The Market for Corporate Tax Knowledge', *Critical Perspectives on Accounting* 22(1): 39–52.

Hasselström, A. 2003. 'On and Off the Trading Floor: An Inquiry into the Everyday Fashioning of Financial Market Knowledge', Stockholm: Department of Social Anthropology, Stockholm University.

Heckscher, E.F. 1935. *Sveriges ekonomiska historia från Gustav Vasa: delen. Före frihetstiden* (2 v.). Stockholm: Bonnier.

Herskovits, M.J. 1952. *Economic Anthropology: A Study in Comparative Economics*. New York: Alfred A. Knopf.

Heuts, F. and A.-M. Mol. 2013. 'What is a Good Tomato? A Case of Valuing in Practice. *Valuation Studies* 1(2): 125–46.

Holmberg, S. and N.O. Tryggvason. 2014. *Svenska folkets bedömning av offentliga myndigheters verksamhet*. Göteborg: SOM-institutet.

Holmberg, S. and L. Weibull. 2006. 'Swedish Trends 1986-2005', Göteborg: SOM-institutet.

Holmes, D.R. 2014. *Economy of Words: Communicative Imperatives in Central Banks*. Chicago & London: University of Chicago Press.

Holmes, D.R. and G.E. Marcus. 2005. 'Cultures of Expertise and the Management of Globalization: Toward the Re-functioning of Ethnography', in *Global Assemblages. Technology, Politics and Ethics as Anthropological Problems*. Malden: Blackwell, pp. 235–52.

———. 2006. 'Para-ethnography and the Rise of the Symbolic Analyst', in M.S. Fisher and G. Downey (eds), *Frontiers of Capital: Ethnographic Reflections on the New Economy*. Durham: Duke University Press Books, pp. 33–57.

———. 2008. 'Collaboration Today and the Re-imagination of the Classic Scene of Fieldwork Encounter', *Collaborative Anthropologies* 1(1): 81–101.

———. 2012. 'Collaborative Imperatives: A Manifesto, of Sorts, for the Re-imagination of the Classic Scene of Fieldwork Encounter', in M. Konrad (ed.), *Collaborators Collaborating: Counterparts in Anthropological Knowledge and International Research Relations*. Oxford: Berghahn, pp. 126–43.

Ingold, T. 2008. When ANT Meets SPIDER: Social Theory for Arthropods', *Material Agency* 209–16.

James, M. 2010. 'Humpty Dumpty's Guide to Tax Law: Rules, Principles and Certainty in Taxation', *Critical Perspectives on Accounting* 21(7): 573–83.

Jareborg, N. 2008. *Mening, värde och rationalitet: Cuvée 1974 i ny tappning*. Uppsala: Iustus Förlag AB.

Johansson, O. 2003. 'Från undersåte till kund', in *Deklarationen 100 år och andra tillbakablickar*. Solna: Skatteverket, pp. 111–18.
Johnsson, M., S.-A Bergkvist and M. Schömer. 2013. 'Skatteverket agerar utan stöd i lagar och praxis', *Dagens Nyheter*.
Keohane, R.O. and J.S.J. Nye. 1998. 'Power and Interdependence in the Information Age', *Foreign Affairs* 77(5): 81–94.
Kjellberg, H. and C.-F. Helgesson. 2006. 'Multiple Versions of Markets: Multiplicity and Performativity in Market Practice', *Industrial Marketing Management* 35(7): 839–55.
Knack, S. and P. Keefer. 1997. 'Does Social Capital Have an Economic Payoff? A Cross-Country Investigation', *Quarterly Journal of Economics* 4: 1251–288.
Kornhauser, M.E. 2007. 'Tax Morale Approach to Compliance: Recommendations for the IRS', *Florida Tax Review* 8(6): 599–634.
KPMG. 2009. 'KPMG's Individual Income Tax and Social Security Rate Survey 2009'.
Latour, B. 2005. *Reassembling the Social: An Introduction to Actor-Network-Theory*. Oxford: Oxford University Press.
———. 2010. *The Making of Law: An Ethnography of the Conseil d'État*. Cambridge: Polity.
Latour, B. and S. Woolgar. 1986. *Laboratory Life the Construction of Scientific Facts*. Princeton, NJ: Princeton University Press.
Laurin, U. 1986. *På heder och samvete: Skattefuskets orsaker och utbredning*. Stockholm: Norstedts.
Law, J. 1992. 'Notes on the Theory of the Actor-Network: Ordering, Strategy, and Heterogeneity', *Systems Practice* 5: 379–93.
———. 2009. 'Seeing Like a Survey', *Cultural Sociology* 3(2): 239–56.
Law, J., E. Ruppert and M. Savage. 2011. 'The Double Social Life of Methods', CRESC working paper no 95.
Leigh Star, S. 1999. 'The Ethnography of Infrastructure', *American Behavioral Scientist* 43(3): 377–91.
Leonard, M. 1998. *Invisible Work, Invisible Workers: The Informal Economy in Europe and the US*. London: Macmillan.
Lepore, J. 2012. 'Tax Time. Why we Pay', *The New Yorker*, 26 November.
Levi, M. 1988. *Of Rule and Revenue*. Berkeley: University of California Press.
Lewin, L. 2008. 'Samling kring folkhemmet', in L. Bennich-Björkman and P. Blomqvist (ed.), *Mellan folkhem och Europa*. Stockholm: Liber, pp. 20–39.
Lezaun, J. and L. Soneryd. 2007. 'Consulting Citizens: Technologies of Elicitation and the Mobility of Publics', *Public Understanding of Science* 16(3): 279–97.
Lin, Y.-H. 1948. *The Golden Wing: A Sociological Study of Chinese Familism*. Oxon: Routledge.
Lindbeck, A., Nyberg, S. and J.W. Weibull. 1999. Social Norms and Economic Incentives in the Welfare State', *Quarterly Journal of Economics* CXIV(1): 1–35.
Lindvert, J. 2006. *Ihålig arbetsmarknadspolitik?: organisering och legitimitet igår och idag*. Umeå: Borea bokförlag.
Locke, J. 1988. *Locke: Two Treatises of Government Student Edition*. Google Books.
Lodin, S.-O. 2007. 'Några kvalitetskrav på en god skattelagstiftning', *Skattenytt* 9: 477–90.
———. 2011. *The Making of Tax Law: The Development of the Swedish Tax System*. Iustus Förlag AB.
Löwnertz, S. 1983. *De svenska skatternas historia:* [en artikelserie av Susanne Löwnertz tidigare publicerad i RSV Info åren 1982-83]. Stockholm: Riksskatteverket (RSV).
———. 2003. 'Skattereformer för 100 år sedan', in *Deklarationen 100 år och andra tillbakablickar*. Solna: Skatteverket, pp. 59–70.

MacKenzie, D.A. 2008. *An Engine, Not a Camera: How Financial Models Shape Markets*. Cambridge, MA: MIT Press.
———. 2009. *Material Markets: How Economic Agents are Constructed*. Oxford and New York: Oxford University Press.
Malinowski, B. 1922. *Argonauts of the Western Pacific*. London: Routledge & Kegan Paul.
Malmer, H. 2003. 'Granskningen av inkomstdeklarationer under 100 år', in *Deklarationen 100 år och andra tillbakablickar*. Solna: Skatteverket, pp. 21–58.
Mann, R.F. 2006. 'Beyond Enforcement: Top 10 Strategies for Encouraging Tax Compliance', *Tax Notes* (May 22): 919–28.
Marcus, G.E. 1995. 'Ethnography in/of the World System: The Emergence of Multi-sited Ethnography', *Annual Review of Anthropology* 24: 95–117.
Marques, R. 2004. 'Fiscal Sociology: Setting a Research Agenda', paper presented at the American Sociological Association. San Francisco.
Martin, I.W., A.K. Mehrotra and M. Prasad. 2009. *The New Fiscal Sociology: Taxation in Comparative and Historical Perspective*. Cambridge: Cambridge University Press.
Mars, Gerald. 1982. *Cheats at Work: An Anthropology of Workplace Crime*. Winchester: George Allen & Unwin.
Maurer, B. 2005a. 'Due Diligence and "Reasonable Man", Offshore', *Cultural Anthropology* 20(4): 474–505.
———. 2005b. *Mutual Life, Limited: Islamic Banking, Alternative Currencies, Lateral Reason*. Princeton: Princeton University Press.
———. 2009. 'From the Revenue Rule to Soft Law and Back Again: The Consequences for "Society" of the Social Governance of International Tax Competition', in J. Eckert, K. von Benda-Beckmann and F. von Benda-Beckmann (eds.), *Rules of Law and Laws of Ruling: Law and Governance between Past and Future*. London: Ashgate, pp. 217–35.
———. 2010. 'From Anti-money Laundering to ... What? The Aftermath of "Compliance" for Offshore Financial Services', in A. Clunan and H. Trinkunas (eds), *Ungoverned Spaces: Alternatives to State Sovereignty in an Era of Softened Sovereignty*. Stanford, CA: Stanford University Press, pp. 215–31.
Maurer, B. and S.D. Mainwaring. 2012. 'Anthropology with Business: Plural Programs and Future Financial Worlds', *Journal of Business Anthropology* 1(2): 177–96.
Mauss, M. 1990. *The Gift*, trans. W.D. Halls. London: Routledge.
Merry, S.E. 1990. *Getting Justice and Getting Even*. University of Chicago Press.
Miller, D. 2002. 'Turning Callon the Right Way Up', *Economy & Society* 31(2): 218–33.
Miller, P. and N. Rose. 2008. *Governing the Present: Administering Economic, Social and Personal Life*. Cambridge: Polity Press.
Mintz, S.W. 1985. *Sweetness and Power: The Place of Sugar in Modern History*. Harmondsworth: Penguin.
Möller, T. 2007. *Svensk politisk historia: Strid och samverkan under tvåhundra år*. Lund: Studentlitteratur.
Muñoz, J.-M. 2010. 'Business Visibility and Taxation in Northern Cameroon', *African Studies Review* 53(2): 149–75.
———. 2011. 'Talking Law in Times of Reform: Paradoxes of Legal Entitlement in Cameroon', *Law and Society Review* 45(4): 893–22.
Murphy, K.M. 2013. 'A Cultural Geometry: Designing Political Things in Sweden', *American Ethnologist* 40(1): 118–31.
Narotzky, S. 1997. *New Directions in Economic Anthropology*. London: Pluto Press.
Neyland, D. 2013. 'Against Performativity?', MISTS working paper no. 3.
Nordblom, K. 2008. *Svenska skatters legitimitet i en tid av globalisering*. UnderlagsPM till Globaliseringsrådets skattegrupp, Stockholm.

Nyqvist, A. 2008. 'Opening the Orange Envelope: Reform and Responsibility in the Remaking of the Swedish National Pension System', Stockholm: Department of Social Anthropology, Stockholm University.
Oats, L. 2010. *Taxation. A Fieldwork Research Handbook.* Oxon: Routledge.
Odén, B. 2008. 'Naturaskatter och finanspolitik - ett finansiellt dilemma', *Scandia: Tidskrift för historisk forskning* 33(1):1–19.
OECD. 2008. *Monitoring Taxpayers' Compliance: A Practical Guide Based on Revenue Body Experience*. Forum.
———. 2010. *Overview: Evaluating the Effectiveness of Compliance Risk Treatment Strategies*. Forum.
Pardo, I. 1996. *Managing Existence in Naples: Morality, Action, and Structure.* Cambridge: Cambridge University Press.
———. 2000. 'Introduction – Morals of Legitimacy: Interplay between Responsibility, Authority and Trust', in I. Pardo (ed.), *Morals of Legitimacy: Between Agency and System*. New York: Berghahn Books, pp. 1–26.
———. 2004. 'Introduction: Corruption, Morality and the Law', in I. Pardo (ed.), *Between Morality and the Law: Corruption, Anthropology and Comparative Society*. Aldershot: Ashgate, pp. 1–17.
Picciotto, S. 2007. 'Constructing Compliance: Game Playing, Tax Law, and the Regulatory State', *Law & Policy* 29(1): 11–30.
Polanyi, K. 1944. *The Great Transformation: The Political and Economic Origins of Our Time.* Boston: Beacon Press.
Porter, T.M. 1995. *Trust in Numbers: The Pursuit of Objectivity in Science and Public Life.* Princeton, NJ: Princeton University Press.
Power, M. 1999. *The Audit Society: Rituals of Verification.* Oxford: Oxford University Press.
———. 2000. 'The Audit Society—Second Thoughts', *International Journal of Auditing* 4(1): 111–19.
Påhlsson, R. 2006. 'Skatteverkets styrsignaler – en ny blomma i regelrabatten', *Skattenytt* 56(7–8): 401–19.
Rawlings, G. 2003. 'Cultural Narratives of Taxation and Citizenship: Fairness, Groups and Globalisation', *Australian Journal of Social Issues* (Australian Council of Social Service) 38(3): 269–305.
Riksrevisionsverket. 1997. *Svart arbete 1. Arbetstagare och företagare. Insatser.* Report 1997: 59. Stockholm: Riksrevisionsverket.
———. 1998. *Illicit Work in Sweden: A Report on a Welfare State Dilemma*. Report 1998: 61. Stockholm: Riksrevisionsverket.
Riles, A. 2010. 'Collateral Expertise', *Current Anthropology* 51(6): 795–18.
———. 2011. *Collateral Knowledge: Legal Reasoning in the Global Financial Markets.* Chicago: University of Chicago Press.
Roitman, J.L. 2005. *Fiscal Disobedience: An Anthropology of Economic Regulation in Central Africa.* Princeton: Princeton University Press.
Rosenberg, G. 2002. 'The Crisis of Consensus in Postwar Sweden', in N. Witoszek and L. Trägårdh (eds), *Culture and Crisis. The Case of Germany and Sweden*. New York: Berghahn, pp. 170–201.
———. 2013. 'Sweden: The Reluctant Nation', in C. Fieschi, M. Morris and L. Caballero (eds), *Populist Fantasies: European Revolts in Context*. London: Counterpoint, pp. 151–209.
Rothstein, B. 1992. *Den korporativa staten: intresseorganisationer och statsförvaltning i svensk politik.* Stockholm: Norstedts.
San Juan, E.A. 2013. 'Cultural Jurisprudence', *Asian-Pacific Law & Policy Journal* 15(1).

Savage, M. 2013. 'The "Social Life of Methods": A Critical Introduction', *Theory, Culture & Society* 30(4): 3–21.
Schneider, F. and D. Enste. 2000. 'Shadow Economies around the World Size, Causes, and Consequences', *Journal of Economic Literature* 38(1): 77–114.
Schumpeter, J.A. 1954. 'The Crisis of the Tax State', *International Economic Papers* 4: 5–38.
Scott, J.C. 1990. *Domination and the Arts of Resistance. Hidden Transcripts*. New Haven: Yale University Press.
———. 1999. *Seeing Like a State: How Certain Schemes to Improve the Human Condition Have Failed*. Yale University Press.
Seabra Lopes, D. 2011. 'Making Oneself at Home with Numbers: Financial Reporting from an Ethnographic Perspective', *Social Anthropology* 19(4): 463–76.
Sjöström, O. 2002. *Svensk statistikhistoria: en undanskymd kritisk tradition*. Hedemora: Gidlunds förlag.
Skatteverket. 1983. *Skatter och skattekontroll – Förutsättningar*. Stockholm.
———. 1985. *Ännu bättre service!* Stockholm.
———. 1995. *Den nya servicen. Serviceprojektets delrapport 1*. Solna.
———. 1997. *Service med kvalitet*. Solna.
———. 1998. *En plan för RSV-koncernens service 1999-2004*. Solna.
———. 2000. *Vår förvaltning år 2010 - I globaliseringens spar*. Solna.
———. 2005. *Riskvärdering*. Solna: Skatteverket.
———. 2006a. *Compliance Costs of Value-Added Tax in Sweden*. Solna.
———. 2006b. *Svartköp och svartjobb i Sverige. Del 1: Undersökningsresultat*. Solna.
———. 2007a. *Regionenkäten - Medborgarnas synpunkter på Skatteverkets sätt att arbeta. Resultat från en riksomfattande undersökning hösten 2006*. Solna.
———. 2007b. *Svartköp och svartjobb i Sverige. Del 2: Möjliga åtgärder mot svartarbete och bidragsfusk*. Solna.
———. 2008a. *Företagens synpunkter på Skatteverkets sätt att arbeta*. Solna.
———. 2008b. *Skattefelskarta för Sverige. Hurtogs den fram och hur kan den användas?* Solna.
———. 2009a. *Handledning för beskattning av inkomst vid 2009 års taxering*. Solna.
———. 2009b. *Slutrapport uthyrning av arbetskraft. "Svartarbetsutredningen" 2006–2008*. Solna.
———. 2011a. *Konsumenterna kan skapa schysst konkurrens och minska skattefusket*. Solna.
———. 2011b. *Om rot och rut och vitt och svart*. Solna.
———. 2012. *Medborgarnas synpunkter på skattesystemet, skattefusket och Skatteverkets kontroll*. Solna.
———. 2013a. *Företagens synpunkter på skattesystemet, skattefusket och Skatteverkets kontroll*. Solna.
———. 2013b. *Skatteverkets inriktning*. Solna.
———. 2014a. *Analyshandboken*. Solna.
———. 2014b. *Effekter på skatteundandragande av sänkt restaurangmoms Rapportering av ett regeringsuppdrag*. Solna.
———. 2014c. *Skattefelets utveckling i Sverige 2007-2012*. Solna.
———. 2014d. *The Development of the Tax Gap in Sweden 2007–12*. Solna.
———. 2014e. *Verksamhetsplan för Skatteverket*. Solna.
Slemrod, J. 1998. 'On Voluntary Compliance, Voluntary Taxes, and Social Capital', *National Tax Journal* 51(3): 485–92.
———. 2007. 'Cheating Ourselves: The Economics of Tax Evasion', *The Journal of Economic Perspectives* 21(1): 25–48.

Smith, A. 1776. *An Inquiry into the Nature and Causes of the Wealth of Nations*. Chicago: Encyclopædia Britannica.

Sørensen, P.B. 2010. 'Swedish Tax Policy: Recent Trends and Future Challenges'. Report 2010: 4. Stockholm: ESO.

Steinmo, S. 2002. 'Globalization and Taxation Challenges to the Swedish Welfare State', *Comparative Political Studies* 35(7): 839–62.

Stridh, A. and L. Wittberg. 2015. *Från fruktad skattefogde till omtyckt servicemyndighet*. Stockholm: Skatteverket.

Svallfors, S. 1995. 'The End of Class Politics? Structural Cleavages and Attitudes to Swedish Welfare Policies', *Acta Sociologica* 38(1): 53–74.

Taleb, N.N. 2007. *The Black Swan: The Impact of the Highly Improbable Fragility*. New York, NY: Random House.

Tarschys, D. 1988. 'Tributes, Tariffs, Taxes and Trade: The Changing Sources of Government Revenue', *British Journal of Political Science* 18(1): 1–20.

Taylor, N. 2003. 'Understanding Tax Payer Attitudes through Understanding Taxpayer Identities', in V.A. Braithwaite (ed.), *Taxing Democracy: Understanding Tax Avoidance and Evasion*. Aldershot: Ashgate, pp. 71–92.

Thärnström, B. 2003. 'Broschyren dags att deklarera under 30 år', in *Deklarationen 100 år och andra tillbakablickar*. Solna: Skatteverket, pp. 119–28.

Tilly, C. 2009. 'Foreword', in I. Martin, A.K. Mehrotra and M. Prasad (eds), *The New Fiscal Sociology: Taxation in Comparative and Historical perspective*. Cambridge: Cambridge University Press, pp. xi–xiii.

Torgler, B. 2002. 'Speaking to Theorists and Searching for Facts: Tax Morale and Tax Compliance in Experiments', *Journal of Economic Surveys* 16(5): 657–83.

Tuck, P. 2010. 'The Emergence of the Tax Official into a T-shaped Knowledge Expert', *Critical Perspectives on Accounting* 21(7): 584–96.

Valverde, M. 2003. *Law's Dream of a Common Knowledge*. Princeton, NJ: Princeton University Press.

Valverde, M., R. Levi and D. Moore. 2005. 'Legal Knowledges of Risks', in *The Law Commission of Canada*, ed. Law Risk. Vancouver: University of British Columbia Press, pp. 86–120.

van Schendel, W., and I. Abraham. 2005. *Illicit Flows and Criminal Things: States, Borders, and the Other Side of Globalization*. Bloomington: Indiana University Press.

Wallace, D.F. 2011. *The Pale King*. London: Hamish Hamilton.

Webber, C. and A. Wildavsky. 1986. *A History of Taxation and Expenditure in the Western World*. New York: Simon and Schuster.

Weber, M. 1978. *Den protestantiska etiken och kapitalismens anda* [Die protestantische Ethik und der Geis des Kapitalismus](Swedish translation by A. Lundquist, 1934). Lund: Argos.

Williams, C.C. 2007. 'Small Business and the Informal Economy: Evidence from the U.K', *International Journal of Entrepreneurial Behaviour & Research* 13: 349–66.

Wise, N. 1995. *The Values of Precision and Exactitude*. Princeton, NJ: Princeton University Press.

Woolgar, S. 2014. '18 Struggles with Representation: Could It Be Otherwise?', in C. Coopmans et al. (eds), *Representation in Scientific Practice Revisited*. Cambridge, MA: MIT Press, pp. 329–32.

Zaloom, C. 2006. *Out of the Pits: Traders and Technology from Chicago to London*. University of Chicago Press.

Glossary

Where available, translations for legal terms have been taken from the official Swedish-English glossary for Swedish courts, available at: http://www.domstol.se/Publikationer/Ordlista/svensk- engelsk_ordlista.pdf.

agencement	A combination of physical agency, technical devices and different types of knowledge creates different agencement, 'arrangements endowed in the capacity of acting in different ways depending on their configuration' (Callon 2007: 320).
allmän självdeklaration	General income tax return. In the text it is colloquially referred to as tax return, självdeklaration.
arbetsgivaravgift	Employers' contribution.
beställning and *beställardialog*	Order. A task given to the Analysis Unit to investigate. The task should be performed through dialogue between the manager issuing the order and the analysts performing it.
bevillning(ar)	Taxes extracted when needed. In use in Sweden from the very start of taxation as we know it, from the thirteenth century to modern times.
brännvin	Potato schnapps. Formerly the most common alcoholic drink in Sweden.
diarie	Registry, where public *tjänsteanteckningar* are stored.
Dramaten	Swedish national theatre scene located in Stockholm.
egenavgift	Employers' contributions for self-employed.
fika	Coffee break. Most, if not all, Swedes take a *fika* sometime during the day; an institution in all Swedish workplaces.

F-skatt nummer	Corporation tax registration number. It is obligatory to have such a number when/if issuing invoices.
Generaldirektör	Director General. The highest placed manager in Swedish bureaucracies.
grundskatt(er)	Ground tax; taxes that are based on property owned.
jämkningsregler	Mediation, adjustment rules for tax.
Jordebok(en)	A book where all taxes collected were noted. Introduced by King Gustav Vasa in the sixteenth century.
jordeboksränta(n)	Formerly, tax collected was referred to as interest paid by the people who lived on the land *(jord)* that belonged to the king.
kund	Customer.
länsstyrelse	Provincial/county council.
Nöterian	Formerly the coffee hall at the Agency. A literal translation is 'the Nut Place'.
Överdirektör	Deputy Director at the Agency.
påpekande	Missive.
Regleringsbrev(et)	Appropriation directives. A yearly letter of instructions that governs all Swedish governmental authorities.
Riksdag	Swedish Parliament.
Riksrevisionen, formerly Riksrevisionsverket	Swedish National Audit Office.
roter	A small group of landowning households that among other obligations had to provide a small estate for a soldier.
schablonbeskattning	A flat rate tax amount.
skatt	Tax AND treasury.
skatta	To estimate, guess, gauge or value something.
skattebetalare	Taxpayer.
Skattenämnd(en)	Tax boards that handled issues that had been contested by taxpayers. The members of a tax board were elected but the board was chaired by an employee from the tax authority. It was replaced by the *taxeringsnämnd* in 1991 and ceased to exist in 2012.

Skatteskrapan	Tax-scraper. A high-rise building in Stockholm, which for many years housed its regional tax office.
Skatteverket	Swedish Tax Agency; in the text it is referred to as the Agency.
skattskyldig(e)	Tax indebted individual, tributary. NB: in the official glossary for Swedish courts the translation is taxpayer. See http://www.domstol.se/Publikationer/Ordlista/svensk- engelsk_ordlista.pdf
skönstaxering	Discretionary assessment.
slumpkontroll	A random audit control (RAC).
svart arbete	Literally black work; exchanges of work evading taxes and/or rules and legislation.
Svenskt Näringsliv	Confederation of Swedish Enterprises.
synpunkt(er)	(Citizens') views/opinions.
Taxeringslagen	The Tax Law section is one of several legal sections that address taxes within the Swedish constitution.
taxeringsnämnd	Taxation board. Instigated in 1902, it developed from being a truly lay body to being increasingly staffed by experts. It disappeared in 1991 and was replaced with *skattenämnder*.
Tjänsteanteckning(ar)	Official and dated notes regarding events, verbal information, discussions and agreements – obligatory for public employees.
torp	Small estates lent to soldiers and their families in return for military service.
undersåte	Minion.
Uppgiftslämnarbörda(n)	Duty by organizations and corporations to provide information for the government's official statistics.
värnskatt	State tax, for high income earners.

Index

Actor Network Theory (ANT)
  and audit, 28
  critiques against, 23–24, 27
  motivations for applying, 23–27, 35, 37
  of taxation, 63, 66
agencement, 31–35, 109, 117, 138, 165, 173–175
Agency, the The Swedish Tax Agency. *See* Skatteverket.
allmän självdeklaration (General income tax return), 49. *See also* tax return.
analysis,
  the role of, 153–155, 173
  vs. research, 77
  methods, used to acquire knowledge of taxation, 21, 59, 66, 77–78, 88, 90, 92, 105, 123, 145, 151
analysis methods, varities of, 28, 77–78, 112–113, 171, 175
analysts at the Agency
  applying para-ethnography, 30–31, 171, 176
  at work, 21–22, 59, 77–82, 95, 122–124, 134–135, 139, 146–147, 154–155
  skills and education of, 29, 77–79
anecdotes and stories
  about taxation, 24–25, 81, 100, 176
  as a method, using, 29, 81, 176
annual tax return, *See* General income tax return
anonymity
  of (audited) taxpayers, 34, 90, 97–99, 103, 111
  of informants, ix, 33
ANT. *See* Actor Network Theory
Appropriation Directives. See *regleringsbrev*
appropriation(s). See *bevillning(ar)*
arbetsgivaravgift (Employers' contributions), 10
arbetslinjen (the Work Approach), 9
architecture, and impact on tax compliance strategies – or the other way around…, 27, 51–56, 83, 85, 126
assemblage, of knowledge, 22, 31–32
ATO (Australian Tax Office), 36, 62
attitude, vs. practice, 92–94
attitudinal survey (*attitydundersökning*), 23, 36, 75, 78, 89–90, 112, 120
attitydundersökning. *See* attitudinal survey
Audit
  and tax compliance, 36, 58–59, 62, 66–67, 72–73, 85, 169
  desk, 121, 141n
  in practice, 34, 53, 57, 70, 127–132, 159, 173
  methods, 79, 84, 116, 119, 121, 174
  procedures, 5, 45–46, 50–51, 58, 65, 127
  Random Audit Control, chapter 3,
  vs. control, 150–151
  what gets audited?, 108, 150, 153, 156
audit society, 76, 149–150
auditee, who gets audited?, 69, 82, 108, 147, 160
auditor, role of, 19, 34, 49, 58, 66, 70
auditor, views on, 2, 45. *See also* tax collector
Australian tax system, views on, 18–19

balancing act
  shaping taxpayers or being shaped by taxpayer values, 58, 73, 85, 136, 179

Balancing act (*cont.*)
licit vs. legitimate actions, 6, 34, 39, 65, 135, 150
behavioural economics, 76
Bergman, Ingmar, 1–2, 4, 57–58, 76
beställardialog (instigation dialogue), 79
beställning (order), 81
bevillning(ar) (appropriation(s)), 46, 71
Boll, Karen, 19, 22, 63, 66
bookkeeping, 49, 95–100, 104, 117, 121, 123, 128, 150, 161, 164
Braithwaite, Valerie, 36, 61–65
brännvin (Potato schnapps), 48
buildings, impact of, 27, 51–56, 83–85, 126

calculation
of cost deductions, 130–132, 180–181
of percentage, 135
vs. valuation, 130–133, 139
call centre, 110–112
Cameroon, 17–18
categorization
of taxpaying activities, 123
of taxpayers, 65, 78, 80, 92–94, 112, 122, 146–148
category, 102, 155, 174
cattle, taxable, 10, 17–18
centennial tax reform (*Århundradets skattereform*), 12, 51
consequences of, 49, 151–152, 168
citizenship, and tax, 3, 9, 13–15, 19–21, 26, 28, 48–50, 60–62, 71–72, 85
COEN (commercial entities)
definition of, 21, 87n, 98, 102, 171, 181n
specific tax code for, 143–144, 148–150, 158, 163, 165
views on tax compliance of , 80–82, 93, 99–100, 123, 149, 153, 157–158, 161–163, 172–174
commensuration, of activities subject for tax, 38, 152, 158
common knowledge, 27, 30. *See also* tacit knowledge
communicability, 141, 156, 165, 175
communication strategies, 5, 33, 35, 64, 66–67, 71, 139, chapter 4, 177
compassion, 45, 85, 156
competition
on markets, 99, 105, 157,
tax, 15
confidential information. 34, 99, 128, 155. *See also* secrecy
Conseil d'Etat (French Council of State), 26–27
consequential analysis (*konsekvensanalys*), 78
considerate, 132
consultant, 130–131, 147, 164, 177
container, as a category, 33, 102, 115–116, 144, 164
controllability, 36, 46, 141, 149–150, 156, 159, 162, 165, 175
cooperation
as compliance strategies, 61, 67, 128–129, 138–139, 161, 164, 177
with taxpayers, 61, 128–129, 173, 177
corporation tax registration number (*F-skatt nummer*), 148
cost deduction
and law, 37, 123, 133, 138, 144
definition of, 21, 81–82, 99–100, 112, 143, 153, 158, 171, 180
erroneous, 99, 134–135, 139, 148, 159
in practice, 96, 98, 133, 143, 150, 162, 176
questionnable, 46, 80, 88, 92, 102, 112, 132, 151–152
counterperformative, 103, 116
creolize, 26, 28, 176, 181
criminal activity, 148
CSR (Corporate Social Responsibility), 73–74, 84–85, 170
curiosity, as a research approach, 3, 20–21, 32, 128, 158

Dags att deklarera ('Time for tax return'), 67–68
Dahomey, 18–19
deduction. *See* cost deduction
Denmark, 19, 70, 80
devices
theoretical concept, 28, 31–32
to increase tax compliance, 17, 117, 165
used in audit, 136, 149
diarie (registry), 128

Director General (*Generaldirektör*)
impact of, 57, 73–74, 165
participating in this risk assessment project, 22, 29, 38, 83–84, 99, 139, 141–146, 152–153, 156–157, 161, 163, 165, 174
disbursement, of tax paid, 69, 181
Disney, 43
Dramaten, Swedish national theatre, 1

economic anthropology, 20, 40
economics, 25, 30, 60, 76–77
effektanalys. *See* impact analysis
egenavgift (Employers contribution for self-employed), 10
empathic. See *empati*
empati (empathy), 136, 139, 177, 181
Employers' contributions. See *arbetsgivaravgift*
equality, 8–9, 18–19, 23, 27
in treating taxpayers. 38, 60, 74, 83, 103, 116, 177–178
See also equitable
equitable, equitability, treatment of taxpayers. 13, 35, 37–38, 61–62, 133, 170, 176–178. *See also* equality
E-services, 161
ethnography. 22, 27, 35, 51, 91, 135. *See also* para-ethnography
of taxation, 17–21, 27, 51, 126–134
Eurobarometer, 91
Excel spreadsheet, 116, 125–126, 134

fairness
in tax system, 61, 164
treating taxpayers, 15, 18–19, 62, 137–139, 149, 177, 180
FAR (the Professional Institute for Authorized Public Accountants), 161
Finansdepartmentet. *See* Ministry of Finance
fiscal anthropology, 6, 19–20, 180
fiscal sociology, 15–17
flat rate tax amount. 92, 104–110, 112–116, 172, 174. See also *schablonbeskattning*
Folkhemmet (the People's home), 8
forest farmer, 131
forms, information on tax, 121, 140n, 147, 161
French Council of State. See *Conseil d'Etat*
fringe benefit, 69, 143, 152, 163
F-skatt nummer (corporation tax registration number), 148. *See also* corporation tax registration number

GDP (gross domestic product), 48, 71
gender, 74, 95
General income tax return. *See* tax return
Generaldirektör. *See* Director General
gift, 14, 51
as tax, 18
ground tax (*grundskatt*), 46–48
grundskatt. *See* ground tax
Gustav Vasa, King, 46–47, 86n

Hadenius, Axel, 17, 103
Hannerz, Ulf, 26
Hansson, Ingemar, 86n
Hedqvist, Per, 51
Herskovits, Melville, 18
historical studies of taxation, 18
Holmes, Douglas, 29
household, 152

impact analysis (*effektanalys*), 78
indicators, 64–65
informal economic activies, 22, 65, 75, 77, 80, 147
instigation dialogue. *See beställardialog*
intelligence analysis (*omvärldsbevakning*), 77–78
intention vs. practice, 2, 29, 70, 78, 93, 114, 142–143, 147–150, 159–160, 162, 174
intentional error/cheating. *See* intention vs. practice
Internal Revenue Service. *See* IRS
IRS (Internal Revenue Service), 45, 64, 69, 123
IT solutions, for increased tax compliance, 66, 83, 149, 171

jämkningsregler (adjustment of tax rules), 152
jordeboken (medieval land register), 46, 48

jordeboksräntan (tax on land owned), 10, 46

konsekvensanalys. *See* consequential analysis

lagom (just enough), 7, 70, 134
länsstyrelse (Provincial council), 50
Latour, Bruno, 23–24, 26–28, 138, 168
law, interpreting, 133–134, 150–153, 168–170
Law, John, 41, 84, 90, 113
legal anthropology, 20
legitimacy
in tax system, 4–5, 18, 57, 59, 107, 135, 143, 153
obtaining and maintaining, 3, 5–6, 18, 20–23, 26, 81, 101, 103, 113–116, 132, 138, 150–151, 162–166
values, 136–137
Lutheran ethics/values, 9, 52

Malmer, Håkan, 28, 50, 66
Mann, Roberta, 64, 69
Marcus, George, 29
marginal tax, 9, 40
market, 15, 25, 157
taxation of, 48
value, 144, 181
marketization, 109
Maurer, Bill, 15, 133
Ministry of Finance *finansdepartmentet*), 21
missive (*påpekande*), 98–100, 106–107, 110–113, 132, 172
Moderaterna (Moderates – the Swedish Conservative Party), 73
modernization of tax laws, 48–50
mottos and slogans, in practice, 14, 85, 156–157, 159, 169, 173
mottos and slogans, 13, 72–74, 179
mutate, 25, 92, 116

numbers
as a way of communication, 13?, 119, 135
persuasiveness of, 28, 71, 82, 134–135, 139, 141, 173–174, 179–180
numeracy, 173

OECD, Forum on Tax Administration's Compliance Subgroup, 64–65, 70
omvärldsbevakning. *See* intelligence analysis
Örebro, Tax Agency regional office in, 34, 123–127, 135–137
Överdirektör (Deputy director), ???

Panama Papers, 19
para-ethnography, 29–31, 176
payment of tax, in kind, 46–47, 51
performativity, 25, 90, 92, 103, 116
Polanyi, Karl, 40n
polymorphous engagement, 41n
pragmatism, 75, 149
praxis, 37, 51, 84, 119, 132–139, 145, 151, 165
progressive taxation, 40, 48
psychological/behavioural tax theory, 62

quantification, 21, 28, 81, 90, 120, 137. *See also* commensuration

RAC. *See* Random Audit Control
Random Audit Control, (RAC)
method, 121–122, 131–132, 137
and tax compliance, 120
department, 123–124, 126–130
purpose of, 119, 121, 137
sampling taxpayers for, 124–125
using results of, 123, 135–136
rätt skatt (the 'right' tax), 56–57, 72, 78, 115, 121, 157
RC, Research Consultancy, 22, 98, 102, 104, 106, 110–113, 172
reasonable
tax decision, 100, 104–105, 129–134, 168, 173
tax system, 133, 177
value, 137–138
Reasonable man, 133
reciprocity, in taxation, 14, 60, 178
registry. See *diari*
regleringsbrev (Appropriation directives), 56, 71, 77, 166
relation
Agency and citizens, 2–3
Agency and COENs, 101–103, 127–130, 149–151

Agency and interest organizations (as an example), 105–109, 146
citizens and state through taxation, 14–17
study taxation as creating, 14–19
tax collector and taxpayers, 2–3, 46–47, 49–51, 71–72
re-organization, of Swedish revenue collectors, 46–51, 55–57
research on taxation
critical, 63–64
economic, 60
legal, 60–61, 64
psychological-behavioural, 62–63
revolving door employment at the Swedish tax arena, 86n
Riksdag (Swedish Parliament), 50, 56, 67, 108
Riksrevisionen, formerly *Riksrevisionsverket* (Swedish National Audit Office), 58
risk assessment project, 21–25, 33–37, 76–79, 122, 145–146, 154
Robin Hood, 44
Roitman, Janet, 17
romanticism, in categorization, 91
ROT – reparationer, ombyggnad, tillbyggnad (repairs, refurbishing, attachments), 69, 87n
roter, 47
Rumsfeld, Donald, 179
RUT – renhållning, underhåll, tvätt (cleaning, maintenance, laundry), 69, 87n

Sahlin, Mona, 73, 117
säkert (secure), *resultat*, 102, 112, 120, 123–126, 134–136, 172–173
samarbetsrummet (cooperation forum), 137
SCB – Statistiska Centralbyrån (Statistics Sweden), 92, 98, 106–110, 113–115, 172
schablonbeskattning (flat rate tax amount), 152–153
Schlingman, Per, 73
Schumpeter, Joseph, 6, 15, 20, 61, 73, 169
Scott, James, 15, 90
secrecy, of information on General Income Return Statement, 34, 99
secure, value, 137–139
self-employed, 69, 79, 146–149, 163
service-mindedness, 57, 67,72–73
Sheriff of Nothingham, 43
SIE file, 127–130, 138
skälig (reasonable), 13, 100, 104–105, 129–134, 138, 168, 173, 177
SKAT (Danish Tax and Customs Administration), 19, 66, 79
skatt, etymology, 9–12
skattenämnd (tax boards), 49–50, 131–132
Skatteskrapan (The Tax-scraper), 51–53
Skatteverket
Analysis Unit at, 21, 51, 59, 76–79, 151–157
buildings and locations, 51–56, 126–127, 142
Management structure, 56–57, 76–79
Mottos and slogans, 13–14, 72–74, 85, 156–157, 159, 169, 173, 179
organization of, 56–57
strategies, 2, 4, 6, 38, 56–60, 64–66, 70, 82–85, 121, 139–142, 155–158, 164–165
skattskyldig(e) (tributary), 49, 71–72
skönstaxering (discretionary assessment), 49–50
slumpkontroll ('random control'). *See* RAC
SME (small medium enterprises), 108–109, 158
SNI-code (Swedish Industrial Sector Classification), 140n
SNO – *Skattenämndsordförande* (Tax Board chair), 131–132, 138
snowplough, 99–100, 149, 165, 178
Social Democrats, 8, 39n, 73
social image of taxpayers,
socio-technical agencement, 31–35, 41n, 84–85, 117, 138, 158, 165, 173
Södermalm, 52
Solna, 22, 53
SPSS file, 112–113, 116, 171
statist individualism, 7, 30n
statistics
about taxation, 77, 84, 160, 172
as a knowledge about taxation,
as a method about taxation,
marketization of, 109, 172
role in society, 28, 105, 109, 114
Statistics Sweden. *See* SCB

Steen, Anitra, 73
Sträng, Gunnar, 54
survey
  archaeology of, 91, 100, 113
  attitudinal, 23, 36, 75, 89–90, 112, 120
  choosing method for conducting a, 92–93, 97–99, 107, 113
  conducting a, 110–113
  making questions for, 94–97, 99
  objective and subjective answers in a, 102, 107, 109, 112
  performativity of, 92, 103–104, 113–114
  political subjectivity in a, 104–109
  social life of a, 100, 114, 117
svart arbete, black work, 6, 77, 80, 99
Svenskt näringsliv (Confederation of Swedish Enterprises), 146
Swedish Parliament. See *Riksdag*
Swedishness, 1–2, 6–9, 163, 176

tacit knowledge, 24, 134
tax collector, ideas of a, 1–3, 43–45,
tax compliance
  and CSR, 73–74, 84–85, 170
  tand psychological experiments, 62–63
  as a tit-for-tat relation, 3, 60, 62, 178
  research on, 17–20, 59–65
  strategies to increase, 66–76, 143–145, 155, 158, 162, 170–174
  varieties for explaining, 30–31, 59–65
tax evasion, 108
tax faults, finding, 138
tax gap, 56, 70–71, 77, 81–82, 135, 157
tax law
  inconsistency in, 143, 165–166
  interpretation at the Agency, 26, 36, 75, 84, 107, 120, 123, 163. *See also* praxis
  interpretation in court, 51, 75
  Swedish, 12–13, 51
  taxpayer interpretation of, 61, 65, 177
tax return, 9, 12, 49–50, 53, 55, 67–69, 72, 74, 76, 82, 108. *See also* General income tax return
  and its impact on tax compliance, 67–69, 174, 176–178
  and nationalism, 9, 53
  audit of, 121–124, 131–135, 159–161, 170, 179–181
  cost deductions on, 99, 154, 161, 171
  making errors on, 142, 147–148, 161, 164–165, 173
  simplifying, 49–50, 64, 67–69
tax system
  definition of, 5–6, 18, 20
  in practice, 51, 105, 162–163
  qualities of fair, 28, 34, 51, 61, 64, 93, 135, 143
tax, varieties of
  capital tax, 14
  etymology, 9–12
  excise, 48
  flat rate tax, 152–153
  ground tax, 46–48
  houses, 39n
  income at source, 39n
  income tax, 3, 9, 12–14, 48–49, 60, 68–69, 72, 143–144
  värnskatt (state tax), 10, 40n
  VAT (*moms*), 12, 14, 62, 77–78, 125, 136, 143–144
taxation
  as a relation, 6, 13–16, 19–20, 62–64, 139, 179
  cheating vs. making errors. *See* intention vs. practice
  fair. *See* fairness
  information about, 28, 58, 66–70, 84
  simplifying, 56, 76, 94, 121, 161, 170
Taxation board (*taxeringsnämnd*), 49
Taxeringslagen (the Tax Law section), 122
taxeringsnämnd. *See* Taxation board
taxpayer
  as cheater, 2, 58, 70, 91, 101, 109, 113–115, 163, 172
  as customer, 51, 72
  values held about, 143
  as ignorant/unknowledgable, 29, 63, 65, 142–143, 146–147, 162
the People's home. *See Folkhemmet*
tjänsteanteckningar (official notes), 128
Toblerone, 96
Torgler, Benno, 30, 63
treasure, 10–11
trust
  in society, 7–8, 16

tax system, 163
in the Agency, 57–58, 74–75, 176–177, 179
Tuck, Penny, 70

undersåte (minion), 71
uniform, value, 124–125, 137
uppgiftslämnarbördan (the duty of public enities to provide information), 105

valuation, vs. evaluation, 180
valuation, 17, 35, 179, 181
values
held and pronounced by the Agency, 10, 21, 35, 37, 56, 120, 136–139, 156, 170–173, 177–181
organization of taxation makes,
practicing, 14, 17–19, 136, 170–173
Swedish, 7, 35, 73, 152, 177
taxpayer, 93
van der Rohe, Mies, 51

Wallace, David Foster, 45
welfare state
and taxation, 5, 9, 12–16,40n, 48, 53, 62
Swedish, 7–10, 39n, 71–73
Wittberg, Lennart, 58
Woolgar, Steve, 23, 32
Work Approach, the. See *arbetslinjen*

Zambia, 133

www.ingramcontent.com/pod-product-compliance
Ingram Content Group UK Ltd.
Pitfield, Milton Keynes, MK11 3LW, UK
UKHW021838100926
8556IPUK00004B/420

9 781785 334108